ALL THE
GOOD ONES
Aren't
TAKEN

ALL THE GOOD ONES Aren't TAKEN

Change the Way You Date and
Find Lasting Love

Debbie Magids, Ph.D., and Nancy Peske

 ST. MARTIN'S GRIFFIN ✠ NEW YORK

www.stmartins.com

Design by Sarah Gubkin

Library of Congress Cataloging-in-Publication Data

Magids, Debbie.
    All the good ones aren't taken : change the way you date and find lasting love / Debbie Magids and Nancy Peske.
        p. cm.
Includes index.
    ISBN-13: 978-0-312-37006-0
    ISBN-10: 0-312-37006-7
    1. Mate selection. 2. Dating (Social customs) 3. Single women. I. Peske, Nancy K., 1962– II. Title.

HQ801.M2335 2006
646.7'7082—dc22

2006042553

First St. Martin's Griffin Edition: May 2007

10 9 8 7 6 5 4 3 2 1

TO MY PARENTS, Robert and Toby Magids, whose complete unconditional love, guidance, and wisdom allowed me to fulfill my greatest potential;

TO MY BROTHER AND SISTER-IN-LAW, Eli and Jennifer Magids, whose love, honesty, and friendship I cherish;

IN LOVING MEMORY of Harriet Alper, whose spirit I carry in my heart always

—DEBBIE MAGIDS

TO MY FATHER, G. Richard Peske, who sees the glass as more than half-full

—NANCY PESKE

Contents

Acknowledgments   ix

Introduction: Creating a Lasting Love   xi

Part I: Why Love Has Eluded You

1. Are You a Dissatisfied Single?   3

2. Thinking Right for a Change   24

Part II: Eight Styles of Dating

3. The Old Faithful   47

4. The Whirlwind Dater   63

5. The Standstill   80

6. The Forbidden Fruit Hunter   99

7. The Compassionate Rescuer   118

8. The Wanderer   135
9. The Uptown Girl   155
10. The Runaway Bride   175

Part III: Change Your Behavior and Your Life

11. Learn New Dance Steps: Understanding and
Changing the Family Dynamics That Influence You   195
12. Build Boundaries and Bridges: Forging Healthier
Relationships with Family, Friends, and Lovers   214
13. Experience All Your Feelings: Recognizing and
Processing Your Hidden, Difficult Emotions   241
14. Embrace *What Is:* Achieving and Maintaining a
Spiritual Perspective on Your Singlehood   264

Part IV: Dissatisfied Single No More

15. Happily Ever After: Success Stories   287

Index   297

Acknowledgments

Debbie and Nancy thank Faith Hamlin, for her professional guidance and wise counsel—and most of all, for bringing the two of us together. We thank Rebecca Friedman, for her insightful comments and careful tending of this project. We also thank Sheila Oakes, for her editorial guidance and enthusiasm.

Debbie's acknowledgments
First and foremost, I want to thank Nancy Peske, for sharing in the journey of creating this book. She brought life to my vision through her exceptional writing and insight as a person. It was truly a joyful experience.

I thank Dr. Patricia Strasberg, my therapist, mentor, and role model, who helped me transform my life and follow my dreams.

I thank Shani Berman, my friend, who assisted me every step of the way during this endeavor. She responded to my needs at a moment's notice. I am so very grateful.

I thank Larry Conroy, my media coach in name, my wonderful advisor in reality. With wisdom and expertise, he helped me to make very wise choices, the first was to find a writer. I will always be appreciative.

I thank my inner circle of friends and family, who know who they are and what they mean to me. My life would not be complete without their love, friendship, connection, and support. I love you all.

And last but not least, I thank my clients and my students, who afforded me the privilege of entering into the most private parts of their lives. They helped me realize that I could make a real impact on people, and help to change their lives for the better. In turn, they became my greatest teachers.

Nancy's acknowledgments

I thank Debbie Magids, whose intelligence, terrific sense of humor, and genuine compassion for others inspired me and made the writing process great fun.

I thank Adam Rader, Sally Powell, Carol Peske, Betsy Shanahan, Richard Derus, and Stephanie Gunning for their advice, encouragement, wisdom, and reassurance.

I thank Neeti Madan, who is not only a trusted advisor but a dear friend.

I thank Dr. Tanya Bannister, for four years of challenging conversations and tough homework assignments that brought me to a new level of serenity.

I thank Charyl Burke, whose love and friendship I value so much. Your willingness to help me find and create my family's new home was an extraordinary gift.

I thank my friends and family, whose support has been so valuable.

I thank George Darrow, my husband, whose love transformed me from a dissatisfied single to a very happy wife, and my son Dante, whose mischievousness, creativity, and kindness never fail to uplift me and remind me of what's really important.

Introduction

Creating a Lasting Love

As a therapist, I specialize in helping single women whose dream of having a permanent, committed, loving relationship with a man eludes them. These women come from all walks of life, and they range in age from their twenties through their fifties. Many of them are very anxious and upset about how difficult it has been to create the lasting love they desire, but they have run out of hope of achieving their goal.

The bookstore shelves are filled with guides on how to attract a man and get a ring on your finger, as if finding true love with a person who is right for you was as easy as following a simple formula. I can't offer you a six-month, guaranteed plan for living happily ever after. What I *can* do is help you to maximize your chances of creating a lasting love that is deeply fulfilling.

Whatever your current situation is, this book can help you

turn your dating life around. Maybe you just broke up with your boyfriend, or maybe you're stuck in a relationship that you know is going nowhere. Maybe you can't move on from a past love, or maybe you've never been in love. Perhaps you date constantly, hoping to find the man for you, or maybe you can't bear to think about dating again if it's just going to lead you down the same old road. This book is for the woman who falls in love with her best friend, only to be rejected, as well as for the one who falls in love with someone who says he thinks of her as his sister. It's for any single woman who wants to know why she keeps ending up a dissatisfied single, and it explains how she can change that pattern.

It's very frustrating to be single when you don't want to be. Every day in my practice, I meet women who are sad, angry, ashamed, and confused about why their relationships never work out the way they want them to. Many of my clients have spent much time and energy doing all the right things to find eligible men, and perhaps have had long-term relationships or even gotten married, and yet, they are still unable to achieve that relationship they desire. I tell the women who come to me, "You don't have to give up, or force yourself to stay optimistic when you don't really feel very hopeful. I believe it's possible for you to change your romantic fortune. But to do that, you need to change yourself."

That might be difficult to hear, but if your relationships are consistently not working out, it's time to stop looking outside yourself for reasons why and look inward at behaviors you might not even be aware of. We all have hidden patterns of behavior, and yours might be making it very difficult for you to create the relationship you want.

When I tell my clients this, they often say, "Dr. Debbie, you're so wrong. I know I want to be married. I am doing everything I can to get there. The problem isn't me." I tell them, as I will tell you, "I want you to take a leap of faith with me and just try something different. What have you got to lose? Aren't you tired of running the personal ads, going on the blind dates, working at a relationship and getting your hopes up, only to have him stop calling? Maybe it's time to take a different approach."

As you work with the ideas and techniques I present in this book, you won't always be comfortable. Change, even when it's change for the better, is always difficult. The good news is that the changes you make, even the smallest ones, will result in some major shifts. Every time you discard an unproductive belief or behavior and replace it with a more productive one, you will notice the effects. You'll start attracting available men who are not afraid of commitment, and you'll stop being attracted to men who can't give you what you want. Most important, you will come to know just how wonderful you are, and how much you deserve the loving partnership you've been looking for. You'll learn to embrace your right to happiness, and even if you find yourself without a romantic prospect on the horizon, you won't feel panicky or depressed. Instead, you'll feel confident that you'll find a very special man and create a committed, lasting relationship with him, because you'll know something deep inside you has shifted.

Commit yourself to looking inward and discovering your romantic backstory. You are ready to write a new script for yourself and your life.

PART I

Why Love Has Eluded You

1.

Are You a Dissatisfied Single?

There's nothing wrong with being single. Many people are very happy in their singlehood, and that's what I want for you, too—for as long as you are single. If you often say to yourself, "All the good ones are taken," "I'm too busy for love," or "I guess I'm just destined to go through life without a mate," then you may be what I call a dissatisfied single: someone who is in search of a lasting, committed relationship and is frustrated because she can't seem to achieve it. I want you to answer the following questions honestly.

Do you feel as if there is no match for you?

At the end of a date, can you rattle off a long list of his flaws?

Do you consistently get involved with unavailable men?

Do you find that you're not attracted to men who pursue you, especially those you know would make great lifelong partners?

Do you continually find yourself with the same ending to romances that looked very different in the beginning?

Are you convinced that there are no wonderful, available men out there?

Do you have an endless list of reasons why you're not married?

Have you been unable to find a satisfying relationship since your last relationship didn't work out—or since your marriage ended?

Do you feel like damaged goods after you've experienced a disappointing date?

Do you feel a sense of shame about yourself, especially when others ask you about your romantic life and you have nothing positive to report?

If you've answered yes to any of these questions, this book is for you.

I have worked with many dissatisfied singles like you who can't figure out why they haven't been able to create the relationship they want, and I've discovered that they tend to fall into one of eight styles. Each style has its own behavior pattern that makes it more difficult for a dissatisfied single to find love, although they all share some fundamental beliefs and behaviors that aren't working for them. Whatever your pattern is, you are probably unaware of it, but in this book, you will not only learn about it, you'll also begin changing it and maximizing your chances of achieving the intimacy and commitment you desire.

The Eight Styles of Dissatisfied Singles

Let me introduce you to eight women, all dissatisfied singles, whom we'll be following on their journey to changing their patterns of behavior and becoming open to love.

The Old Faithful, who longs for the one she can't have and gets "stuck":

RACHEL, a thirty-year-old physical therapist, is everyone's favorite go-to gal. Given her friendly and generous nature, it's no surprise that Rachel has had a number of boyfriends over the years. But there was always something "off" with all of them: either he ultimately decided he just wanted to be her best friend, or vice versa. Rachel is reluctant to date because she thinks no one can possibly measure up to her old flame, Adam.

The Whirlwind Dater, who is busy all the time, and constantly dates whoever she can but has difficulty finding a permanent mate:

CAROLE is proud to be a successful woman in her own right:

She is an events planner for a museum and a well-respected member of the community. A take-charge person, Carole has read all the dating guides and makes sure she has a date every weekend. She was even married once, in her twenties. But now that she has turned forty, she's tired of "all these wonderful men slipping through [her] hands."

The Standstill, who has done a lot of work on becoming the best woman she can be, but never dates and has a difficult time relating to men on an intimate level:

All her friends think JULIE, thirty-nine, is a great catch: She's pretty, smart, successful, and a great friend. Julie seems so confident that no one would guess she is secretly embarrassed that she's never had a long-term, committed relationship, and is scared that no man will be interested in her. She buries herself in work, never letting on how lonely she is.

The Forbidden Fruit Hunter, who gets involved with men who are married, already have a girlfriend, or are still stuck on an ex and therefore emotionally unavailable:

ALYSSA, forty-two, a vivacious woman from Long Island, is a little embarrassed that she's never been married. She once lived with a boyfriend who was still hopelessly in love with his ex, and she has been involved with three men who were either married or living with a girlfriend. Alyssa admits she is deeply ashamed of her behavior.

The Compassionate Rescuer, who always dates the guy who has problems, putting her energy into "fixer-upper" boyfriends:

Thirty-three-year-old NICOLE has been dating Jonathan for two years, and she's miserable and feeling utterly trapped. Jonathan has an excellent record as a salesman and sales manager, but he's constantly losing jobs, and Nicole believes it's because he is too angry and sarcastic. Nicole has learned to tread lightly around her moody boyfriend, but she feels too guilty to leave him and too burned out to stay.

The Wanderer, for whom just one man is not enough to fill the void, so she always has a lover or potential boyfriend on the side:

Thirty-year-old AMY's ready smile and job as a publicist make it easy for her to find boyfriends, and she always has one. Currently, she is dating Brian, a freelance journalist, and says she's madly in love with him, but she has a dark secret: She is cheating on him. Amy feels horribly guilty, hates her behavior, and is utterly baffled by it—but says she can't help herself.

The Uptown Girl, who is attracted only to those men with money, prestige, and looks:

LUCY, thirty-five, always dresses to the nines because she feels she's got to look her best to attract the right man. Her family expects her to marry well, and she's got a nice boyfriend, Michael, who comes from a wealthy family and has a pretty good job himself. But Lucy is worried that he doesn't match up to her family's very high standards of wealth and prestige.

The Runaway Bride, who is good at relationships until asked to commit—then she finds a way to end the relationship, pronto:

ELIZABETH, twenty-eight, is sweet-natured, quick to laugh, and has had several serious boyfriends. But as soon as he proposes, or asks her to move in with him, somehow, it falls apart. Lately, she has been thinking a lot about her past relationships, and is convinced that she has ruined her life by walking away from some terrific guys, but says she really doesn't know what went wrong.

You may feel that one of these types sums up your entire romantic history, or maybe you fit into two or three types. Perhaps as you read one of these descriptions you recognized a friend of yours, whose romantic history has also been an unhappy one. As you read this book, you will learn more about each of these types, discover how these behavior patterns came about, and get practical guidance on how to change them so that you can stop being a dissatisfied single and instead, create a lasting love.

The Challenge of Being Single When You Don't Want to Be

Many of my clients come to me because they are frustrated by their inability to find a long-term relationship that works for them. Some of these women date a lot, determined to follow the advice of so many dating guides that promise "it's all about numbers, so just keep your datebook filled." Some of them have given up on dating altogether, convinced that it's hopeless. Some get themselves into relationships that fall apart quickly or dramatically. Others have had a long-term relationship—even a marriage—that ended badly, and they are convinced they ruined their only chance for love.

Some of my clients alternate between despair and determination, depending on their confidence level that week. All of them are plagued by feelings of guilt and shame.

Many of my clients genuinely try to enjoy their singlehood and their unattached state. They embrace life with a positive attitude, whether or not they have a date lined up for the weekend. A lot of them have rich friendships, strong relationships with their family, a good sense of community, and fulfilling careers, yet despite the positives in their lives, they experience feelings of shame, regret, and inadequacy about being single.

It isn't easy to be single in a culture that so values couplehood and marriage, especially when most women do want a long-term commitment. When a leader of the feminist movement that sprang up in the sixties and seventies claimed, "A woman without a man is like a fish without a bicycle," the sentiment didn't convince many women for very long that they'd be happier going through life solo. When you're the one who hasn't gotten married yet, despite your efforts to achieve that dream for yourself, it's really hard not to slip into believing there's something wrong with you.

If you're unhappy with your single status, or starting to panic about never finding the love you want, I promise you that there is nothing to feel guilty or ashamed about, and you are *not* damaged goods. Here's the great news: You do *not* have to spend years in therapy working on yourself before things turn around. If you make the smallest shift in your beliefs and behaviors, it will greatly improve your chances of creating the relationship you want and deserve.

Four Ways of Changing

I will help you to truly understand why you find yourself alone when you don't want to be, or in a relationship that isn't working for you. To create the relationship you really want, you will need to examine and make changes in your beliefs, behaviors, emotions, and spirit.

BELIEFS

Your beliefs, which are probably far too negative, may actually be driving your emotions. For example, you are waiting for a man who was supposed to meet you only to realize, after a while, that he is very late. You try to call, but there is no answer. Your thoughts—*He's so disrespectful!* and *He's never going to show up, because he doesn't like me* or even *Something terrible happened to him*—probably cause you to feel furious, despairing, or frightened. When he shows up and apologizes profusely, explaining that his cell phone went dead and he got caught in traffic, those emotions fall away very quickly, don't they? The emotions fade because they were driven by beliefs that turned out to be false.

BEHAVIORS

If you can't reach the man who is late for your date, you might storm out of the restaurant and call your girlfriend to complain about how he's treating you. When you learn the real reason he was late and hear his apology, you realize that your behaviors were totally unproductive. I will show you how to stop simply reacting to situations, and consciously decide on the actions you want to take. It's important to break out of your comfort zone and push yourself to behave in a way that's unfamiliar, but that you know is healthier for you, because it will start you on the road toward feeling completely natural and comfortable in that behavior. I call this *acting as if,* because you're acting as if this way of operating doesn't make you feel self-conscious and anxious, when it does! I find it's far more effective to *act as if* than to wait until you feel totally comfortable with an action and then take it. I would hate to see you turning down a date because you're nervous about it, or not saying no to a man who isn't right for you because it will be uncomfortable to do so. Too often, people get stuck waiting to feel different before they change their lives, and I think that is not productive.

Altering your behavior is difficult. It takes vigilance, perseverance, and courage, because many times, changes are painful. At the end of the day, however, the change is well worth it.

EMOTIONS

While you are *acting as if,* you will be feeling some strong emotions, so I will teach you better ways to handle them. Instead of repressing your feelings, you are going to experience them, no matter how intense they are, and yet they won't overwhelm you.

SPIRIT

Finally, there's no guarantee that you will create the relationship you want, because that's not how the universe works. That's why I will guide you on ways to get in touch with your spirituality, however you define it, and take a philosophical approach to the unpredictable, baffling, and sometimes frustrating journey toward lasting love.

How to Use This Book

I'll take you through the process of discovering where you are and why you behave the way you do, and give you the tools to change your behavior and achieve your relationship goal. You'll start by learning the important skill of uncovering and analyzing your hidden beliefs, which I'll explain in chapter 2, "Thinking Right for a Change." Then, by reading the eight chapters on the individual styles, you will begin to see how you, like other dissatisfied singles, are subconsciously following behavior patterns that originated in childhood, viewing yourself through a distorted lens, and having trouble managing your feelings and attaining intimacy. In chapter 11, "Learn New Dance Steps," and chapter 12, "Build Boundaries and Bridges," I'll teach you more about how your family influenced and continues to influence you, and how to start changing the role you play with them—and with your romantic partner—which is hindering you in your quest for a loving, committed relationship with a man.

In chapter 13, "Experience All Your Feelings," you'll learn practical ways to manage the strong, challenging emotions you will experience on this journey, and in chapter 14, "Embrace *What Is*," I'll help you get a spiritual perspective on your single-hood that will keep you feeling positive, and will actually make it more likely that you'll find what you're looking for. In chapter 15, "Happily Ever After," I will provide inspiring follow-ups on each of the eight central women profiled in this book, give you guidance on how to write your own success story, and help you to recognize when you've finally broken out of the old behavior patterns and are truly open to a loving, intimate relationship.

If you've just about given up on your dreams, I want you to start over, by getting rid of the self-protective excuses you've made for not finding love so that you can begin thinking positively. I call these excuses *red herrings*.

Red Herrings

It's human nature to talk ourselves out of wanting something we think we can't have. If you dearly want a romantic, loving relationship that lasts, but you fear you can't have it, you have probably come up with many red herrings—that is, seemingly sound excuses for why you are still single.

Red herrings are excuses you create to explain why you are single when you don't want to be. They are very effective at distracting you from recognizing your hidden beliefs that are very distorted, create painful emotions, and interfere with your ability to form a permanent, satisfying relationship. It feels more empowering to say "I'm just too busy to focus on romance" than to admit that deep down, you think, *I'm much too needy for any man to stick around me for long.* When you flippantly tell your girl-friends, "All the good ones are taken," it's less frightening than admitting your hidden belief: *I'm just too emotionally damaged to find a lasting, loving relationship.* As painful as it is to think, *I'm not thin enough to attract someone,* even that red herring is less devastating than the hidden belief, *I'm not worthy of love.*

Those self-protective excuses can make you feel strong in the moment, but if you tell yourself that you don't care, be-cause it's hopeless anyway, your dark feelings of sadness, de-spair, anxiety, shame, and inadequacy won't go away—they'll just be suppressed. Then, the next time a guy you started seeing tells you, "It's just not working for me," or you get an invitation to yet another friend's wedding, those feelings will pop right back up.

Stripping off this top layer of excuses can be a painful pro-cess. You may find yourself resisting it, and wanting to believe that you really aren't sad that you are single and unattached. You may suddenly get inspired once in a while and convince yourself that if you just try again with another personal ad or give your ex-boyfriend another chance, you'll solve your prob-lems. But you know that's not the answer. If it were, you would have found lasting, committed love long ago.

I am sure you have tried very hard to find and foster a lov-ing relationship. You've gotten your hopes up many times, and have gone out into the dating scene with optimism and enthusi-asm, but were disappointed yet again. You might be wonderful "girlfriend material," but until you move past your red herrings, uncover your hidden beliefs, and start replacing them with more productive ones, your unconscious habit of sabotaging yourself will continue. It's time to do the work of getting back on track to your dreams.

There seems to be no end to the number of excuses dissatisfied singles make for not having the relationship they want, and yet when you look at them closely, you can see that they just don't stand up. Here are some red herrings my clients have come up with, and the reasons they aren't true:

- *"All the good ones are taken."* If so, why are there new wedding announcements in the paper every week, month after month, year after year? Any statement that begins with the word *all* is a result of *black-and-white thinking* (a type of distorted thinking in which you look at everything as all or nothing). The "good ones" will start showing up more often in your life when you make changes to your internal beliefs.

- *"My boyfriends have all been sweet, but their sweetness feels smothering."* If a lover's attention and affection always feel smothering instead of nurturing and loving, it might be that you are deeply uncomfortable with the attention and affection you want and deserve. When you change your deep-rooted beliefs about yourself, you'll be able to feel at ease in a relationship with a man who expresses his affection, and you'll be able to create a deep, emotional connection with a partner.

- *"All men have a lot of emotional baggage. . . . All men drink."* *All* is a sweeping generalization. It is an excuse for why the men you get involved with have these problems. There are men without emotional baggage and who don't drink to excess.

- *"There's something wrong with all the men out there—none of them can commit!"* You could date a thousand men, but if you don't truly believe you are deserving of love, you will continue to attract, and be attracted to, men who can't commit, and it will seem as if you're proving yourself right. When you change your deep-seated beliefs, you will start to see there are many men who are available for loving, committed, intimate relationships.

- *"Men aren't interested in women my age."* There are men who date older women, men who date women their age, and men who date women younger than they are. You can attract someone who is interested in you, no matter what your age. This is one of the most popular excuses used, and those of you who are older would be surprised to know that even twenty-five-year-olds feel this way. Then again, maybe you aren't surprised, because at twenty-five, you thought you were too young to interest a good man!

- *"I'm too busy with my career for a romantic detour."* Even very busy people will make time for dating, but if you are strongly attracted to someone and slam on the brakes suddenly, using work as an excuse, you're sabotaging yourself. Love is energizing, not draining, so when we really want it and we have the potential to get it, we create room for it in our lives. You may be rejecting potential mates, or you may be creating an imbalance in your life, putting all your energy into work and not following up with men you find interesting, in order to avoid getting rejected. This excuse is especially common because it seems totally legitimate and it can be embraced without shame.

- *"I'm too picky—I'm so special (different) that it's hard for me to find someone I can 'connect' with."* You may be casting about for that intangible reason why you're not connecting, whether it's that you're particular about how tall your partner has to be, or you feel your sense of humor is so different that you will never find a guy who makes you laugh, or that it's impossible to find a guy who can match your dedication to the arts. Those are all excuses; what's really going on is that, internally, you aren't ready for that someone you can be truly intimate with.

- *"He doesn't share my intellectual or cultural interests."* Many of the happiest, longest marriages are between people who are very different as individuals and who have very different interests. While you may wish you could change his involvement or interest in something you enjoy, it isn't enough to make or break a relationship, so it is an excuse for not being open to love.

- *"He is not rich enough, handsome enough, or successful enough."* Plenty of rich, handsome, successful men are not capable of commitment, and plenty of plain-looking men of modest means are great catches. You may be looking for reasons not to be attracted to someone who could give you the relationship you want, when the real reason is that, deep down, you are afraid of having it.

Discovering Your Red Herrings

You're at a big family wedding or an anniversary party. You are looking your very best, you're having fun talking to people you haven't seen in ages, everyone is clearly engaged by you, and you are feeling your most confident. Then, one of your female relatives—maybe your mother, maybe your aunt—comes up to you and says lightheartedly, "So, when are *you* going to get married?"

This question may upset you, and you may stammer out an excuse and then try to compose yourself and ignore the difficult feelings it brought up. Or you may have become so accustomed to defending yourself that your excuse readily pops out of you. What is it? "I guess I'm too picky," "I'm too busy for romance," or "Just haven't found the right guy yet"?

If you're not sure what you would say, fill in the following sentences, and see if they don't elicit some red herrings you've been embracing in order to explain to yourself why you're still single when you don't want to be.

I never make it to a third date with a man because

———————————————————— .

I've been single for so long because —————————— .

(Continued)

If I'm not married by the time I'm age thirty (or forty), it means_____ .
My relationships never work out because_____ .
I really want to get married to the right man for me, but I haven't been able to do that because _____ .

In the next chapter, you'll learn about cognitive distortions, which is what red herrings are. When you're finished reading chapter 2, come back and review your responses in this exercise, and see if you can identify why these thoughts are distortions.

Projection

Like red herrings, which protect us from our painful hidden beliefs, *projection* serves as a defense mechanism that protects us from painful feelings. Projection occurs when we take our own attributes that we're uncomfortable with and convince ourselves that we don't actually have them, but that the other person does. The most common form of projection that dissatisfied singles engage in is projecting onto their significant other their own inability to be intimate and committed.

We've all heard the stand-up comics joke about men who can't commit, and many of you may embrace the idea that the only real intimacy you can have is with your girlfriends and family, not with a man you're emotionally involved with. It's much easier to think that our relationship problems are outside of us. If he has the intimacy issue, you don't have to look at your own inability to open up to a man. If he is a "commitmentphobe," you don't have to think about how deeply uncomfortable you are locking into a long-term, exclusive relationship with any man.

In our culture, women are thought to be the ones who nurture relationships, create the intimacy, and hold the marriage together. We're supposed to want to be married. If on a very deep and hidden level, you are uncomfortable with being intimate or committed to a relationship, you end up subconsciously projecting that onto the men you get involved with rather than acknowledging the painful truth you suspect: that it's you who struggles with these issues.

At the core of this projection is embarrassment at not living up to your own and other people's expectations of you, and feelings of low self-worth that make it painful to look at your role in the relationships that don't work out. When you get past your excuses and discover your own discomfort about intimacy and commitment, you can start identifying the hidden beliefs that are creating that discomfort. Deep down, you may believe that being intimate opens you up to being betrayed, for instance, or you may believe that if you commit to a man, you will somehow be betraying your parent or parents. If you can find the courage to face your own issues instead of projecting them, you can begin to change them, which I'll show you how to do.

Of course, it's entirely possible that he, too, has difficulty being intimate and committing to a relationship. Even so, it's important to recognize that you've attracted a mirror who reflects back to you your own issues.

Mirroring

Sometimes we are surprised by which men we attract or are attracted to, but once we get involved, we realize that our relationship with them feels oddly familiar. All of us subconsciously choose to get involved with men who *mirror* our issues. This is not always a bad thing, because within your relationship, the two of you can work on your issues and help each other to take risks, stand up for yourselves, or make whatever other changes you need to make. Having the support of someone who truly accepts you as you are makes it easier to deal honestly with your shortcomings. However, when your mutual issues prevent the two of you from accepting, trusting, and supporting each other, it's a big problem.

If you fear intimacy, it feels right somehow to be in a relationship with a man who, one way or another, has an issue with intimacy. He might fear closeness or try to establish it far too quickly. It's as if you and he were both given scripts to follow, and you're playing your assigned roles beautifully. Perhaps he keeps you at arm's length, and you feel you have to win him over, which makes you feel inadequate—and yet, it's as if you've played this part before, so you hang in there, feeling oddly comfortable in this situation. Or, he comes on too strong and you quickly reject him, because this makes you feel safe and in control. In both cases, you've attracted and been attracted to someone who mirrors your issues.

Sometimes in mirroring, you attract and are attracted to someone who isn't your opposite so much as your twin. You both fear commitment, so neither of you takes the risk to talk about marriage, and each of you secretly blames the other for the relationship not moving forward. Or, neither of you can truly open your heart to the other, and you assume that the other person is the problem, instead of recognizing that you both fear intimacy.

When you begin to face and work through your own fears of intimacy and commitment, replacing them with a faith that you deserve and can achieve the close, loving relationship you say you want, you will find partners who will mirror you—it's just that now, they will mirror your new comfort with being intimate with and committed to another person. When you can change your unhealthy hidden beliefs, the men who mirror you will reflect back to you your new, healthy beliefs.

What You *Can* Change

You've probably heard the old saying, "You can't change anyone." It's true that you can't actually change other people, but you can always change yourself. If you're a dissatisfied single, you have to be the one who changes—not your ex, not the man you're seeing right now, not the man you'd like to get involved with, but you. It's not him; it's you—*and that's okay.*

Some of my clients have gone to extraordinary lengths to "fix" the men they're dating, wasting energy that they should have spent healing themselves of the painful, hidden beliefs that are holding them back and making them feel terrible about themselves. You truly deserve the relationship you want, but you won't get it until you begin focusing on yourself instead of on him. I promise you that whatever beliefs you hold about yourself deep down, if they are making you unhappy and sabotaging your search for love, you can begin to dismantle them, no matter how long those beliefs have been stuck inside you.

As you begin to change your thoughts, feelings, and behaviors, the people around you—the men you're involved with, your family, and your friends—will respond. Some of them will be unsettled by the new you, because you no longer mirror their issues. Some of them may reject you. Others, too, may be inspired to change, and you will also start drawing into your life people who are attracted to the new, healthier you. You'll attract and be attracted to men who, like the new you, can tolerate a high level of intimacy, and who aren't frightened by commitment. Ultimately, you will maximize your chances of creating the relationship you want with the one who is right for you.

Hidden Beliefs

I see dissatisfied singles in their twenties, thirties, forties, and fifties, from all walks of life. What they have in common are the deep-rooted, unhealthy beliefs they hold about themselves, which are based in low self-worth.

SOME COMMON UNHEALTHY BELIEFS

I'm unlovable.
I'm not sexually desirable.
I'm repulsive.
I'm undeserving and unworthy.
I'm damaged goods.
I'm damaging to those I love.
I'm too needy.
I'm just not good enough to be loved.

It's sad, but because of their experiences (particularly as children), many women, at their core, truly buy into these soul-crushing beliefs, whether they realize it or not. In the next chapter, we'll take a look at distorted thoughts that cover up these beliefs. By deconstructing those unproductive thoughts and replacing them with more positive ones, it will be easier to face and let go of the hidden beliefs that are holding you back.

2.

Thinking Right for a Change

When your thoughts are negative and unproductive, it can be very difficult to achieve the relationship you want. Red herrings are great examples of distorted thinking. At times, there is a sliver of truth in these thoughts, but that truth has been stretched so much that it has turned into a falsehood. For example, take the excuse that you can't find love because you are overweight and too busy. If a dissatisfied single who is over her ideal weight and working ninety hours a week at a computer tells me that these are the reasons she is single when she doesn't want to be, I know she's distorting the situation. I have seen many overweight women find the relationship of their dreams, and many workaholics adjust their lives to fit in time for romance with someone they're strongly attracted to.

The reality is that acting in ways that make it more difficult for you to meet eligible men, or to spend time getting to know them, is its own line of defense. These behaviors allow you to avoid the risk of getting involved with a man and getting hurt or rejected. What's really going on is an underlying hidden belief that is so painful that you construct a red herring to cover it up. If you want to create a lasting love, you must start looking closely and rejecting these unproductive beliefs that are causing you pain and holding you back from what you want.

Here's how it works: If you hold the subconscious belief that you are unlovable and no man will ever truly accept you, you can avoid the deep discomfort of exposing that belief by coming up with an excuse like "There isn't a man for me, so it's pointless to bother dating." You can reinforce that red herring by making it difficult to date. When you neglect your health and do nothing to work on the reasons you overeat and don't exercise, and you engage in behaviors that cause you to be very overweight, it's considerably easier to avoid dating. If you fill every minute of your time with work and other obligations, you do the same thing, and you also steer clear of experiencing quiet moments in which your hidden, deeper feelings might surface. While these thoughts and behaviors protect you from rejection, they also prevent you from finding love.

When you first start looking at your thoughts, it might take some effort to get past your strong feelings to uncover what you're actually thinking. Let's say you're feeling shame. What is the thought connected to that feeling? Is it *I am unattractive*? or *Everyone around me is getting married and I'm not. There must be something really wrong with me*? Each of these thoughts represents a different type of flawed thinking. They do not foster your ability to feel hopeful and confident and do what you need to do to achieve your dream of finding a loving, committed relationship.

Nine Common False Assumptions of Dissatisfied Singles

You probably don't realize it, but like all of us, you make assumptions about the unknown, whether it's what someone else is thinking or feeling or what the future holds. When your assumptions are mostly negative, your perspective is unbalanced and you become pessimistic. If you examine all your negative thoughts, you'll realize that many of them are distorted, irrational beliefs your mind creates. Instead of weighing all the evidence, good and bad, you downplay or ignore the good and play up the bad. When you assume that other people are thinking negatively about you, that only awful things are going to happen down the road, and that the worst, most hurtful explanation for an event has got to be "the" explanation, you're engaging in distorted thinking, or what therapists call cognitive distortions.

As someone looking for an intimate, healthy, committed relationship, you can't afford to be continually engaging in unproductive thoughts. They will make you feel hopeless about yourself, men, dating, relationships, romance, and the future. They can also cause you to subconsciously sabotage a situation with a man you deeply love and who is wonderful for you.

Let's look at the nine most common types of false assumptions that dissatisfied singles make about themselves and their relationships.

FORTUNE-TELLING

The past can inform us about the future, and it's good to learn from your mistakes and to be able to look at a new situation and say, "This is familiar, and I can see where it might lead me." However, judgments about what the future might hold are not sound when you assume that one or two past incidents determine the outcome of all future incidents. Because you've had disappointing dates or relationships, you might think, *This is going to be a horrible date; they all are,* or *Men always end up leaving me. That's what has happened to me in every relationship.* In your rational mind, you know that you can't predict how that blind date will go, or whether a relationship will end and in what way. *Fortune-telling* causes you to give too much weight to the past, and to dismiss all the positive possibilities in your future.

Fortune-telling can be a self-fulfilling prophecy because you set yourself up for the failure you're certain is coming. Very often, I hear clients say, "If I don't get married by the time I'm thirty, it's hopeless—I'll never get married." They are unknowingly setting themselves up to be single at thirty, and maybe at forty and fifty, as well. Or they might avoid intimacy by saying, "My relationships always fall apart when I let down my guard, so I'm going to play it cool and not let him know how much I care about him." This thinking sets you up for failure because intimacy requires sharing; you can't create it by avoiding being vulnerable.

One of my clients was convinced that she's not like other women, that she's just not sexy and that no man will ever be attracted to her physically. She became best friends with men she was interested in, but never achieved intimacy with them. Because she insisted that she couldn't find what she wanted or attract the right partner, she almost gave up on love. Whenever she had an opportunity to meet men at a party, bar, or play, she would wear black, plain clothing that was unflattering, or business clothes, and she wouldn't bother with makeup, perfume, or jewelry. She was very uncomfortable dressing or behaving in a feminine or sensual way because it didn't feel "natural." Her belief that men wouldn't look twice at her resulted in her not making any effort to draw their attention, and as a result, her belief was validated.

Whenever she was around a man she found very attractive, she got nervous and became very serious, uncomfortable, and even cold—which is not her natural personality. On a very deep level, she couldn't accept that she *is* sexy and attractive, and she was unaware that she was very afraid of intimacy. The thought that she wouldn't attract the man she wanted made her subconsciously prevent herself from connecting with him.

MIND READING

Mind reading involves the irrational belief that you have almost magical powers of awareness. You can try to read between the lines of what your partner says, observe his behavior, and hash it over with your girlfriends, but you can never really know what a man is thinking unless he chooses to tell you. Thoughts like *I'm sure the reason he didn't call is because he thinks I'm too needy,* or *He says he doesn't think I'm too old for him, but I know that deep down he's uncomfortable with my age,* are examples of mind reading.

The singles who engage in mind reading often drive themselves crazy trying to analyze other people's unspoken thoughts. A few years before she came to see me, one of my clients dated a man she thought might be "the one," but she became utterly convinced that her boyfriend thought she was too needy. She felt very vulnerable and anxious, and talked herself into thinking, *I know he's going to reject me because he thinks I am draining and neurotic.* To alleviate her anxiety, she began calling him frequently, asking for reassurance that he loved her, and grilling him about his activities in order to make sure he wasn't cheating on her. After a couple of months, he ended the relationship, saying that her clingy behavior made him feel so suffocated and mistrusted that he couldn't be with her.

Another variation on mind reading is expecting someone else to know what you are thinking or feeling. You may have caught yourself saying the following to a girlfriend: "If he really loved me, he'd know what behavior makes me angry," "Can't he see I don't like it when he jokes about my family? I shouldn't have to tell him how offensive that is," "I can't believe he would buy me a car safety kit for my birthday instead of something romantic and personal," and so on. I guarantee that if you keep your real thoughts and feelings bottled up, waiting for him to figure them out, you won't achieve the intimacy you desire. The dissatisfied single who engages in this type of mind reading usually gets deeply frustrated and even incensed at her partner's behavior, often to the point where the relationship falls apart. Yet even when this happens, she won't clear the air and explain to her ex why she was unhappy, because she feels she shouldn't have to spell it out for him.

BLACK-AND-WHITE (ALL-OR-NOTHING) THINKING

As human beings, we take comfort in our ability to identify and group things. Being unsure about whether a decision is right or wrong can be very anxiety provoking, and yet most of the time, we can't know whether a decision was truly "right" or "wrong," even after we've experienced the consequences. If you learned something from your last relationship, which ended painfully, was it wrong to have gotten involved in the first place? Was it wrong to have stayed involved for three months? Six months? The answer is never all or nothing; there was good and bad, so that relationship falls somewhere into the gray zone.

It's unsettling to be in that gray zone, unsure of whether a situation leans more toward the good or the bad. Consequently, it's our nature to distort our experiences and categorize them as black or white. We use extreme words like *everyone, everything, always,* and *never,* saying, "I just found out he's gay. These things *always* happen to me," or "*All* men are just out for one thing. They don't want marriage and commitment." When you look at these extremes, your rational mind can laugh at how foolish and simplistic these thoughts are. However, the comfort of feeling that you have a clear, flawless perception of what the situation is gives you a false sense of control. That's why it's so easy to fall into *black-and-white thinking.*

One of my clients couldn't get past the distorted thought that "all men are critical." No amount of evidence that her friends provided could sway her to believe otherwise. When she was growing up, both her parents were hypercritical, and eventually, she became this way, as well. Because making cutting remarks felt familiar to her, she would often become attracted to men who were very sarcastic. Over time, however, she became increasingly uncomfortable with any partner who mirrored her hypercriticism, and she would end the relationship. Very often, rather than owning up to her problem with being too disparaging and working on it, she would project this behavior onto the men she dated who actually weren't very critical. Anything they said that might possibly be construed as negative or judgmental, whether it was "Hmm, I can see why you're doing it, but I'm not sure if I'd be comfortable buying a car that's not on warranty," or "Are you sure you want to get a studio apartment instead of a one-bedroom?" she interpreted as an example of them disrespecting her and telling her how to live her life. She was either attracting men who were her mirror or projecting her critical nature onto her current partner—and she was engaging in a cognitive distortion about men. For a long time, she ignored the reality that there are a lot of guys, even among her former boyfriends, who are not hypercritical.

Maximizing (Catastrophizing) and Minimizing

When you take the negative possibilities in a situation and blow them way out of proportion, you are *maximizing*, also known as *catastrophizing*. For example, if you pretend to love sports to please your boyfriend, and are afraid to be honest with him about not wanting to regularly attend basketball games with him because you think, *If I don't love sports, he won't love me*, you're maximizing. It's as if you take the worst-case scenario and assume it's the most likely scenario instead of a pretty unlikely one. (How many men would reject a woman just because she doesn't share his love of sports?) Of course, that is an example of mind reading, as well. Maybe he wouldn't have a problem with your not going to so many games with him—you really can't know unless you have the conversation.

Minimizing is similar in that you downplay all the positive possibilities in a situation, giving yourself a distorted picture of reality. A lot of red herrings are examples of minimizing, such as, "He says he really loves me and wants to spend the rest of his life with me, and he's a wonderful guy, but he's not a vegetarian, and I could never live with that." It's true that you don't want to ignore conflicts and differences between you, but when you stretch them out of proportion, especially if you also downplay the positive, you talk yourself out of some great opportunities that might result in the love you're looking for.

It's common to make both these cognitive distortions at the same time. If a client tells me, "I know he called me the very next day, but I didn't like his tone of voice, so I don't think I'm going to pursue this relationship," I know she's both maximizing (making a big deal out of his tone of voice) and minimizing (dismissing his obvious eagerness to pursue a relationship).

One client of mine had been involved in many relationships that failed. Often, men left her because she minimized her partner's behaviors that should have been deal breakers—they were immature and volatile and blamed her for all the problems in the relationship, and sometimes, for their own problems. She would accept fault, but these men would leave her. She is now in a relationship where everything is great—she and her boyfriend laugh together, he takes an interest in her hobbies, and he's kind to her. However, she's always finding signs that this relationship might not work out. She's maximized a minor trait of his—he is shy and takes a while to warm up to people—and wonders if she should leave him because of this. Unless she puts his behavior in perspective, she may unknowingly sabotage this relationship.

PERSONALIZING (BLAMING)

When you believe that a problem is all your fault or all his fault instead of recognizing that both of you contribute to your dynamic, you are *personalizing*. You're assuming that you or your partner has an extraordinary amount of power and influence over the situation, which isn't the case. Every relationship involves two people who both do some things that are good for the relationship and some things that are not so good. You're personalizing if you say, "The breakup was all my fault" or "The breakup was all his fault." Both of you contributed to the dynamic, and even if you wanted to keep trying and he didn't, you were a part of the reason the relationship didn't work out in the first place. As long as you were in the relationship, you were a factor.

Blaming him or yourself or even both of you isn't productive and healthy. Taking a more objective attitude and seeing what worked and what didn't will help you to move on and create a relationship that will work.

I worked with a couple whose marriage was on the brink,

and it was clear that the man felt all their problems came down to the fact that she didn't want to have sex with him. He insisted that if she'd just "get over whatever it is that's making her uninterested," the relationship would be perfect. But if she didn't, he said, he would leave. She bought into his assessment 100 percent, and in fact, she had brought them to therapy in order to "fix" herself and thus "fix" the relationship. As I worked with them, it became clear to me that they had major issues. He was very controlling and often belittled her, and she had great difficulty standing up for herself or making her own decisions. Their relationship did not last, but I'm happy to say that she continued in therapy, and eventually let go of her habit of personalizing.

SHOULDING OR MUSTING

In this cognitive distortion, you believe there are certain rules everyone should or must follow. If you break these rules, you feel guilty or unworthy, and if someone else does, you feel angry and cheated. In fact, people have their own ideas about how to express love and what is acceptable behavior and what isn't—ideas that don't always match up with their partner's. I remember one client who actually wanted to break up with a boyfriend simply because he sent a dozen long-stemmed red roses to her office—she was incensed as she told me, "It was a total violation of my privacy to send those roses to my workplace!"

When you are *shoulding or musting,* it's common to use the words *should, must,* and *ought,* for instance, "He should have called before coming over," and "If he really loved me, he ought to have proposed to me by now, because it's been six months since we met."

One of my clients has a long list of *shoulds* and *musts* based on her idealized view of her father. Her father is apparently a very handsome, charming, and loving man, who showers his wife with flowers, jewelry, and thoughtful little gifts, and who treats his daughter like a princess. Her parents are wonderful people, but they have always felt it is not appropriate to talk to their daughter about their problems. As a result, she came to believe that her father is perfect—even though, of course, no man could live up to that standard. As a result, at forty-two, this woman has always had many male suitors, but she always breaks off her romances, claiming that she's dissatisfied because they just can't compare to her role model for how a husband should be, so they're not good enough for her.

LABELING (NAME CALLING)

Singles often engage in *labeling* (or *name calling*) because attaching harsh descriptive words to a person or situation allows them to avoid looking more deeply at it. It's easy to dismiss a man, or yourself, by making pronouncements such as "He's a jerk!" and "I must be crazy." It's okay to vent about a situation, but your venting should be a tool for further exploration. What is it about his behavior that upset you to the point where you called him a jerk? What did you do that makes you feel you must be crazy, and why did you do it? These are the kinds of questions you need to ask when you find yourself labeling.

Labeling is often used when someone has been hurt, yet again, in her search for love. Instead of fully feeling her pain and trying to figure out what is really going on, she resorts to this kind of distorted thinking.

One client of mine has a pattern of entering relationships that are ambiguous. She flirts, and the man flirts back inconsistently, so she's never quite sure if he's really interested. Usually what happens is that he is with her when he wants to be, then he pulls away, and then she agonizes until he calls out of the blue wanting sex again. Eventually, either he stops calling or she is in so much emotional pain that she cuts off the relationship. Afterward, she beats herself up mercilessly, saying, "I saw it coming. I'm so stupid and weak and pathetic." Judging herself harshly and labeling herself prevents her from going deep inside herself and working on the reasons she continues to get involved with men like this.

EMOTIONAL REASONING

Often, we confuse our emotional reality with the larger reality, engaging in the cognitive distortion of *emotional reasoning*. It's almost like the child who thinks that if he closes his eyes, you can't see him. Being unable to see, he assumes he can't be seen—he thinks his momentary reality (everything is dark) is the same as yours.

If you feel hopeless about a relationship, you might say, "This relationship is hopeless," not realizing that your feeling doesn't dictate the circumstances. In fact, the relationship may be a very good one. Another common example I hear a lot is, "Our relationship is working; I can feel it. Why doesn't he see it?" If it's working for you, it's not necessarily working for him, and vice versa.

You can't necessarily determine whether a relationship is good or not just by considering the feelings that you're aware of at the moment. You may not be acknowledging the emotion or feeling that will help you to assess what's really happening. Often I see clients who reveal a lot of clues that their relationship is not going well: They've caught the man in several lies, he's unavailable a lot, and he ends phone calls very suddenly. In short, the signs point to him cheating on her. Yet because the woman is feeling cherished by him or because she's feeling proud to be hooked up with such an eligible bachelor, she isn't considering her more uncomfortable, deeper feelings—like mistrust, embarrassment, and shame.

One client I work with keeps ending up in relationships with men who don't want to commit and who treat her badly, even being downright mean to her. When she started seeing me, she was about to turn thirty and was miserable about being alone. Shortly afterward, she came into my office and said she didn't need to come anymore, because she had met a guy. They'd been together for only two weeks, but she said this relationship felt different from any other she'd ever been in. She had been with him every night, and he was calling her and e-mailing her all day long, so she was confident that she had broken her behavior pattern. When I tried to take a more realistic look at the situation, she got angry and said she knew how she felt, and that was that. Two months later, she came back to therapy and admitted that she'd been ashamed to call me and reveal that the relationship had ended a week after she'd last spoken to me. She was finally ready to look at how she was using emotional reasoning to assess a situation, and her progress in therapy began.

COMPARING

Singles with low self-esteem often engage in *comparing*, measuring themselves against others or against what they think they ought to be. Of course, they never measure up, and they'll say things like, "I'm just not like other women, who know all the tricks of pleasing a man, so I'll never find a boyfriend." Measuring yourself against others is completely pointless. Distortions like "At least my man doesn't cheat on me, like my sister's husband does" do not help you to find a loving, committed relationship.

Comparing can help you to feel soothed temporarily because you can always find someone in a worse situation than you are in, but eventually, your unhappiness in your own relationship can't be brushed aside with excuses like "It could be a lot worse. All men drink—at least my guy's a happy drinker, not a mean one." Comparing also works to help you talk yourself out of risking a relationship and the possibility of getting hurt.

One client constantly comes up with pronouncements like, "My hair is frizzier than anyone else's—no wonder men don't hit on me at clubs," and "I'm just too ordinary to compete with all the beautiful, successful women in this city." Another of my clients was constantly using her weight as an excuse for why she couldn't find a relationship, but then her best friend, who is much heavier than she is, fell in love with a wonderful guy who treated her beautifully. This helped her stop believing in the old distortion "Men are only attracted to skinny girls."

Five Traps for Dissatisfied Singles

The distorted beliefs that dissatisfied singles engage in run the gamut, but I have found that there are five traps that they fall into as a result of these beliefs, which prevent them from finding satisfying relationships.

THE TRAP OF BELIEVING YOU CAN BE IN CONTROL AT ALL TIMES

From the time we're about two years old, we tend to fall into the trap of thinking that if only we were in charge of everything, we'd be happy. Of course, if we were honest with ourselves, none of us would really want the responsibility of determining everything that happens to us and to those around us. It can be frightening not to know what our future holds, and to think that at any minute everything we love could be taken away from us, so we try to manage this fear by taking control of our lives as best we can and believing that we can have control.

We all need some sense of control over our lives and our relationships. If you want to find love, you do have to take control of some aspects of the dating process. However, it's of the utmost importance to be able to relinquish some of your need for control and experience the anxiety of the unknown. If you do, you open yourself up to far more possibilities. Taking all the control actually works against you—it impedes your chances for finding a lasting relationship.

When your beliefs are distorted, and you attempt to control how your relationship will turn out, it is self-defeating. For example, if you're going to go on a date, and after one phone conversation you decide that while this person sounds nice, you probably won't click with him, you will try to figure out how the night will go and how quickly you can get home (knowing exactly what will happen gives you the illusion of control). Having talked yourself into believing that, of course, tonight will be yet another boring evening, you've already closed yourself off from an opportunity. You won't approach the date with curiosity and openness but with pessimism and negativity. In short, because you try to take control of the situation in order to prevent rejection, you actually set yourself up to be rejected!

If you are willing to surrender your desire to be completely in control of the evening, you'll be open to however the date unfolds. You'll let yourself feel a little nervous and remember that all great adventures begin with a positive attitude and a willingness to feel the fear and take the plunge anyway. You'll pick out an outfit and do your hair and makeup so that you feel your most confident and attractive, and remind yourself that if he doesn't find you lovely, or if you really don't like him, it's okay. As long as you approach the date with an open, positive attitude, and maximize the possibility that it will go well, you will open yourself up to new possibilities. Instead of making a quick exit, you can say yes to that after-dinner drink—and maybe discover that your date was worth getting to know.

THE TRAP OF BELIEVING THAT EXTERNAL CIRCUMSTANCES DRIVE RELATIONSHIPS

When we don't feel a sense of control over our ability to find love, we tend to cling to simplistic excuses and talk ourselves into believing that if we could change our circumstances, Mr. Right would suddenly show up, and we'd soon be setting a date for the wedding. There's a certain comfort in believing that "If I just didn't have to deal with my demanding mother all the time/my terrible job/my financial problems/my difficulty losing weight, and so on, I could find just the right man, and our relationship would be fabulous." After all, any of these problems is indeed a significant challenge that requires work and can be very distracting, making it harder to focus on your search for a romantic partner.

However, even as you're working on these external problems, there is internal work you can begin to do that will have a *much* more significant impact on your ability to find the loving relationship you desire. Thinking that a change of outer circumstances will result in a change in your romantic fortune is setting yourself up for disappointment. There are thin, gorgeous women with great jobs and supportive families who have trouble finding the love they want, and overweight, plain women with awful careers and demanding families who find the man of their dreams and create the relationship they've always desired. What they really have going for them are *internal* circumstances: namely, the fact that they aren't accidentally short-circuiting their chances for love. As you work with this book, you, too, will change your internal circumstances and better your chances of finding an intimate, committed relationship.

THE TRAP OF BELIEVING THAT YOU NEED A MAN TO BE HAPPY

I know it's difficult to be single when you don't want to be, but it's too easy to overemphasize the negative aspects of being single. Many women talk themselves into believing that if they could just find the perfect partner, all their problems would be over. He would make them feel happy, and good about themselves. He would give them emotional security, and probably financial security, too. He would be a constant reminder that she is a lovable, worthy person. If you believe any of these statements, you have expectations of a relationship that can't possibly be met.

If you're looking outside yourself for happiness and feelings of self-worth, you are doomed to failure. You can only create happiness yourself, and you are the one responsible for how you perceive yourself. Moreover, there is no lasting security in any relationship, emotional or otherwise, because life is fragile. Even the most loving man might leave tomorrow, through no fault of his or yours. If you're dependent on a man for happiness, your happiness will be very precarious.

In our bridal-happy culture, it's easy to forget that "getting the ring" is no guarantee of happily ever after. If you have personal problems, regardless of your relationship situation, it's your responsibility and your privilege to change your life for the better.

THE TRAP OF BELIEVING THAT WORRYING IS PRODUCTIVE

Worrying creates anxiety, and when you're anxious, you don't have the creativity or the clarity to solve problems. I recommend being concerned about a problem rather than worrying about it. *Concern* simply means taking note of a problem, but *worrying* involves obsessive thinking that causes stress, which clouds your perceptions. Working through your feelings of anxiety and fear will allow you to access your creativity and achieve clarity. These are the real tools for change, not giving in to worrying or obsessing.

When you engage in distorted thinking, it's easy to become anxious and start worrying constantly. Thoughts like *If I don't put out, I know he'll reject me* and *If I approach him, he'll think I'm desperate* can send you into an obsessive spiral as you try to resolve a situation your head. The best cure for worrying is a combination of evaluating your negative thoughts, working with your emotions such as fear, and taking a spiritual attitude toward the outcome of any particular date or relationship. (You'll learn more about managing emotions and developing a spiritual perspective later in the book.)

THE TRAP OF BELIEVING THAT HANGING IN THERE ALWAYS RESULTS IN A REWARD

I see a lot of dissatisfied singles who were taught as children that the only true rewards are in heaven, or "Good things come to those who wait." Because they hold that core belief, they convince themselves that very delayed gratification is acceptable and that it's even noble to wait for it.

I don't endorse pursuing instant gratification, but if you are waiting for some distant reward for your behavior, you can easily begin playing the martyr, letting others take advantage of you and staying in situations that are not healthy or productive. It is very unhealthy to take the attitude, *If I just keep trying to do everything perfectly, my boyfriend will stop being unappreciative of me and will start treating me well.* Love is not painful. It's not a chore, or a burden. Love energizes and uplifts you most of the time. If you're in a relationship and you can barely remember the last time it made you feel energized and uplifted, and you're just slogging along waiting for the situation to change for the better, it's important to consider whether you are falling into the trap of waiting for a far-off reward instead of dealing with the problems in your life today.

You may be so used to engaging in negative, distorted beliefs that you don't recognize them. The following exercise will help you become more aware of this unproductive thinking, deconstruct your thoughts, and help you to consciously change your habit of being pessimistic.

Identifying Your Distorted Thoughts

Throughout the course of a day, as negative thoughts pop into your head, jot them down in a notebook, leaving a blank line between each thought. Also, if you find yourself feeling angry, sad, ashamed, or frustrated, take a few moments to ask yourself, *Is there a thought connected to this feeling? What is it?* Once you've identified the thought, write it down.

At the end of the day, look at your list of negative thoughts. As you review each one, ask yourself whether it is a particular type of distorted thought. It might even fall into two categories. On the line below, write in what type of distortion or false belief it is.

Here are some examples:

"I can't believe I'm running late. I am so irresponsible."
(Labeling)

(Continued)

"He sounded so tense when I called him at work. I think he's mad at me." (Personalization) (Mind Reading)

"Another Friday night alone. I'll never have a boyfriend." (Black-and-White Thinking) (Fortune-telling)

"Ugh, my hair is just hideous. I look horrible." (Maximizing)

As you look over your list, you may notice that your faulty thinking tends to fall into the same few categories. Notice whether you're engaging in black-and-white thinking or minimizing or another type of distortion.

Next, try to come up with more positive variations of these thoughts, for example—

"I can't believe I'm running late. Oh well, these things happen. Next time, I'll remember that the traffic is bad this time of day."

"He sounded tense at work, but I could be wrong. I'll ask him later if he was upset and, if so, why."

"Another Friday night without a date. I think I'll call my girlfriend and ask her if she wants to do something fun, or maybe I'll go check out that live blues jam I read about in the paper, or see a movie."

"Ugh, my hair is really not working in this weather. I guess I'll just try to style it differently or wear a hat and forget about it. After all, I hardly notice it when other people are having a bad hair day."

(Continued)

Try to come up with as many positive substitutes for your negative beliefs as you can. Consider writing them in a journal and reviewing them, so that it becomes easier to catch yourself in negative, distorted thoughts and replace them with more productive ones.

If you did the exercise of identifying red herrings on pages 17–18 in chapter 1, go back, review them, see if you can determine what kinds of distortions they are, and think up more positive thoughts to replace them.

In my office, whenever a client says something that's a distorted thought, I say, "Let me re-language you," and I reword what they said, using more positive language. After a while, they will stop themselves after expressing a distorted thought and will automatically correct it. By taking the time to recognize your anxiety or discomfort and actually say your thoughts aloud to yourself, or write them out, you, too, can start recognizing your distortions and correcting them. It will become automatic with practice.

Whatever your typical distorted beliefs are, they are rooted in your past. In part 2 of this book, you'll learn about each of the eight styles of dissatisfied singles and their particular backstories, behavior patterns, distorted beliefs, and hidden beliefs. You may find yourself identifying with one style, or possibly you'll find a little bit of yourself in several styles. As you read each chapter, you'll become more adept at identifying the types of thoughts and feelings that you experience, and you'll improve your ability to recognize your hidden behavior patterns, start changing them, and begin turning the tide of your romantic fortune.

PART II

Eight Styles of Dating

3.

The Old Faithful

The Old Faithful makes a wonderful friend, daughter, sister, and coworker, because no matter what happens, she'll be there for you. She's the one who always remembers your birthday, who answers the phone in the middle of the night when you call to cry about your latest romantic misadventure, and who rushes to your bedside when you're in the hospital. Old Faithful is often an overachiever, yet she's the last person to brag about herself.

You'd think these terrific women would be snapped up by fantastic guys as soon as they step out into the dating world, so why do so many of them find themselves approaching their thirties, or even their forties, without the committed, happy, fulfilling relationship they dream of?

Like all dissatisfied singles, the Old Faithful can't seem to find lasting love. She may successfully hook up with a nice guy who loves her madly, and she may love him, but she doesn't feel any chemistry and she can't figure out why. Or she becomes intoxicated with a man who thinks she's a great pal, but who either never shows a sexual interest in her or in the end does not fall in love with her. She may secretly pine for a man and obsess over him, but will keep silent, hoping that someday he'll want to turn their friendship into a romance. Very often, the Old Faithful gets stuck on a past love and can't let go of the relationship even when it's obvious that there's no hope of rekindling it.

Half the Package

The Old Faithful always seems to end up with half the package. She will become extremely close with a guy she considers an excellent catch: She may be his "best buddy," the "go-to girl" he can really talk to, or a girlfriend who is supportive, nurturing, and understanding. Although she has long, intimate conversations with this man, and he thinks she's the best, she can't achieve that *When Harry Met Sally* ending. She has passion or emotional intimacy with a man, but never both.

The Old Faithful is buying into some hidden beliefs that are preventing her from having the whole package: an emotionally intimate and passionate relationship with one man. For years, she has covered up her hidden beliefs with self-protective excuses like, "I guess I'm just too picky," or "The timing is always off with me and guys for some reason."

Are You an Old Faithful?

1. Do you have trouble letting go of past relationships, spending an unusually long time pining for your ex?

2. Do you feel you missed out at your one chance for true love?

3. Are you uncomfortable showing any affection toward your boyfriend when your father or mother are in the room?

4. Do you fall in love with your best friends?

5. Do you find you're sexually incompatible with guys you feel very emotionally connected to?

6. Do your friends, partners, and family all seem to confide in you and come to you when they have problems?

7. Do you have difficulty revealing your vulnerabilities and deepest dreams to your friends or your romantic partner or both?

8. Do you dread going out on dates and looking for the next "one"?

9. Are you your mother's or your father's "special girl"?

10. Do you always put other people's needs first?

The more of these questions you answered YES to, the more likely it is that you are an Old Faithful.

Stuck on a Lost Love

Despite the problems she's had in past relationships, the Old Faithful is trapped in longing for her past love. Whether he broke it off or she did, whether or not they both felt they were in love with each other at the time, now she is thinking that he was "the one," and she was just too blind to see it—and it's too late. Or she feels that she simply has to make her ex see that they were meant for each other and ought to get back together.

Rachel was thirty-six when she came to see me in the hopes that I could help her get over her ex-boyfriend and move on with her life. She was optimistic, fun-loving, and sociable, and she had many close friends. Meeting men was not a problem for her, she explained, because she worked as a physical therapist, treating many handsome athletes who had sports-related injuries. But after four years of trying to forget about Adam, whom she'd hoped to marry, Rachel was steeped in regrets and very depressed about her future prospects.

Rachel said she really wanted to get married, but she was very reluctant to go out into the dating scene because, and as she explained to me, she just couldn't let go of her strong feelings for Adam. Rachel was still in love, but Adam had no interest in rekindling their romance. He thought Rachel was a wonderful girl and told her so often, and encouraged her to believe she'd find the right guy for her, but he just wasn't it. When she had tried to date, Rachel compared every man to Adam, thinking that Adam wouldn't have acted that way or expressed that opinion, or remembering that Adam had owned a shirt just like the one her date was wearing.

Rachel felt she was wasting her time and her date's because she couldn't imagine herself falling in love again. With Adam unavailable and her heart set on him, she felt destined to be single and unattached forever. She wanted to know why she couldn't let go of Adam and be attracted to another man. What's more, she recognized that Adam wasn't the first man she got stuck on despite his inability to return her strong feelings of passion. Like many of the dissatisfied singles who come to see me, she felt as if she'd been in this relationship before, and she wanted to break her relationship pattern.

Rachel's Backstory: The Origins of the Old Faithful

Rachel came from a Jewish immigrant family, and her father, Alan, had done his best to make the American dream come true for them. As a child, Rachel watched both her parents struggle to make ends meet, and to help out their large extended family.

Playing a caretaking role with others came easily to Rachel. She had a natural talent for helping people and making them feel good about themselves. She had great role models for this behavior—her parents, Alan and Sarah. Rachel knew that they were overburdened by attending to the needs of their many relatives, making themselves available to every aunt, uncle, and cousin, and offering advice, emotional support, or money, but she very much admired them, and followed their example.

Watching her mom and dad nurture their loved ones without complaint, Rachel got the message that she should focus on other people's needs, and as a result, she dismissed the importance of her own needs. She never let on that when her family moved to a new neighborhood when she was ten, the other kids picked on Rachel in school, ridiculing her discount store clothes, her frizzy hair, and the foods she brought in her lunchbox. Instead, Rachel worked hard to earn the approval of these children, buying them candy, doing their homework for them, and eventually winning them over.

While her brother, Josh, felt free to talk to his parents about the difficulties he had adjusting to school, or making friends in their new neighborhood, Rachel felt that it was her duty to protect her parents from having to hear about her own unhappiness—particularly since they were so concerned about Josh. What's more, Sarah sent clear signals that she was deeply uncomfortable with anyone around her being scared, depressed, or emotionally upset. She would be visibly stressed, offer a quick platitude about how surely everything would be okay, and avoid a heartfelt conversation. So, just as Rachel's mom would cry alone in the bathroom (as Rachel later discovered), Rachel would cry alone in her bedroom at night rather than "burden" anyone with her sadness or fears.

Sarah had been the caretaker in her own family at a very young age. She had learned to repress her heartache and frustration, only letting it out in small moments, such as when she broke a dish. She would allow herself to get very upset over this type of minor mishap, but she'd be a rock of reliability and calm in a real crisis. Unbeknownst to Rachel, her mom was afraid of getting in touch with her daughter's fears and disappointments because she knew that if she did, she would get in touch with her own, which would be too painful.

Rachel was much more emotionally connected to her father. Alan would share with Rachel that he'd had a frightening nightmare, and he'd come to her when he wanted to reminisce about a special memory. Rachel was the one who knew his favorite song and that he felt sad about his troubled uncle. So while her parents were close and would go out dancing together, or take vacations without the kids, it was Rachel—not Sarah—who was privy to Alan's greatest vulnerabilities and sentimental musings.

To Alan, Rachel seemed mature, caring, and eager to be

"Daddy's best girl." He enjoyed being a soothing force in her life. Rachel reveled in how loved and cherished he made her feel, but despite feeling secure in her relationship with her father, she wasn't comfortable confiding in him. Alan had no idea she was sad, and it didn't occur to Rachel that she should share this with him. She thought their relationship was wonderful. Rachel wished she could feel as close to her mom, who was warm and loving, but not emotionally connected to her daughter in the way Rachel's dad was.

Sometimes it's the mother who is the Old Faithful's confidante. Another Old Faithful, Candace, recalled that as a little girl, she would often see her mother break down into tears, and she felt it was her job to comfort her. Candace's mother, Dinah, felt that only Candace could truly understand her, because her husband was a gruff, hypermasculine man, as were their four sons. Candace's mom told her all about her disappointment in the people who had let her down over the years, and her dream of one day being able to not worry about money. She used to joke, "Who needs a therapist when I have my little Candy to be my sounding board?" Although Candace was very uncomfortable with the burden of being aware of her mother's secrets, and having to be discreet in order to protect them, she thrived on her mother's attention, so she accepted this role.

Hidden Beliefs

"DAD/MOM DESPERATELY NEEDS ME AND MY LOYALTY IF HE/SHE IS TO SURVIVE."

One of the reasons the Old Faithful is unavailable for the relationship she longs for is that she holds the very unhealthy, distorted belief that a parent desperately needs her as an emotional confidante. This belief takes hold when she's a child and she begins edging out one parent to be the other's confidante. Even a small child can sense there is something wrong with playing this adult role that rightly belongs to her father (or mother). However, she is encouraged to play this role, even if the parents aren't conscious of it. On some level, Candace felt it wasn't right for her to be let in on her mother's deepest secrets and vulnerability, but she loved her mom, and she loved the validation she got for listening, so she never spoke up. Sarah resented the easy intimacy between Alan and Rachel, but felt too guilty about her resentment to acknowledge it and deal with it. Because she'd never learned how to create a deeper bond of intimacy with her romantic partner by confiding in him, she had no idea how to go about it. Rather than allowing her daughter to simply be a child, unburdened by the emotional needs of her father, Sarah quietly repressed all her difficult feelings, so she was quite unconscious of the position she was putting Rachel in. Meanwhile, Rachel couldn't help wondering why her mother didn't act as Alan's confidante, leaving Rachel to do it instead.

"I'M NOT WORTHY OF LOVE."

The hidden belief that most frightens the Old Faithful is the belief that she is not worthy of love. Many dissatisfied singles believe they are not worthy, but for the Old Faithful, it stems from her confused dynamic with her parents when she was a child. When a child assumes the role of one parent's confidant, that child subconsciously steps into a spousal role on an emotional level. Whether or not the child or her parents are aware of it, this extra burden creates an unhealthy family dynamic of guilt and inappropriate emotional intimacy.

Rachel was very defensive when I suggested to her that she

felt unworthy of love. After all, she felt very much loved by both her parents, although she admitted she wished she felt as close to her mother as she did to her father. But as we discussed how she never revealed to the people she most cared about just how sad or frightened she was, keeping these feelings inside, she realized that she had never trusted that a man could accept and love her if she wasn't constantly upbeat, loving, and giving. Because no one had attended to her emotional needs when she was a child—in fact, they weren't even aware of them—Rachel got the idea that she wasn't worthy of having her needs taken care of. If she were lovable, her childish mind reasoned, someone would be *her* confidant, nurturing and reassuring her. This hidden belief got buried deep inside her, and was influencing her behavior as an adult.

In addition, Rachel had felt Sarah's resentment over usurping her role as Alan's closest confidante, and this influenced Rachel's belief that she was a bad person. After all, it appeared as if she had pushed her mother out of her rightful role (when actually, her mother simply hadn't taken it on). Rachel felt that replacing her mother made her unworthy of love. Keep in mind that none of these thoughts ever came to the surface for her; they remained in her subconscious.

Sadly, the Old Faithful grows up to be confident and fun-loving on the outside (because after all, this attitude pleases everyone around her), but on the inside, she feels so ashamed, guilty, and unlovable that she can't open herself to true love. She hides her dark feelings from herself as best she can, and shields her closest friends from them, as well. Candace, for example, had a breast biopsy that caused her to cancel lunch with her best friend, but she gave a vague excuse for rescheduling lunch rather than risk having her friend learn just how frightened she was. She told no one about her experience, and mentioned it to me only in passing, as if it weren't appropriate for us to talk about an experience that any woman would find upsetting. Candace was so used to locking up strong feelings inside of her that it actually didn't occur to her that she could share her fear with her friend or her therapist.

Say Good-bye to the Past

If you are an Old Faithful, you need to learn how to experience your emotions, and let them out, so that you can work through them and finally close the door on the past. Unless you make this break, you won't be open to a future that presents opportunities for emotional intimacy with a lover. You need to say good-bye to the ex you've been pining over, and good-bye to the role of confidante to your parent.

Saying good-bye to being "Daddy's little girl" or "Mom's best friend" requires you to draw boundaries, change those problematic and distorted hidden beliefs to healthier ones, and start creating a better, more functional relationship with your family. To finally get over a romantic relationship, you must allow yourself to grieve. You also have to change your behavior so that you don't keep an ember burning just in case he "comes around."

The idea that a relationship is truly over and that rekindling it is completely hopeless can be very difficult to embrace. Sometimes the belief that "maybe he'll change and it'll work out between us" gets taken to extremes: Candace had great trouble accepting her on-again, off-again boyfriend's admission that he was gay. He was not going to magically transform into the sexually and emotionally available mate she hoped for.

Remaining loyal to your ex reenacts your emotional marriage to your parents: It seems that if you move on, you will hurt your ex, just like making a break for emotional independence from your parent will hurt him or her. Despite your pain, you may be more concerned with sparing your ex or your parents. It doesn't matter if your ex or your parents would actually suffer should you move on to a healthy, fulfilling relationship that contains the whole package: emotional intimacy and sexual attraction. It seems like you can't have this type of relationship without hurting them—but of course, now you realize just how distorted this belief is.

Are you still fantasizing about how you might get back together with your ex? Do you analyze your former relationship endlessly, looking for ways in which you could have acted differently and made it work? My guess is that the least of your problems was how dedicated, nurturing, and supportive you were. After all, you learned at an early age to tend to other people's needs. You are probably talking yourself into an old relationship so that you can avoid starting a new one, and that's not going to get you where you want to go.

It's very hard to let yourself feel the full force of your grief over the fact that your relationship with your ex is over, period. As an Old Faithful, you've gotten so good at presenting a happy face to the world that you may even have forgotten how to feel your own emotions. Facing your grief head-on can be frightening and deeply uncomfortable.

As you are doing this, you will also have to just say no to the emotional intimacy you have with your ex. This does not mean you can never speak to him again, or that you can't be friends. It means you have to lower the intensity of the relationship so that you can heal and then become available for a healthier romantic relationship.

Rachel realized she needed to stop being emotionally married to Adam. For instance, whenever she was about to board a plane, she would call him on her cell phone to say, "I just want you to be the last person I spoke to if the plane should go down." She decided she would stop doing this, and stop phoning him so often, or talking so intimately with him about matters like his fears and frustrations. As she began to reveal her difficult feelings to her friends more often, she also stopped expressing to Adam just how special he was to her. The emotional "marriage" was dissolving.

Setting boundaries with your ex may not sit well with him. If he reacts with hurt or anger when you tone down the friendship, explain to him that you are doing this for both of you, so that you can move on and find new partners. After all, how can he, or you, have genuine intimacy with a new partner when both of you are half in this relationship with each other? Allow him to be angry without you feeling guilty. Remember, you are doing what's in your best interest, and his, as well.

When you feel as if you've lost your soul mate, you may find yourself constantly sentimentalizing your relationship. It's very important to take off those rose-colored glasses and remember the bad times, too. You learn from them—you can be clearer about what you want in a romantic partner—and it will also help you to stop pining for a relationship that is long over.

Think about your ten worst memories with your ex. Remember a particularly painful argument, an uncomfortable time you spent together when you felt you were not connected to him, and so on. Candace was able to recall that although they had been together for nearly three years, the ex-partner she romanticized had never known anything about her most deeply held spiritual beliefs, which informed her life and her worldview. It hadn't occurred to her that as long as she kept something so important hidden inside, she would never attain the intimacy she sought. In retrospect, she realized that part of the reason she'd never given him a hint about her beliefs was that he had given her many signs that he didn't respect people who were very spiritual. Remembering that, her perspective shifted, and she stopped believing that it was only bad timing that had doomed their relationship.

Correcting Distorted Thinking

The Old Faithful is prone to minimizing the evidence that a past relationship was not what she had hoped it would be, and maximizing the evidence that it was. She also engages in labeling ("I was an idiot for letting him go") and personalizing ("It's all my fault that he left"). Her thoughts about the new men she meets can become just as distorted, because she hopes to protect herself from becoming too intimately involved with a man.

When it comes to her relationship with her parent, she tends to fall into all-or-nothing thinking ("If I'm not his/her confidante, no one will be). While it's possible that Mom or Dad won't find a replacement confidant should the Old Faithful change her relationship with her parent, it's very likely that he or she has someone to turn to other than the Old Faithful (and in any case, the role of confidant rightfully belongs to the parent's romantic partner). Also, deep down she fears that if she has the whole package with a romantic partner, she'll be betraying her parent and her mother or father will, in return, be furious or devastated and simply fall apart. She's both maximizing this parent's potentially negative reaction and personalizing, believing she has more power over her parent's mental and emotional state than she actually has.

The Old Faithful also has difficulty being optimistic about her future because she tends to engage in fortune-telling, thinking *I'll never find a lasting love* and *I'll never find another man as wonderful as my last boyfriend.* This mires her in sadness instead of helping her to work through her grief over past relationships, and her past inability to find the love she wants, which would free her up to embrace the future with hope.

Just Say No

One of the most important things you need to do as an Old Faithful is to draw boundaries with your parents. When you stop being your parent's "special girl," you will stop feeling so uncomfortable having the whole package for yourself.

Over time, Rachel also came to see that her father's true love was, in the end, his wife: *They* were the couple. She even came to see that her mother, who had been her own father's confidante, had unconsciously felt undeserving of the whole package of a relationship, as well. This, she learned, was why her mother had had such difficulty opening up to her husband—and why it was so easy for her to let her daughter slip into that kind of relationship with him in her place. Rachel also discovered that in Alan's childhood, he had also played the role of confidant to one parent, and that's why he gravitated toward emotionally relying on his daughter instead of his wife. By changing your dynamic with your parents, you free them up to have "the whole package," too.

Work at finding common interests with your parent who has been shut out, and try to build a bridge of intimacy with this parent even as you draw boundaries with the other one. Rachel, for example, began spending time with her mom going to garage sales and flea markets, and she started to open up about herself and encourage her mom to talk about her deeper feelings. Urge your parents to reconnect with each other: bring them both into the conversation that the parent who is closer to you starts. Encourage them to talk about the bond between them and to spend time together. As your parents become closer and you pull away from your confidante role, it will be easier for you to focus on working through your difficult emotions that you've been repressing for too long, and healing yourself at last.

New Beliefs, New You

As you get rid of the old beliefs, you need to replace them with healthier ones that will serve you on your quest to find an intimate, committed relationship. You may decide that your new beliefs are, "My parents would be thrilled if I had a committed, intimate relationship with a man," "Dad is just fine even when I'm not around," "I deserve the whole package," and "I am lovable and worthy of nurturing." Changing your beliefs doesn't happen overnight, but the more you actively discard the old ones and reinforce the new ones, the sooner it will happen.

It's important, too, to act in accordance with your new beliefs. Now that you believe you're lovable and worthy of nurturing, prove it to yourself! Think about what really makes you feel happy and good about yourself, and make sure you get it. Rachel realized that instead of spending her evenings on the phone with her friends, talking as she cleaned her kitchen, she needed to go out more. She asked her friends to accompany her to bars, restaurants, concerts, and shows. This way, she could enjoy the nightlife of the city, feel alive and vibrant, and have a chance to meet people.

As an Old Faithful, you've spent a lot of time attending to other people's needs. It may feel strange, even selfish, to ask them to attend to yours. Letting people you love know that you are sad, angry, or frustrated is not imposing on them; it's allowing them to give to you and feel closer to you. Think of how good it feels for you to help someone else cheer up, or work out their emotions. Wouldn't your friends and family want to be able to experience that wonderful feeling of having helped you?

As you work toward changing the behavior patterns that have been hindering you, don't forget to be gentle with yourself. It's terrific that you are able to appreciate the men in your past and stay on friendly terms with them, and it's great that you're close with your parents. By setting some boundaries and letting go of what was, however, you open yourself up to so many more possibilities for love.

4.

The Whirlwind Dater

The Whirlwind Dater is not a woman who lets life pass her by. If she wants a date, she can get one—but it won't necessarily turn into a relationship. The Whirlwind Dater has read every singles guide on how to snag the perfect man in thirty days or less, and it would take a natural disaster to keep her from circulating at some party or event this weekend where she hopes to find Mr. Wonderful. But no matter how many men she goes out with, the Whirlwind Dater can't sustain a fulfilling relationship for long.

She has plenty of red herrings, of course, like "I guess I just haven't found the right one yet," "It's a numbers game. If I date enough, I *will* find him," and, when she's just been left by her latest partner, "Men can't commit!" Her friends are baffled by her inability to create the lasting love she says she really wants for herself. It's not for lack of trying. It's certainly not for lack of opportunities. The Whirlwind Dater makes herself seen wherever the men are, and she is attractive, vivacious, and interesting. She can talk about a variety of subjects and is always up on the latest trends. No wonder it's easy for her to strike up a conversation with a man. If he's a reasonably nice guy, that's enough for her—she's not picky. She's usually the pursuer, and men initially are drawn to her, but then things fall apart.

Rarely does the Whirlwind Dater end a relationship. Instead, the man is usually the one to leave. Afterward, she may realize that despite any sexual chemistry or common interests they shared, they didn't quite have that emotional, soul connection—but she can't figure out why. At those rare times when she's without any romantic prospects, or she strongly suspects her current mate is about to end the relationship, the Whirlwind Dater quietly admits to herself that something isn't working. Once again, she's ended up in the same place—still single, still looking.

Are You a Whirlwind Dater?

1. Do you date constantly and never seem to find a lasting relationship?

2. Will you drop everything to make time for a date?

3. Are you always on the go—scheduling all your free time?

4. Is it hard for you to relax and do nothing?

(Continued)

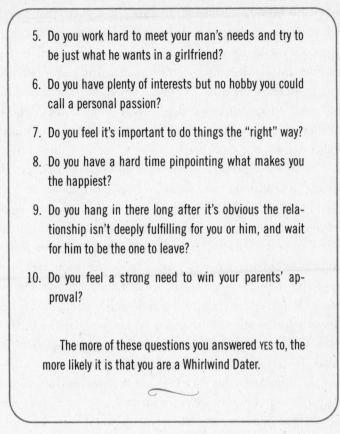

5. Do you work hard to meet your man's needs and try to be just what he wants in a girlfriend?

6. Do you have plenty of interests but no hobby you could call a personal passion?

7. Do you feel it's important to do things the "right" way?

8. Do you have a hard time pinpointing what makes you the happiest?

9. Do you hang in there long after it's obvious the relationship isn't deeply fulfilling for you or him, and wait for him to be the one to leave?

10. Do you feel a strong need to win your parents' approval?

The more of these questions you answered YES to, the more likely it is that you are a Whirlwind Dater.

The Woman Underneath

As a therapist, I always enjoy hearing about the exploits of the Whirlwind Daters in my practice. They are as far from boring as can be. Usually, they are vibrant, successful women with great social skills. If you met them at a party, you'd think, *What a fascinating woman!* And yet, they are closed off from their deepest feelings. I often find that underneath their confident exteriors, they don't know who they really are and what they truly want from life. It's as if they are chameleons, blending in with their environment, adapting to the expectations of others. Often, they're afraid to be on their own, and their self-esteem can take a dive when they don't have a partner or a potential partner. At the same time, however, they seem to be very confident and controlling, wanting things done "just right"— meaning, their way. No one would ever really know how unsure of themselves they really are.

Carole was a prime example of the Whirlwind Dater. She was the adventurous sort, ready to hop a private jet to Paris when her new, wealthy boyfriend suggested a romantic weekend in the city of love or to immerse herself in the athletic life when she began dating a salesman who had a passion for cycling. She told me she was proud about the wide variety of wonderful men she has known in her life. Whenever she was with a new man, she immersed herself in his world. As a result, she was an extremely well-rounded woman who knew a little bit about nearly everything, from wine to restoring Victorian homes, from politics to saltwater fishing.

Carole traveled a lot with the men she met but also enjoyed living a New York City lifestyle. She was a very successful events planner for a museum, and had a reputation for being on top of every detail. She kept herself very busy and very scheduled— every weekend or evening was booked with activities, many of them dates or events at which she hoped to find her next boyfriend. I had spoken to Carole twice on the phone over the last three years, but both times she'd canceled our initial meeting. She apologized, saying that she'd found a fantastic guy and didn't think she needed therapy to help her deal with her feelings about being single after all because she was hopeful this guy was different. Finally, however, she made an appointment and kept it, because she was ready to do some work. Carole's boyfriend of six months had just written her a Dear Jane e-mail when she got a phone call from her best friend, Brianna. Brianna's husband of sixteen years had left her, and this brought up a lot of painful feelings for Carole about her own inability to maintain a relationship.

Like many Whirlwind Daters, Carole had even been married once in her twenties. She explained to me that she hadn't been especially attracted to this man, but he was a nice guy, and her parents and friends adored him. The lack of connection was something she took for granted, but she guessed that it might have been the reason why he had left her after less than ten months. That was her longest relationship to date. Now, she was forty, and tired of watching what she called "all these wonderful men just slipping through my hands." She told me she was starting to think she would never stop finding herself in this situation, no matter how many men she dated. She was ready to consider the possibility that maybe there was something she was doing that was contributing to her unhappiness.

After a few sessions, I could see what Carole couldn't: that these men were slipping away because they were never really hooked into her emotionally, and vice versa. She had a serious problem with intimacy that I knew we had to delve into if we were going to get her to a place where she could maintain a loving, committed, and emotionally enriching relationship with a man.

Carole's Backstory: The Origins of the Whirlwind Dater

Like a lot of Whirlwind Daters, Carole grew up in a family where at least one parent was very exacting and had high standards of behavior. Carole's father, Joe, was a stern but fair man who had very clear ideas about how to do everything from answering the telephone to making a sandwich. Carole explained that he always liked things "just so," and thrived on routine and discipline.

Joe was very happily married to Carole's mother, Lila, who deferred to Joe and tried her best to make him feel like the master of the household. Like her husband, Lila believed in living your life a certain way. However, their seeming confidence in their strong beliefs about the way things ought to be covered up the fact that Lila and Joe both tended to be anxious. When Carole got in trouble at school for talking during a fourth grade assembly, they took away her bike for a month, hoping that what they called "tough love" would keep Carole on the straight and narrow. When Carole was caught smoking with her friends in junior high, her parents got scared and quickly enrolled her in a private Catholic school, an intense overreaction that made her frightened of offending her mother and father again.

Even so, Carole was a very well-behaved child. She got a lot of praise for being mother's little helper, and was determined to become a woman her parents could be proud of, so she was as obedient as she could be.

Most Whirlwind Daters, like Carole, had a relatively happy childhood with loving parents, but grew up feeling insecure about what might happen if they didn't meet Mom and Dad's expectations. The Whirlwind Dater may admire her parents for having demanded the best of her, and may credit them for making her the way she is: a responsible, successful, reliable person who can interact well with a wide variety of people.

These are all great qualities to have. However, because the Whirlwind Dater took to heart the belief that she had to measure up in order to secure her parents' love, she internalized the belief that to be lovable, she had to work very hard and make the grade. Her parents may have expected her to be a straight-A student and an Ivy League graduate, or to be the ever-dutiful daughter, never causing any emotional turmoil at home. Often, the Whirlwind Dater feels pressured to stifle her true personality. She may be a very physically active and outgoing girl, but her parents pressure her to be reserved and quiet, or she may be introspective and intellectual, but her parents wish she were extroverted and more social. She feels she has to be something other than she is if she is to have any hope of getting her parents' validation and attention.

One Whirlwind Dater, Suzy, had parents who utterly adored each other, but they were so wrapped up in their relationship that they weren't as strongly connected to their children as they could be, and were rarely emotionally present or supportive to Suzy. Suzy tried to get their attention and affection by being as good as she could be, always overachieving, thinking that if she could become the best daughter in the world, their behavior toward her would change and they would reassure her that they felt she was special and delightful. Unfortunately, her plan never worked. Her parents never made the time to come see her science fair exhibit or attend her National Honor Society induction. They urged her to get a nose job and breast implants, and although Suzy resisted and told them she was happy with the way she looked, this pressure took its toll on her self-esteem. Over time, in therapy, she came see that her parents' inability to appreciate how terrific she is had nothing to do with her.

The Process of Self-Discovery

I wondered what would have happened if Carole had rebelled against her parents and engaged more fully in the process of self-discovery. As I worked with her, I tried to get Carole to talk about her mother and father, but it was difficult, because she was very defensive about them. She felt they had taught her the social graces that allowed her to thrive in the world. Carole was devoted to raising money for the museum she worked for because she really believed in funding for the arts to benefit the entire community, including those who are underprivileged. However, I sensed that she was doing this more out of a sense that it was the right thing to do than because it was her true passion.

I knew that if Carole didn't start discovering who she was and what made her feel most alive, she would continue being chameleon-like in her relationships as well as in other aspects of her life. She could fit in with anyone. She always seemed to know just what accessory she ought to be donning this season and just what book she ought to have read and have a thoughtful opinion on, yet when I asked her questions like, "Did you have a hobby as a child that you were really enthusiastic about?" or "Is there anything you do that you seem to have endless energy for whenever you pursue it, because you just love it so much?" she would draw a complete blank.

Finally, Carole admitted to me that as a girl, she had genuinely loved going on nature hikes with her Girl Scout troop. As she described what it was like to walk through the woods and identify different trees and birds, and smell the pine needles underneath her feet, I could see her eyes light up. It was as if I were talking to the real Carole for the first time.

I asked her when she stopped going on those nature hikes she so loved, and she explained that her father had spoken to her Girl Scout leader and suggested that the girls focus more on community activities than exploring nature. The woman was swayed, the girls began learning about local government and helping entertain nursing home patients, and Carole stayed in the troop and earned her badges, but the joy of scouting was gone for her. She was already doing those activities as part of her church, and when she wasn't doing her homework, she felt compelled to do her civic duty.

When she explained to me what had happened all those years ago, I realized that Carole had internalized some very powerful beliefs about herself that she needed to recognize if she was going to be able to be her true self in a relationship.

Hidden Beliefs

"IF I DON'T FOLLOW THE RULES, I'M BEING SELFISH AND IRRESPONSIBLE. I'M A BAD PERSON FOR WANTING TO BREAK THE RULES."

Rules give us structure, which we humans thrive on. They help prevent us from offending each other and make us feel secure. However, rules should be based on common sense and mutual benefit. When too much weight is given to the rules, we start to define our worth by whether or not we're following them.

In Carole's case, her parents needed a lot of rules in order to feel secure, to manage their anxious tendencies, and to feel in control of their lives. Carole had picked up on her parents' anxiety about her, and had learned to be placating and reassuring toward her parents and toward other people. Whenever she got in touch with her discomfort with herself, she grew nervous, and her adherence to her own set of rules made her feel less panicky. Interestingly, she was open to other people acting in daring or nontraditional ways, but when it came to her own behavior, she was very conservative and even rigid.

"NO ONE WILL LOVE ME AS I AM. I'M
NOT GOOD ENOUGH, SO IN ORDER TO
BE LOVED, I HAVE TO BE WHAT OTHERS
WANT ME TO BE."

A childhood marked by conditional love from her parents creates in the Whirlwind Dater the belief that she isn't good enough as is; there are things she needs to do and ways she needs to behave to please her parents and hence gain love and approval. Eventually, she transfers this need for approval, seeking acceptance from other people. If someone approves of her, she's so happy about it that she minimizes anything she doesn't like about them. When it comes to men, she isn't picky: If a guy likes her, that's enough for her. She can be a good girlfriend to just about any man. The question is, does she want just any man, or does she want a man who will fully love the real her?

When you play the chameleon, you cheat yourself as well as your partner. You make it impossible to achieve intimacy—that deep, emotional, soul connection that can come only when you let yourself be vulnerable, open up, and reveal your insecurities and dreams. Yes, there is the possibility that you will be rejected, but if you don't open up, your relationship will remain on the surface. Until you know yourself, you can't truly love yourself. Until you can truly love yourself, and be yourself around other people, you can't attract the intimacy you long for.

Breaking the Rules

If you're a Whirlwind Dater, you need to get rid of the pattern of behavior you've created to avoid getting rejected. To start, I want you to break a few rules.

Breaking the rules and hurting other people is very different from breaking the rules and merely disappointing other people. People who have expectations of you are not always thinking about your best interests. They might be focused on their own need to feel comfortable with what you're doing. If you often stop yourself from pursuing an activity because that voice in your head is whispering, *What would Mom and Dad think?* or *What would people say?* it's time to start separating out the functional rules in your life and the rules that are holding you back from being happy. Keep the ones that serve you, and start breaking the ones that don't.

Carole was very much married to all the rules she had for herself and concerned about doing things the way they "should" be done. Whenever she was at a spa, she wouldn't rest—she would get up at six and exercise. Whenever she was in Manhattan, she would visits the museums, and whenever she was in Philadelphia, she would break her diet and eat a cheese-steak sandwich because "that's what you do in Philadelphia." It would be good for her to rebel a little.

In one of our sessions, Carole mentioned to me that she was feeling compelled to finished the latest acclaimed literary novel because she believed in her father's rule that you should always read fine literature in order to become a more enriched person. By this point in her life, Carole was clearly culturally well-rounded, but there was nothing she did that was just for her—something that simply gave her pure pleasure. I encouraged her to put down the book that was "good for her" and gave her the homework assignment of not following her rule of reading a fine novel every day after work for twenty minutes. Instead, her job was to spend those twenty minutes doing something fun that she knew her father wouldn't approve of.

The next week, Carole reported that she had spent a good ten minutes standing in her apartment that first day, clueless about what she might enjoy doing—she was that out of touch with her own likes and dislikes. Finally, she decided to take a walk in the park, because it was a beautiful night. She savored the smells of the flowering trees and found herself wondering what their names were, and remembering how much she'd loved to be in nature when she was a girl. She wandered into a bookstore and bought a guidebook to trees, and went back the next night after work to see if she could identify any of them. Each night following, she made an effort to appreciate and learn more about the foliage in the park, and happily reported to me at her next session that she'd discovered that the park sponsored educational nature walks. Carole was clearly very excited to have rediscovered her childhood passion, and vowed to participate in the park's official nature walks and learn as much as she could about the local plants and animals.

I told her that this was a great beginning, but I didn't want her once again feeling she had to follow the rules and commit to every nature walk and learn what she was "supposed to" learn. I urged her to check out the ones she was most interested in and then continue to explore nature on her own without pressuring herself to meet a certain goal of doing every walk that was offered, or learning the name of every tree. Carole saw my point and promised she would try not to make her enjoyment of nature into a project with a lot of rules for her to obey.

Correcting Distorted Thinking

Carole had to rethink the rules she lived by, and she needed to start correcting some of her distorted thinking, too. I wanted her to break her habit of catering to her boyfriends.

Carole met Eric at a party and soon realized he loved the

nightlife. As a record producer, he was used to going out late and didn't have to be in his office until late in the mornings. Rather than assert that she didn't want to stay out until 1 a.m. on weeknights socializing when she had to get up early for work, Carole just went along with Eric's plans.

I asked Carole what she thought would happen if she told Eric that she would prefer to cut their evenings a little short, and leave the late-night activities for the weekend. "I wouldn't want him to think I'm a stick in the mud," she said. I asked her to explore this example of mind reading. What evidence was there that he would think less of her if she stuck to a schedule that was more in tune with her work hours? In fact, Carole couldn't think of any. She even admitted that he'd expressed admiration for the work she did. I asked her if that wasn't evidence that in fact he would interpret her need to have earlier evenings as a sign that she was devoted to her job, rather than a sign that she was boring. Carole was able to admit that she was minimizing the evidence that he might respect her need to get to sleep earlier on weeknights in order to be fully alert at her job, and engaging in mind reading instead.

In fact, when Carole did finally get up the courage to confront Eric about her needs, he was very understanding and even apologized for not recognizing that he was keeping her out too late.

Often, the Whirlwind Dater is afraid to stand up to her latest partner and tell him what she wants, whether it's more time to herself, more affection, or a change in their sexual dynamic. She fears he'll get angry and defensive, and won't be willing to listen, or alter his behavior. The Whirlwind Dater will often modify her own sexual behavior to please a man, engaging in acts that make her feel uncomfortable, or going for long stretches without sex because her partner's libido is low. Whatever the case, it's his sexual appetite and preferences that determine their sex life. When the Whirlwind Dater does speak up, sometimes she can't find common ground with her partner, but sometimes he's willing and able to meet her halfway so that she's more sexually satisfied.

Usually, the Whirlwind Dater has difficulty achieving intimacy with a man, and she remains emotionally disconnected from her closest friends, keeping her conversations focused on topics and activities rather than matters of the heart. She probably has many girlfriends that she socializes with, but she engages in mind reading, assuming that if she were to reveal her true self, her friends would reject her. She'll listen to her friend's most intimate confessions but won't reciprocate because of this fear. Her hidden belief that she won't be loved if she doesn't meet with others' approval combines with her mind reading to keep her feeling she has to be very cautious and not let people get too close, lest they disapprove of her and leave.

Most Whirlwind Daters bend their behavior and even their beliefs in order to placate their partners and friends, and meanwhile they are still trying to please their families, as well.

Discover Yourself

Because the Whirlwind Dater learned to please Mom and Dad to earn their love, she probably did not spend enough time getting to know who she is and what she wants from life. Many women, like Carole, knew when they were children what it was that they loved to do, but in an effort to conform to others' expectations, they stopped indulging in their pleasures and stored them away. You may have dreamed of having a particular career but felt pressured to give up that dream. Even if you don't switch careers, you might be able to pursue that dream in some other way. Carole, for example, needed to spend more time in nature, which had given her so much joy in the past. You might be able to volunteer, take a class, or begin a part-time job doing something you love. If you adore books, you could join a writer's group or a book club, take a creative writing class, or work in a bookstore a couple of evenings a week. Reconnect with what you love.

If you can't identify something that really makes you feel energized and happy, then do some exploring. Try something that simply sounds intriguing, and let go of any thoughts you have about being good at it.

Take a Hiatus from Men

It may sound counterintuitive, but if you, as a Whirlwind Dater, want to find the loving, committed relationship you desire, you are going to have to do the difficult and uncomfortable work of stopping yourself from making your hunt for the next man the focal point of your life! I want you to commit to taking a hiatus from dating for three months. No going on a blind date just because you think it wouldn't be fair to your friend not to go out with a guy she really thinks would be right for you. No giving a man your number at a party or club. Instead, tell him, "You're a great guy, but I am not looking for a relationship right now."

Is this assignment making you feel uncomfortable? Believe me, my Whirlwind Dater clients have a very, very tough time with this one. They'll swear up and down that they'll do their best to stay away from a relationship, and then they'll come into my office, beaming, saying, "Dr. Debbie, don't be mad, but I started going out with this guy and I *swear* to you, he is the one.

I just couldn't let this opportunity pass." Before you go on dating hiatus, I want you to finish reading this book and pay very close attention to my advice about managing difficult emotions, which you'll find in chapter 13, "Experience All Your Feelings." I am not underestimating how hard this hiatus may be for you, but I believe you can handle the discomfort if you work with the techniques I provide to manage your feelings of anxiety, fear, sadness, and so on. If you know another Whirlwind Dater, by all means, make a pact that the two of you will not break your hiatus, no matter what men come along, no matter how uncomfortable you feel. It will make a difference.

The first thing you'll start noticing is that you have more time on your hands. Rather than spend this time productively—and I know you are a very productive person who hates downtime—I want you to become a woman who is comfortable in her own skin even when you aren't doing anything at all. That's right: just spend some time doing nothing. Ride a bus across town and back, sit in a café and watch people but don't strike up a conversation, walk along the beach or through the park. Don't put on a pedometer and set a goal for yourself, or take out a pad and start scribbling a to-do list, even if it feels like having no agenda is a total waste of time. I want you to spend at least two hours a week doing *nothing*. If you have to put it into your PDA—"Do Homework: Veg"—do so. This is an appointment with yourself that you aren't going to break.

Some of you might suspect what will happen when you allow yourself this downtime. Feelings you don't want to face are going to come up. Thoughts like *No one is going to really love me. I don't even know who I am,* are going to pop into your head. Painful memories might come back to you. It won't be comfortable, but allowing these feelings and thoughts to surface and then dealing with them is a crucial part of your journey of growth.

New Beliefs, New You

Once you've started getting rid of the unhealthy, unproductive, and distorted beliefs that have held you back, you need to start embracing new beliefs that will help you get where you want to go. You might choose beliefs like, "While I make different choices than my parents do, they are good choices," "My parents, family, and friends may be disappointed in my choices, but they will still love me," and "I am worthy of spending some of my time simply doing what makes me happy." I believe that when you deny yourself pleasure, it's as if you're putting a big box over the light inside you that wants to shine, and denying everyone the joy of getting to know who you really are. Until now, you've been cheating yourself and the men you've been involved with. You've probably been cheating your friends and family, too. As you start to get to know yourself better and work on loving yourself more, it will be easier for you to shut out the voices of disapproval that come from other people and from inside you.

As you work on the special challenges of being a Whirlwind Dater, you'll experience the excitement of getting to know the fabulous woman you really are. You'll probably surprise yourself as you explore all your many talents and desires. Over time, you'll see more clearly which men you can have a deeper connection with, and at last, you will be able to make that connection.

5.

The Standstill

The Standstill often appears to be a very confident woman who has accomplished just about everything she has ever set out to do, with the notable exception of finding a romantic, committed relationship. When asked if she'd like a life partner, she may laugh or shrug, claiming that the last thing she has time for is to go on a manhunt, and that she's satisfied with her career, her friends and family, her sense of community, and her lifestyle. She says that while a relationship would be nice, she really doesn't give it much thought, because she doesn't need a man to feel fulfilled. Her excuse, "I'm too busy to get into the dating scene," seems very plausible to the people around her; after all, she does spend a lot of time working.

However, the Standstill is extremely skilled at keeping her

true emotions and beliefs well hidden. Even her closest friends would not guess that a major reason she is devoting so much time to her career, her extended family, or her volunteer commitments (or all three!) is to avoid having to think about dating, and that she is secretly embarrassed that she's never had a long-term relationship and scared that no man will be interested in her. The Standstill never lets on how lonely she is, or that deep down, she feels unattractive, unsexy, and unworthy of male attention. That insecurity makes it very difficult for her to take the risk of dating.

Are You a Standstill?

1. Do you rarely, if ever, date?

2. Are you insecure about how few relationships with men you've had over the years?

3. Are you still a virgin, or do you rarely have sex?

4. Do you put on a happy face for the world?

5. Does intimacy with men feel scary to you?

6. Did you feel awkward with your femininity when you became an adolescent?

7. When you were growing up, were you rewarded more for your accomplishments and smarts than for your femininity?

(Continued)

8. Do you have a hard time feeling comfortable with wearing makeup and dresses, flirting, or engaging in other traditionally "feminine" behaviors?

9. Is it difficult for you to express feelings of vulnerability?

10. Do you often compare yourself negatively to other women who you think are more attractive and charming?

The more of these questions you answered YES to, the more likely it is that you are a Standstill.

The Standstill's Bravado

The Standstills I've met usually insist to their friends and family that they aren't bothered by the fact that they haven't had a long-term relationship in years, or that they have never had one. Or, they might admit that they wish that weren't the case, but they're accepting of the situation and not upset by it. Some of them have not dated in over a decade, while some of them date every few months but it never leads to a relationship. Some of them are virgins, or have had sex only a few times. This is often a painful secret for them.

While the Standstill is very good at hiding her shame, fear, and anxiety, those feelings deeply affect her. For instance, she may become very anxious when a milestone birthday approaches, which reminds her that another year or decade has passed and yet there is still no sign that her situation will change.

One of the biggest struggles for the Standstill is to get past her hidden belief that the reason she hasn't found a man is that she is incapable of attracting one. Standstills usually are very out of touch with their sense of femininity and sensuality, and are extremely insecure about it. They don't allow themselves to feel beautiful, sexy, and womanly. They may even be dismissive of how important it is to feel this way and to express it, because that is a great way to avoid their painful hidden belief that they are not sexy or attractive.

Opening Up

For the Standstill, it's easier to try to be thick-skinned than it is to open up and be vulnerable. Even if she meets a great guy that she has chemistry with, she either doesn't recognize his attraction to her or she shuts down and doesn't let herself be flirtatious and feminine, choosing instead to act almost businesslike in the way she approaches the relationship, or simply getting anxious and uncomfortable. She's much more at ease being in her head than being in her body, or being active instead of receptive. She may love flowers and jewelry, and will buy them for herself, but if a man who is pursuing her buys her these sentimental, personal items, she is a little suspicious, or laughs nervously and thinks, *How hokey!*

Julie is thirty-nine years old and has never had a real relationship. She has had a few guys in her life, but she wouldn't consider any of them boyfriends, because she was with them for only a couple of weeks to a few months. She has had sex with men, and she was very attracted to Tony, one of the men she slept with. She had wanted a relationship with him, but he was only interested in what he called "a little fun" and being friends.

Whenever they hooked up, she was drunk, and they never created an intimate, emotional connection.

After a few months of this awkward dynamic, Tony stopped phoning her, and Julie started to realize that she had established a pattern of getting involved only with men she drank with. Believing that this was not going to lead her to a real boyfriend and marriage, she decided that this chapter of her life was over with. She stopped hooking up with men and quit drinking, but for four years, she didn't date or have sex at all. Then she entered therapy.

When I asked Julie why she thought she had gone for such a long spell without romance, she told me it was probably because she worked long hours as a corporate lawyer and was putting all her energy into moving ahead. She was clearly proud of her success and was well respected in her field. Her parents, particularly her mother, thought she was incredible, and loved to brag about how their daughter had such a great, high-powered, well-paying career. When asked if Julie was seeing anyone, her parents always offered the excuse that men are threatened by dynamos like their daughter, and Julie herself seemingly believed it. She liked to say that men couldn't handle a smart woman with a big paycheck and a corner office, but on some level, she knew it wasn't true.

For all her bravado, Julie was deeply depressed by her single status. She told me she was jealous of her girlfriends who had partners, but the stories she told of her friends and their lovers revealed that some of these were extremely dysfunctional and even destructive relationships. Julie didn't see them that way. She just wished that, like her friends, she could be "in the game."

Another Standstill I worked with, Audrey, told me that whenever she was around people who hadn't known her for a long time, she would make up stories about ex-boyfriends so that she wouldn't have to, as she put it, "feel like a freak." She lived in fear of being caught in her lies, but couldn't help herself, because she felt so ashamed that she'd never had a partner. I reassured her that with all the pressures on women to "have it all," it's no wonder that she felt so compelled to meet everyone's expectations to succeed not just in her career but also in her romantic life, and I could understand why she had taken to lying about her romances.

Both Julie and Audrey reported that everyone thought they were wonderful friends and beautiful, confident, "together" women. They were much admired by the people in their circles. But while the Standstill may have no problem finding a girlfriend to socialize with, or even going to a restaurant or a Broadway show by herself, she is usually terrified to date. She often believes that she can't possibly be the type of woman that a man would be attracted to, much less fall in love with. The Standstill may be physically very beautiful, but will hide that beauty rather than enhance it—for example, favoring severe suits at work and unflattering but comfortable clothes on the weekends, minimal makeup, and no jewelry. If she does present herself femininely, it's because she feels she has to live up to someone's ideas about how she ought to look and behave, and she's uncomfortable in what she wears, unsure of who she is when she's in a dress, or heels, or even makeup. Often, even when she is dressed up for a formal event or a date, the Standstill feels plain, unsexy, and undesirable, because as a child, she was expected to be one of the boys, rejecting "girly" behaviors and values.

Julie's Backstory: The Origins of the Standstill

In Julie's childhood home, being "girly" was something even her mother sneered at. Her mom, Doris, was the powerhouse in the family. She was hard to please and held very high standards for her two sons and for Julie, who was the middle child. The children competed to see who could get the best grades, who could make the most free throws in the driveway where they had a basketball hoop, and who could win their parents' praise, which was rarely given.

Julie described her father as very sweet but also very passive, content to let his wife set the rules in the house and set the tone. In their home, achievement was everything, and Julie's mother defined achievement as success academically and socially. Julie was class president, head of the debate team, a star swimmer, and a top student, and that was just in junior high school. She later went on to be the first in her family to attend an Ivy League university, where she majored in pre-law.

When I asked Julie if she'd always wanted to be a lawyer, she explained that it had been her mother's idea, and that she had been very reluctant to pursue that career. Before applying to law school, she had decided to talk to her father about it rather than confront her mother, and he had given her all sorts of reasons why her mother's plan was a logical, sensible one for her. Rather than stand up for herself, or stand up to her mother, Julie dutifully began to study law.

No Little Princess

What many Standstills never get from their fathers, which other girls get from their dads, is the sense that she is Daddy's little princess. He is uncomfortable with her femininity and as a result, acts as if it doesn't exist. Julie described her relationship with her father as being no different from the one he shared with his sons. In fact, she might as well have been a boy, given the way he interacted with her. While she was not particularly drawn to sports or student government, she knew these activities were highly valued by her father, and she felt that she might get his attention by pursuing them. He did praise her somewhat for these pursuits, but as is typical in a Standstill's childhood home, his attention stopped there.

All little girls act coquettishly with their fathers, basking in the special attention they can get from Daddy; it's their first experience with male love. In short, a girl wants to be Daddy's little princess. The Standstill learns quickly that her father won't respond positively to this feminine behavior. Later, as a teenager, her relationship with her father becomes even more distant. She wants her father's eyes to light up when she enters the room, and to be told she looks lovely in her first truly grown-up dress and pair of high heels. She wants to feel special and protected as he opens the door for her and looks suspiciously at the boys who come around. But the Standstill's father is not able to give her any reassurance that her new, more womanly body and ways are attractive.

The Standstill's father is so uncomfortable in his role as parent to a girl that he either withdraws from her or treats her like one of his sons, or does a combination of the two. As a result, the daughter gets the message that there is something not right about her femininity, that it ought to be ignored or suppressed, or that it doesn't exist. She may react by becoming a tomboy, or she may allow herself to wear makeup and enjoy being "girly," but feel very uncomfortable expressing her femininity around boys and, later, men. When a man responds to her womanliness, she is suspicious or uncomfortable because it feels so unnatural to her. She's had no role model for a man cherishing her as a feminine woman.

Womanly Bodies

A Standstill's discomfort with her femininity does not always come from her relationship with her father—it can be related to her mother, as well. Audrey was an only child whose mother was very competitive with her. In order to feel more secure in her mom's love and prevent her mother from feeling threatened by her, Audrey eventually learned to tone down her flirtatiousness and girlishness. She sensed that if she attracted more masculine attention than her mother did, her mother would reject her. This was reinforced when Audrey was a teenager and her mother would borrow her clothes, saying, "This color looks better on me," or when she would say things like, "I have a date coming over tonight. Here's ten dollars to go to skating with your friends. I'd rather not have you around, distracting us." What Audrey heard was, "I'd rather not have you around, distracting *him*."

A Stiff Upper Lip

In her childhood, the Standstill gets the message that she must reject her femininity. She also learns that her parents are not comfortable with her expressing her emotions. Her mother and father emphasize her independence and self-reliance, and expect her to be thick-skinned. In Julie's home, for example, the children were rewarded with treats if they didn't cry when they got shots at the doctor's office or they skinned their knees. Her parents often ridiculed Julie's flighty aunt Tricia, her mother's younger sister, who was quick to cry or express anxiety, which made Julie uncomfortable because she very much loved her aunt. Like many Standstills, Julie was also taught that physical affection is not something to be publicly displayed, so she would stiffen when hugged and feel awkward when kissed on the cheek. In fact, she told me that she had used alcohol as a social lubricant to help her not feel quite so inhibited around men.

Because she's used to stifling her emotions, the Standstill seems very emotionally strong and steady, and puts on a good front about being unattached. In fact, she may even be unaware of the depth of her feelings of loneliness and low self-worth. When she is with a man, she can become confused and anxious, unsure of how she feels or how to read his expressions of emotion, because it all feels foreign to her.

Hidden Beliefs

"I HAVE TO WORK HARD AND PROVE MYSELF WORTHY OF LOVE BECAUSE I'M JUST NOT GOOD ENOUGH."

Because she had to struggle to get her parents' approval, the Standstill feels she's lovable only if she works hard at earning that love. While she may seem confident, her sense of self-worth is very weak, and she will be very judgmental toward herself. Her drive to continually accomplish more and be better at what she does helps her succeed in her career, and makes her a loyal friend who will really go out of her way for someone she cares about. No matter what rewards she reaps for her hard work in life, or how much her friends tell her she's terrific, she never really believes she's worthy of anyone's love. She feels she can't relax and receive other people's nurturing, as this will only result in her feeling she has to do even more for them to be worthy of the attention they've given her.

"I'm not sexy, sensual, or desirable."

Having gotten no attention (or only negative attention) for being girlish, and having had her more masculine side reinforced when she was a child, the Standstill developed painful hidden beliefs about her femininity. Most notably, the Standstill feels she is not sexually desirable. She might even feel repulsive and have very negative feelings about her body, as well. She feels great shame about her womanliness, and tries to suppress it, which usually results in her not attracting as many men as she could attract. Because men are not approaching her, her feeling that she is not desirable gets reinforced. She may well reject her femininity altogether and convince herself that romance is out of the question for her. Excuses like "I'm just not the marrying type," or "Men are just too threatened by a strong woman like me" prevent her from accessing the deeply hidden belief that no man will ever adore and cherish her.

Your Body, Your Self

As a Standstill, you face the challenge of getting out of your head and your thoughts and getting back in touch with your body and how beautiful, sensual, and desirable it is, whatever its size or shape. Cherish your body. Spend the money on an aromatherapy facial or a deep salt scrub massage. Take baths with essential oils, turn off the lights, and surround your bathtub with tealight candles. Consider taking a class in belly dancing, or sensual stripping. If those activities feel artificial to you, that's okay. Try them anyway, because getting in touch with your senses and indulging them will help you to reconnect with your feminine self and your body.

When I suggested this to Julie, she rolled her eyes, but I continued encouraging her to just do it, even if it seemed silly. She finally got a deep massage and a facial at a spa. She told me that she had done it just to prove me wrong, and was shocked by the strong, difficult emotions that surfaced as a result. Julie said it felt embarrassing to have the massage therapist working on her. That is typical for many Standstills because a massage is so body focused and can be sensual—and it brings to the surface the shame they feel about themselves and their bodies. Also, being physically pampered can be uncomfortable if you're used to relating to your body in a very practical, nonsensual way.

I continued to encourage Julie to get past her resistance to "girly" activities like taking luxurious baths, wearing less tailored clothing on the weekends, and even allowing herself to wear makeup that wasn't neutral and businesslike. Like most Standstills, she needed a lot of time and practice even to begin feeling comfortable with these behaviors.

After working with me for many months, Julie found the courage to take an evening class on the art of flirting. She was embarrassed to attend the class at first, but afterward reported with excitement that she'd found it liberating and empowering. She told me she hadn't realized that she could signal her interest to a man with simple behaviors, such as maintaining eye contact just a little longer, smiling broadly from across a room, and tilting her head. While some of the women in the class—who, like Julie, hadn't dated in years—were cynical about these suggestions and labeled them "phony," Julie was heartened to know that there was a way she could adjust her actual behaviors to reflect her emotions, which she had difficulty accessing. As she put it, it was easier to act as if she were attracted to a man than to let herself feel just how attracted she really was, because that made her feel extremely nervous and vulnerable at the same time.

Eventually she tried out her new skills at a cocktail party, using them on a man she found very handsome and funny. He responded by flirting back, which made her a little nervous, but she didn't back off or become cool and distant. Though nothing came of this interaction after the party, it really boosted her confidence.

Correcting Distorted Thinking

Standstills often feel they have to measure up to a high standard, which was the message they got in childhood. They constantly feel they are falling short, and beat themselves up for not meeting their goals, so they get stuck comparing. Audrey invented fictional boyfriends because she felt so miserable and ashamed whenever she compared herself to other women. She felt she had to compete, and believed she couldn't do it in reality, so she made up stories in which she was able to attract men. If you feel pressured to impress others with a more exciting past than you've had, focus on the future, and simply tell people who inquire, "I'm not with anyone now, but I'm definitely looking!"

If you feel ill at ease about trying to flirt with men, and cling to the distorted thought, *I'm not like other women; I can't attract and charm a man,* I assure you, there are many beautiful, fascinating women who have also felt that way. Remember that it is a distortion, and that there is nothing productive about comparing yourself to other women who you think are more successful at attracting men than you are.

Many Standstills who are not in a relationship, even if they have romantic prospects, tend to believe that they aren't the "type" of woman men are attracted to. They also believe their past dictates their future, so they have no chance of finding love. They engage in fortune-telling. If you find yourself predicting a dire future, make a point of noticing it and reminding yourself that making the smallest shift in your behavior, thoughts, and feelings can change everything. I have heard many wonderful stories about women who went for long stretches without a man but who did the inner work on the beliefs that were holding them back. Then they met the right guy and entered a fulfilling, committed relationship so quickly that they were frankly a little disoriented.

When you make the shift, you might be surprised at how speedily things turn around. Julie told me her long-standing belief, *I will never attract a man,* was shattered that day at the cocktail party, and I was very encouraging of her, but I knew that the habit of fortune-telling was a hard one to break. In fact, she did fall into it again sometimes, but she would catch herself and correct the distorted thinking.

This is where faith comes in: faith in yourself, faith in the process of opening yourself up and making yourself more attractive by sending out signals that you are receptive to a man's attention, and faith in the universe providing someone who is right for you.

Because the Standstill can go for such an extended period of time without a romance, it's easy for her to fall into the trap of believing that external circumstances drive relationships. She thinks she has no control over her lack of prospects. Moreover, with so little experience being in relationships, the Standstill will often idealize what a relationship could do for her. I've heard Standstills say they will never feel beautiful and womanly until they attract a man who sticks with them, but it doesn't work that way. If you are not feeling sexy and desirable, you will be insecure about your desirability, even if men are always telling you that you're totally hot. By not dealing with your own feelings of sexual inadequacy, and expecting a man to make you feel sexy, you set yourself up for failure. No amount of reassurance from him will be enough, and eventually the man may get tired of having to convince you that he finds you attractive. When you work on your distorted beliefs and start believing that you really are sensual, sexy, and desirable, you will start projecting that belief and feeling confident in it, and men will respond.

See Yourself with New Eyes

We live in a world where the media and advertising bombard us with airbrushed images of women with impossible bodies and faces. (In fact, the models don't even look like they do on the magazines, and they often have poor self-images.) Recently, one of my clients showed me a fashion magazine from the 1970s and pointed out how meaty some of the models were compared to today—these were the images she saw as a child, and even then she thought they were impossible to attain, and now, of course, the models are even thinner, with perfect muscle tone. No wonder women have such difficulty feeling attractive.

If you limit how much time you spend looking at idealized images of feminine beauty and balance them a bit with images of more realistic female bodies, it will be easier to perceive yourself as sexy and desirable. Look at yourself with new eyes. If you've focused too much on your thighs or your hair, really look at how beautiful your smile is, or how clear your skin is.

Everyone has physical assets; notice yours, and don't shy away from showing them off.

When you find yourself thinking you're not measuring up to some other woman, stop yourself. Take the time to think through what it is about the other woman that you find intimidating—whether it's a woman you met or know in real life or a celebrity or model you're comparing yourself to. Is it her physical beauty that makes you feel you can't measure up? Her ease in her body as she moves on the dance floor? Her ability to flirt with a man? Whatever the quality is, ask yourself, what is preventing you from having or expressing that quality?

Sometimes closing your eyes and visualizing yourself looking stunning as you exchange witty banter with a man can help you to feel more in touch with your attractiveness. Dancing sensuously, even alone at home in your apartment, can put you in touch with your sexuality, as well, making it easier to embrace this new belief that you are desirable just as you are.

Mission: Flirtation

If you are a Standstill, you probably are thinking, *Well, it's clear that I have a lot of work to do on myself. I can't expect to attract a man right now or put energy into that, when I have to pay attention to myself and do all this internal work.* A zeal for making changes is a very good thing. That said, enough with the excuses. You're going to flirt with a man or go out on a date this week. Not next week, not next month, not when you're feeling truly ready to do so—this week. You have your homework assignment!

Many of you may have gotten into the habit of keeping

yourself so busy that you think, *I can't possibly do it this week. I'll just make a mental note to try this out later.* Resist the temptation to put this off. It's extremely important to stop blocking yourself from moving forward. Believe me, next week you'll have an even better excuse for not getting past your fear and doing this assignment.

What I'm asking can seem very scary, and you might feel a little panicky. Thoughts like, *I don't have any clothes that will make a man notice me,* or, *What if the guy thinks I'm unattractive and gives me the cold shoulder?* may pop up. Trust me, men *love* to be flirted with. If he becomes uncomfortable or gives you the brush-off, that's okay. Some men will reject you, and you'll reject some men; that's part of dating, and it's no reflection on how desirable and attractive you are. Don't start obsessing about why he didn't respond the way you wanted him to. The purpose of this exercise is simply to start getting you over your fear and inertia, not to get into a relationship. Think of this as practice.

You can smile broadly and crack a joke with the guy in the deli who assembles your chicken salad, or with the waiter at lunch or the parking lot attendant. You can flirt with a man in a chat room online, or flirt with a man who posted a personal ad on Match.com or another singles site. It doesn't matter how you flirt or whom you flirt with. The point is to *act as if* this behavior didn't feel artificial and then keep acting that way until it feels natural and comfortable.

When you've completed that task, I want you to find a way to reward yourself, because it is no small feat to break your habit of isolation, get in touch with your sensuality and femininity, and express it through flirting. Then, over the next month, make some specific goals for yourself to build on this foundation. You might decide that every day, you will flirt with some man. Or, you might decide that you'll flirt with a man at least twice a week, and make a point of letting your friends and family know that you are interested in being fixed up with someone. You can start the process of placing a personal ad. Many dissatisfied singles get very uptight about the photo for the ad and exactly what to say. You don't have to do it by yourself. Ask your friends to help you describe yourself and choose an appropriate photo.

I also want you to work on your confidence about your desirability. Again, *acting as if* can go a long way. If you were confident in your body, what kind of clothing would you dress in? If you were confident in your femininity, would you feel comfortable with flowery prints or delicate jewelry, bright colors or a softer hairstyle, and so on? Think about what you would look like and act like when talking to an attractive man, if you felt assured of your desirability. From that picture of yourself, you can start making the changes in how you present yourself and how you act that will lead you to being more attractive, and more confident in your attractiveness.

New Beliefs, New You

As you become more comfortable with your sensuality, let go of your need to have your parents approve of it. They may never feel at ease with your womanliness, but that's their issue to work on, not yours. Continue to embrace this aspect of yourself and validate your feelings, rather than looking outside yourself for confirmation that you are a beautiful, desirable woman. Remember, the images of women you see in advertising and the media are retouched by computer, and those women themselves often have to go to extraordinary lengths to keep up their appearance, which doesn't necessarily make them happy. Don't give in to the temptation of comparing your attractiveness with theirs.

Like my client who bought into the distorted thinking that heavyset women can't find boyfriends—until her girlfriend, who was heavier than she was, got into a relationship with a wonderful guy—you need to be careful not to maximize the evidence that men aren't attracted to women like you, or minimize the evidence that they are. As you make a point of getting in touch with your beauty, vulnerability, and sensuality, you will become more comfortable with these aspects of yourself and because of that, you will attract more men. It will be hard to break the habit of telling yourself, *He's not really interested in me* because you've constantly reinforced the belief that men don't find you sexy and alluring. Every day that you work to reinforce your healthier beliefs about yourself, it will be easier to embrace the romantic opportunities that begin to present themselves—and believe me, they will appear.

6.

The Forbidden Fruit Hunter

The Forbidden Fruit Hunter is usually loads of fun, great at entertaining, and as social as can be. She's a people person who can be the life of the party or the most successful sales associate in the company. Consequently, she finds it easy to make friends. Her friends consider her wonderfully loyal, and this trait makes her valued in the workplace, as well. When it comes to men, she has no problem connecting with them and sparking a romance.

However, in all her relationships, the Forbidden Fruit Hunter has difficulty staying emotionally attached. She has a few people in her life that she is very close to, but she will suddenly pull back from them, needing her space, and leaving them confused about why someone they feel such a connection to would disappear for long periods of time and then come back. The Forbidden Fruit Hunter doesn't know why she is compelled to distance herself, because she's unaware that too much intimacy makes her feel smothered. She thinks she loves having that close connection, but sustained intimacy is simply too uncomfortable for her. When it comes to romantic partners, she unconsciously chooses a man who will not be able to stay connected to her. If the man isn't actually married to another woman, or living with someone, he is the walking wounded, still hung up on his ex, and emotionally unavailable.

The Forbidden Fruit Hunter either doesn't recognize what she's getting into or doesn't want to accept what the situation is, and is far too optimistic about her partner's potential for emotional loyalty and true intimacy with her. When she begins dating a man, she may know he is involved with another woman, but she convinces herself that his relationship with that woman is over and there's a legitimate reason why he's still living with her, sleeping with her, talking to her on the phone every day, and so on. The other woman may be a wife who he claims doesn't understand him and won't agree to a divorce, or a live-in girlfriend who he claims is just a good friend and nothing more. The Forbidden Fruit Hunter may believe that after a short time of being in a new romance, he'll move on from his grief over his beloved wife who died suddenly last year, or his girlfriend who left him after nine years to marry someone else. Or, the Forbidden Fruit Hunter suspects or even knows her new man is bisexual and can't commit to having a long-term, monogamous relationship with her, but she keeps telling herself that somehow his feelings will change.

In fact, often the Forbidden Fruit Hunter continues to pursue a man after he has openly admitted to her that he's married, or living with someone, or feels he'll never get over the wife he lost. If she sees her pattern of getting into relationships with men whose hearts are already spoken for, she'll come up with red herrings like, "I can't help it. All the good ones are taken," "Men are all cheaters," "I just have the worst luck with men," or "With me and guys, the timing is never right." On some level, she may recognize that it's not the timing and the men that are holding her back from finding lasting love; it's something in herself that is contributing to the situation.

Are You a Forbidden Fruit Hunter?

1. Do you find yourself consistently attracted to guys who turn out to be married or emotionally unavailable for some other reason?

2. Are you ashamed or angry at yourself for continually ending up with unavailable men?

3. Do you often reject nice guys who are clearly not involved with another woman?

4. Are you too quick to believe that a man you're dating is really over his ex and devoted to establishing a monogamous relationship?

5. Did you grow up in a single-parent home?

6. Did you feel that your single parent needed your protection and caretaking?

7. Do you feel obligated to call your parent (or a sibling) daily or almost daily to check in and to take care of him or her practically and emotionally?

(Continued)

8. Do you have great difficulty saying no to your parent (or a sibling)?

9. Do you feel you ought to tell your parent (or sibling) everything about yourself, and have no secrets?

10. Do you have a sibling you feel you had to protect from harm because you couldn't rely on your parents to do that?

The more questions you answered YES to, the more likely it is that you are a Forbidden Fruit Hunter.

Two Key Patterns

The Forbidden Fruit Hunter is usually deeply uncomfortable with herself because she is often "the other woman." She is not the type to deliberately try to pry a man away from someone else. Instead, the Forbidden Fruit Hunter consistently finds herself attracted to unavailable men, and she genuinely doesn't know why she has this pattern. She insists that she really does want a partner of her own, and will often point out how hard she's worked at her relationships as evidence of how much she wants a permanent connection. She has extended more trust than most women would extend, she's been understanding, loyal, and incredibly patient, but her partners always remain half in and half out of their relationships with her.

The Forbidden Fruit Hunter has another behavior pattern she usually doesn't recognize: She is overly attached to a parent—or in some cases, a sibling. These are women who call their family member every day whether they want to or not, or who may call less often but feel obliged to tell them absolutely everything, from the details of their sex lives to their emotional temperature of the moment. Sometimes they resent this parent and sometimes they are completely devoted to him or her and defensive about their dedication. The other parent is out of the picture, having left the family long ago through death, divorce, desertion, or illness.

When the Forbidden Fruit Hunter is overly attached to a sibling instead of a parent, she will focus far too much energy on her brother's or sister's life and too little on her own. This attachment to the parent or sibling stands in the way of the Forbidden Fruit Hunter's getting really close to a man.

The Unintentional Affair

She may be naïve, or she may simply have been lied to, but the Forbidden Fruit Hunter usually enters a relationship with a man thinking that he is emotionally available when in fact, he isn't. If he's married and admits it, she will believe his story that he's going to get divorced, and it may be a very plausible one— but she won't press him for specifics. She's unaware that deep down, she is comforted by the fact that with him, she won't achieve true intimacy. If he says he is not married, she is not likely to go looking for clues that he actually is, or that he's got a girlfriend already. If he's still pining for a woman he's no longer with, she will downplay the importance of his connection to her, because again, she knows on a subconscious level that he isn't available, and for her, that feels safe.

Alyssa, forty-two, was a vivacious Jewish woman from Long Island, and a classic example of a Forbidden Fruit Hunter who got involved with an unavailable man quite unintentionally. After it ended, she entered therapy because she was tired of having her relationships end with a whimper or a bang, never with a wedding ceremony. Alyssa had her share of boyfriends over the years, and briefly lived with a partner once, much to the dismay of her mother, JoAnn. When she came to me, Alyssa had just ended a relationship with a married man that lasted for three years, which she had kept secret from her mom and her entire close-knit extended family.

Alyssa explained that she had not known that her boyfriend, Mark, was married until after they'd been going out for four months and were having sex. She'd been ignoring what seemed to me like obvious signs that he was married, such as never being available on weekends for more than a few hours here or there. Alyssa told me she was shocked and hurt by the unexpected news, but continued the relationship because she bought Mark's story that his wife was very religious and wouldn't agree to a divorce, and that he lived with her only for the sake of their kids and because he didn't have enough money to finance an apartment for himself as well as pay child support. He reassured her that as soon as his youngest child finished high school, he would end the marriage and marry Alyssa. Three years passed, the boy graduated, Alyssa confronted Mark about his commitment to her, and he dropped the bomb that he'd decided he could never leave his wife. Alyssa was devastated.

Part of Alyssa's pain came from shame. She felt as if she should be wearing a scarlet letter on her chest for having slept with a married man, and she was beating herself up, saying she deserved this ill treatment—that she'd been stupid and wrong to have stayed in the relationship. She felt very guilty for not letting her mother know what had happened, and she was anxious about her mother's many questions about her recent moodiness and crying bouts.

On top of all of this agony, she still was in love with Mark. She felt there was no one else out there for her, and looking back on her relationships with men over the years, she felt doomed to end up yet again with an unavailable man.

Alyssa's Backstory: The Origins of the Forbidden Fruit Hunter

As a child, Alyssa had been extremely close to her mother, JoAnn, and JoAnn felt that of all her three children, Alyssa was the most like her. She loved to tell people that Alyssa and she were best friends. Alyssa's relationship with her father was not nearly so close. She was afraid of him and his temper; he was stern, cool, and distant, except for when he got angry. Then he became sarcastic and verbally abusive toward the family, but mostly toward JoAnn. Alyssa has vague memories of him taking a belt to some of her brothers once or twice, but mostly she remembers wishing he would just go away so that the tension and pain would stop. When she was thirteen, he died in a car crash, and life was never the same again.

JoAnn worked long hours trying to keep her husband's storage and moving business afloat to support her children and herself after the father died. As the eldest, Alyssa was the child her mom relied on the most. Alyssa felt guilty and responsible for her father's death, partly because he happened to die when he was out buying her a treat (which he rarely did for her), and partly because as a very little girl, she had sometimes wished him dead, and in her young, subconscious mind, she believed that God somehow granted her wish. Because she felt responsible, and because she was by nature a very reliable girl, she took over where her father had left off. She made sure her younger brothers did their homework and their chores, she gave her mother emotional support, and she kept her own fears and sorrow to herself so as not to burden her mom.

Forbidden Fruit Hunters almost always come from family backgrounds with circumstances such as illness, death, or absence of a parent. If either the mother or father is missing, the Forbidden Fruit Hunter assumes his (or her) emotional and other responsibilities, which includes being the best friend, emotional support, and surrogate spouse to the remaining parent. Occasionally, both parents are in the family, but one suffers from mental illness, a disease, or a disability that renders him almost helpless and the other parent is too distracted or distraught to nurture the children. The Forbidden Fruit Hunter steps in practically as well as emotionally, becoming enmeshed with the strong parent and fulfilling an adult role.

Sometimes, the family member that the Forbidden Fruit Hunter is overly involved with is a sibling. When at least one parent neglects his or her role as a parent to the Forbidden Fruit Hunter and her sibling, the Forbidden Fruit Hunter may put aside her own needs in order to nurture her brother or sister. One of my clients, Phoebe, was overly attached to her gay brother. She'd moved to New York City with him after he came out to their parents in a small town in Alabama and their parents had utterly rejected him. Emotionally taking care of her brother, like emotionally taking care of a parent, distracted her from her own hidden discomfort with intimacy.

Phoebe had always been protective of her sensitive brother, so when he came out of the closet at age nineteen and announced he was gay, she felt it was her duty to shield him not only from the pain their parents could inflict upon him, but also from any rejection he might receive from anyone in the community. She got him to move to New York City with her, found him a job, and focused totally on his needs. Her social life revolved around going with him and his friends to gay bars, or talking about gay issues with her two heterosexual female friends, both of whom were involved with gay men themselves. When she finally began meeting men (at her brother's urging), she kept ending up with gay men or men who turned out to be involved with other women. In fact, she came to therapy because her brother insisted that she needed some help, and it was difficult for her to get past the idea that there was a reason she should examine her behavior patterns that went beyond just making her concerned brother happy.

The Caretaking Role

Phoebe's choice to live with the loved one she was so close to is typical of this type of dissatisfied single. Because the Forbidden Fruit Hunter takes over for the missing or unavailable parent, she often lives with the parent (or sibling) in order to take care of them practically as well as emotionally. Or, the Forbidden Fruit Hunter may find some other way to maintain her position as the surrogate spouse and parent to her siblings. Alyssa was teased by her brothers for being the "holiday drill sergeant," because she was so dictatorial about how her mother's birthday should be handled each year. She expected her brothers to prove their loyalty to their mother by gathering in the family home for a "proper" observance of mom's special day, bringing all their children, an appropriately lavish present, and all her mother's favorite foods from gourmet delis and bakeries. If someone couldn't make it, or brought the pastries from the wrong bakery, Alyssa got angry and accusatory.

The Forbidden Fruit Hunter isn't just close to her parent or sibling, she's emotionally consumed by her relationship with them, even if they say they are ready to create distance, as Phoebe's brother insisted he was. She feels that if she pulls away, she'll be abandoning her loved one the way he (or she) was abandoned by the spouse (or parents). In return for her loyalty, the Forbidden Fruit Hunter often receives the love and approval she seeks, which reinforces her behavior pattern. If she does pull away, the parent or sibling will subconsciously try to pull her back into the old dynamic. What they say and how they actually behave are two different things.

That leaves the Forbidden Fruit Hunter emotionally unavailable for a partner of her own, so on a subconscious level, she is drawn to men who give her signals that they are not ready for a loving, committed, monogamous relationship with her. She feels unworthy of that type of relationship, scared that she can't possibly be a good enough girlfriend, and worried that she will be betraying her parent (or sibling) by making her partner a priority over her family. She also feels guilt at the thought that she would be neglecting her parent (or her sibling, if that is the family member she is overly attached to). Thus, the Forbidden Fruit Hunter remains emotionally closed off to the possibility of a committed relationship.

Hidden Beliefs

"IF I COMMIT TO A RELATIONSHIP,
I'LL BE BETRAYING AND EMOTIONALLY
KILLING MY MOM (OR DAD OR SIBLING
—WHOMEVER SHE IS EMOTIONALLY
MARRIED TO)."

The Forbidden Fruit Hunter's loyalty to her parent or sibling runs so deep that she subconsciously believes that replacing them as the primary person in her life with a man she loves is a deep act of betrayal that will cause her loved one great harm. In Alyssa's case, that belief was further reinforced after her father died. Although she never told anyone, Alyssa blamed herself for having somehow caused his death. As an adult, she could see this was completely irrational reasoning—after all, he could've died in a car crash going to get the paper instead going to get ice cream for her, and he certainly didn't die because she had been angry with him a lot and at times had thought, *I wish he were dead!* I was impressed that Alyssa was conscious of this painful, childhood belief, because so often a child will completely repress such a thought. What Alyssa wasn't conscious of was how that thought led her to another hidden belief that was just as destructive: *If I leave mom and cause her pain, she could die too.* This very idea was so terrifying that she was highly skeptical when I suggested that she had internalized it and was still acting on it.

Another variation I've heard is, "I can't marry this man and move across the country. It would kill my mother." Of course, such an action wouldn't actually kill anyone's parent, but on a subconscious level, the Forbidden Fruit Hunter truly believes that it would be devastating to her mother, so she can't allow herself to pursue the relationship.

"I'M NOT WORTHY OF A PARTNER. I'M TOO NEEDY."

Because she is playing the role of a surrogate spouse to the parent, and has been strongly encouraged to play that role, the Forbidden Fruit Hunter feels her value lies only in what she can do for her parent. She did not have her own needs validated and met, so she believes that her needs are a burden to others and not worthy of attention. If she were worthy and her needs were legitimate back when she was younger, she reasons, her parent would have acted like a parent toward her, and would have found a way to meet their own needs without depending so much on their daughter.

Of course, the Forbidden Fruit Hunter doesn't recognize this belief when she is an adult. Instead, she simply is uncomfortable around available men and finds herself avoiding them, while being drawn to men who can give her love without the commitment. She fears that if a man really were devoted to her, he would discover how needy she is, be repulsed, and leave. A man who is already spoken for is a safe partner, because she knows he won't come too close.

Say No to Unavailable Men

If you want intimacy, you have to stop distracting yourself with relationships that stay at a surface level and that allow you to conceal who you really are and never discover who he really is. You can't do that unless you commit to ending any relationship the moment you recognize that the man is not emotionally available to you.

Some men will come right out and tell you that they're not ready for a relationship. If you hear this, take it at face value. Don't talk yourself into believing he's just shy, or feeling vulnerable at the moment, and that he really wants you to ignore what he's saying and reassure him. If he says it, he has a reason for saying it. Respect his self-assessment and move on *immediately*.

Other men will mislead you about their situation, either deliberately or because they aren't sure what it is. A man who is in an ambiguous relationship with a woman will often get involved with a new woman, thinking in the back of his mind that things will sort themselves out eventually but for now he shouldn't deny himself the pleasure of starting up with a new partner who is interested in him.

There are clues that a man is still involved with another woman:

- *He can't stop talking about his ex.* Whether he speaks fondly of her or insists angrily that she ruined his life doesn't matter: if she's a common topic of his conversation, he's still hung up on her, and he's not available to you.

- *He can't talk or get together with you except on his terms, at odd hours.* If a man has many excuses for why he can't take a phone call at the moment, or why he can't spend an important holiday with you, or why he prefers to meet over lunch and on certain evenings, he is not necessarily lying to you. However, if you are a Forbidden Fruit Hunter, and you find yourself in this situation, end it. It's much more likely than not that he's seeing another woman.

After all, getting involved with men who are already taken is your pattern, and you need to start becoming attuned to those signals.

- *He blows hot and cold.* Men who cancel dates at the last minute and then come on strong with invitations for a romantic weekend getaway, or who don't call for weeks and suddenly are all over you, have an intimacy issue. It's likely that when he's not available, he's involved with another woman. Let him go.

- *He lives with another woman.* It might be his best friend from college, and he might get miffed when you suggest that he and she are more than just pals, but you need to assume the worst here because of your pattern. If this woman is his sister or his mother, observe the situation closely and see if he isn't a Forbidden Fruit Hunter, too, overly involved with a family member and unavailable for a committed relationship with you. There are men who are unambiguously available. Hold out for one of them.

If a man is actually married and admits it to you, don't accept any vague excuses he offers for why it's okay for him to start a relationship with you. Ask him some hard questions, right away: "How long ago did you separate from her? Do you still live with her? Where are you in the divorce process? Do you have any children? What is your situation with them?" Don't let yourself get caught up in the romantic notion of "let's see what happens and what fate has in store for us." Yes, those tough questions may kill the romance, but you must know the answers, and once you do, you have to stop yourself from distorting them in order to justify getting involved with him.

If his answers satisfy you, you still need to be very cautious about any man who is legally married. For example, maybe he really is going to court next week and finalizing the divorce, and he is the one who left, and he felt the marriage had been dead for several years. The actual divorce can stir up many different feelings that he's trying to avoid, and on some level he may be thinking that by getting himself into a relationship he can dull the pain of the end of his marriage. Ask questions, pay attention to the answers, and tread very carefully.

Correcting Distorted Thinking

It's very hard for the Forbidden Fruit Hunter not to minimize any bad news that a potential partner tells her about his situation with another woman, but it's crucial that she not engage in this kind of distorted thinking. Be totally honest with yourself about his availability right up front, before you get really stuck on him!

Another common distortion is personalizing. After a relationship ends, because you were aware of the other woman, or his inability to disconnect from his ex, and yet chose to be with him anyway, you're likely to feel terribly guilty and blame yourself. I want you to get past blaming yourself, or him, and recognize that you fell into a behavior pattern that you were unaware of for reasons you were unaware of. Now you know better, and you are going to do your best not to make the same mistake. Don't beat yourself up for the past, and don't start labeling yourself. Labeling will keep you stuck in self-loathing and guilt and prevent you from getting past the hidden beliefs that are causing you to date married, engaged, and spoken-for men. It's far better to solve the problem than get stuck feeling awful about yourself.

The need to be involved with an unavailable man, and to convince herself that he really is available, is so strong that it can lead a Forbidden Fruit Hunter to engaging in emotional reasoning. One of my clients was in a relationship with a guy for two years, and regularly reported that things felt so wonderful, that they'd spent the weekend making love passionately, or picnicking in the country and talking about their future together, or confiding their deepest fears to each other. One day, she came in shell-shocked because she'd found out he had been cheating on her for close to a year, and now he was leaving her. As we explored the situation, we discovered she had been using emotional reasoning all along and had not allowed herself to pay attention to the now obvious clues that he wasn't all that committed to her—for instance, there had been many nights when she couldn't reach him on his cell phone, and he would always give the excuse that he was out with his buddies and couldn't hear the ringer. She had always felt uneasy about this excuse, but then he would show up and it would feel so nice to be with him that she didn't ask any hard questions and she disregarded her suspicions.

I also find that the Forbidden Fruit Hunter is especially prone to falling into the trap of believing that external circumstances drive relationships and the trap of believing that hanging in there always results in a reward. When I urge a Forbidden Fruit Hunter to set boundaries with her parent or give an ultimatum to her boyfriend, she will often insist that if she just helps her mother though this particularly difficult time or offers her boyfriend a little more patience and understanding, everything will get much better. Even when she admits that the relationship is holding her back from what she wants, she feels compelled to hang on to it, because it's difficult to change and scary to think about being truly intimate with an available man, thanks to her hidden beliefs. She will pile on the excuses for why she can't pull away just now, and why she has to keep sacrificing. When that happens, I challenge her to take specific actions to extricate herself from those problematic relationships.

Break Away

In addition to breaking away from the man who is not capable of giving you what you wants, as a Forbidden Fruit Hunter, you face the challenge of breaking away from the parent or sibling you deeply love, and setting boundaries so that you can focus on meeting your own needs and finding the romantic connection you desire.

Making this break requires letting go of a lot of fear. First, there is the fear that if you say no to your parent and let them fend for themselves even in the smallest way, you are hurting them deeply. You know your mother won't die if you don't call her every day, and that if she works herself up worrying about whether you're okay because you didn't check in, that is her issue to deal with, not yours. Reassure her that you do care, and you will check in regularly, but explain that when you have to call every day it takes away from the joy of connecting to her. Setting a small boundary like this may well upset your parent, but it's important to do.

Your parent may surprise you with a willingness to create a little distance between the two of you. When you're benefiting from someone's attention, it's hard to speak up and say, "Really, you don't have to do that for me"—and if your loved one has said this to you, you probably dismissed them, so they gave up trying to get you to stop fussing. Phoebe's brother was very happy that she decided to take my advice, stop focusing so much on him, and work on developing relationships and friendships of her own. He even helped her place a personal ad and encouraged her to date, which she had begun to give up on because she had so often ended up with men who had girl-friends and were hiding it. Alyssa's mother was very resistant to Alyssa's new, stronger boundaries at first, but over the course of many months, she became more accepting, and even began dat-ing herself, which she hadn't done in years. Freed from her en-meshment with her daughter, JoAnn was finally open to the possibility of emotionally connecting with a man again.

You may find that if you pull away from your loved one and focus on yourself that you feel anxious. Because you're no longer distracted by thinking about them or dealing with their needs all the time, your difficult emotions, which you were pushing aside, may emerge. For instance, Alyssa discovered that she was harboring anger and resentment toward her mother and allowed herself to feel these long-repressed emotions. Rather than run away from these feelings, it's important to start think-ing about what sort of boundaries you could set with your loved ones that would make you feel more comfortable and less imposed upon. When you do so, you'll find yourself enjoying them more and resenting them less.

New Beliefs, New You

At first, it can be hard to grasp that your deep enmeshment with your parent or sibling is interfering with your ability to sustain an emotional connection with a lover, but as you set clearer boundaries with your loved one, and stick to them, you will make a huge shift. You'll get rid of the old hidden belief, "My parent (or sibling) can't live without my constant attention" and replace it with the healthy belief, "He (or she) can manage just fine without me," which will free you from feeling guilty when you get close to a romantic partner. An emotionally intimate romance won't make you feel as if you're betraying or abandoning your loved one.

What's more, by acknowledging your deepest, hidden emotions and working through them, and nurturing yourself better than you have in the past, you'll eliminate the old, unproductive belief: "I am not worthy of love because I'm far too needy." You won't be looking for someone or something to fill the void, because you'll be filling it—with positive thoughts and feelings about yourself. Remember to give yourself plenty of credit, kudos, and rewards. Your self-discipline and drive, which have served you so well, are wonderful qualities that will help you to reshape your life to give it more balance. When you stand up for yourself and say no to someone's unreasonable demands, or your own unfairly high expectations of how you should act in order to please and placate other people, be proud, and pat yourself on the back. That is hard work for a Forbidden Fruit Hunter.

When you get in the habit of treating yourself well and valuing yourself, you won't be attracted to a man who can offer you only a certain level of intimacy and no more. You'll be certain that you deserve better, and you won't be emotionally hooked into trying to earn his loving attention. Instead, you'll move on, knowing that the man who can give you what you want is out there, and now you'll be able to recognize him.

7.

The Compassionate Rescuer

The Compassionate Rescuer is dependable and kind, and very understanding and accepting of other people and their failings. She probably has a career in the helping professions, such as nursing, teaching, or social work, and feels compelled to go that extra mile, whether or not she gets paid overtime. She's got a heart of gold and is such a great friend, daughter, aunt, sister, and community member that it seems terribly unfair that she's always winding up with a guy who has serious problems.

Her partner may be an alcoholic or have another addiction, such as gambling or using drugs. In other instances, he has plenty of friends and a great career, but he also has an anger management problem, psychological problems, or a mental illness, and no matter how much the Compassionate Rescuer pleads with him, he won't do what he has to do to address the problem, whether it's get therapy or take medication. He may simply be unable to hold down a job, floating from a friend's couch to his mom's house until the Compassionate Rescuer swoops in to give him shelter, a meal, and a pep talk. She will devote all her attention and energy to him as she tries to help him solve his problems, and yet these men will often turn sullen and resentful toward her. She seems destined to be alone, or hooked up with a guy who's a fixer-upper.

Are You a Compassionate Rescuer?

1. Do you always fall for the guy who "needs" you, whether he "needs" you emotionally, physically, or financially?

2. Is it hard for you to say no to your partner, family members, and friends?

3. Do you feel responsible for ensuring the livelihood of at least one of your parents or siblings?

4. Do you experience a great amount of guilt if you do something for yourself while you know a loved one is unhappy?

5. Do you make excuses for your boyfriends' drinking, gambling, verbal abuse, or other destructive behavior?

6. As a child, were you the one in the family that everyone could count on, not just to do your homework without being told but also to support your parents practically and emotionally?

(Continued)

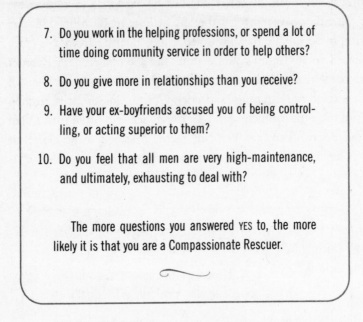

7. Do you work in the helping professions, or spend a lot of time doing community service in order to help others?

8. Do you give more in relationships than you receive?

9. Have your ex-boyfriends accused you of being controlling, or acting superior to them?

10. Do you feel that all men are very high-maintenance, and ultimately, exhausting to deal with?

The more questions you answered YES to, the more likely it is that you are a Compassionate Rescuer.

Wishing, Waiting, and Hoping

Much as we all admire, respect, and appreciate a woman who sacrifices for others and who is compassionate, empathetic, and loving, these wonderful qualities are burdensome for the Compassionate Rescuer. She is so programmed to put other people first that her life is out of balance. She is constantly giving and rarely, if ever, receiving. She buys into the idea that if you want to receive, you need to give even more, and she'll become burned out emotionally, spiritually, and physically trying to earn her reward. Because her entire identity is wrapped up in being a caretaker, she thinks that if she isn't constantly giving, no man will ever love her.

When she does become involved a man, she tends to be extremely optimistic about his potential while overlooking or downplaying his many flaws. She'll hang in there until he ends the relationship, or his behavior deteriorates so badly that she knows she has to walk away. Even then, she feels guilty, wondering if maybe she could have done more for him. She personalizes, telling herself, "It's all my fault."

The Compassionate Rescuer is not a masochist. She really believes that there will be a payoff for her martyrlike behavior, and her life will be great once things change. She has faith that her boyfriend will clean up his act, truly appreciate her at last, and credit her for his amazing turnaround. Despite all the evidence that this isn't likely to happen, she stays in the situation, because she's been programmed to be a caretaker and keep hoping that things will change for the better—and because she thinks she doesn't deserve any better.

Focusing on Him

The Compassionate Rescuer puts all her efforts into caring for the needs of someone other than herself, a man who is very needy and who, for a while at least, gives the Compassionate Rescuer a lot of love and validation for being such a kind, caring, nurturing person. Ultimately, however, she gives so much that she becomes burned out, and his gratitude begins to fade as he becomes more self-absorbed, encouraged by her constantly putting his needs above hers.

Thirty-three-year-old Nicole had been dating Jonathan for just over a year, and was feeling miserable and utterly trapped. Jonathan had a business degree and an excellent record as a salesman and sales manager, but was constantly losing jobs, which he blamed on the boss, or office politics, or anything other than himself. Nicole, however, believed the reason that he was unable to stay employed was that he was too angry and sarcastic. She came to therapy because she felt guilty and anxious whenever she thought about leaving him, but she was too emotionally drained to stay. She told me she had been down this road four times before, with men who were drinkers, or marijuana addicts, or who had emotional problems. She told me she felt she was doomed to play Wendy to some Peter Pan.

Jonathan was thirty-six, and Nicole felt that by this point in his life, he should be settled into his career. When she first met him, she thought he was utterly adorable, with his square jaw, piercing green eyes, and strong shoulders, and he was so charming and seemed so honest that she completely bought into his story of why he was unemployed at the time. Now, however, she could see that he had serious problems with holding down a job.

Nicole, on the other hand, was in a very stable position, working as a special ed teacher in the public schools. The hours were long and the position didn't pay very well, but the children adored her and she was well-respected among her peers. She always had a smile and a ready joke to offer, no matter how tense the situation, and everyone knew they could count on her to solve problems and offer a sympathetic ear. No one would ever guess how bad she was feeling inside and how much emotional abuse she was taking from her boyfriend.

Jonathan had moved in with her shortly after they began a torrid affair. Their living arrangement was supposed to be temporary until he landed a new position. While he did get a new job within two weeks, four weeks later he was fired. It became clear to Nicole that he wasn't going to find his own place anytime soon, but she didn't feel she could ask him to leave, because she couldn't figure out where else he could go. Within a few months, Jonathan's amiable façade slipped, and he became short-tempered. Later, he would apologize and blame it on being under stress. He'd also gotten into the habit of making sarcastic remarks about her low-paying job, criticizing her living habits, and putting her down for almost everything she did, but he did it in a half-joking way and when she complained, he told her she was being far too sensitive.

On top of that, he grumbled and acted hurt whenever she spent time with other people. As a result, Nicole rarely saw her girlfriends anymore and had changed her whole routine to be with him, hoping that would help improve his mood and fuel his enthusiasm for job hunting. She couldn't remember the last time she took yoga, because the class interfered with having dinner with him. And she was spending a lot of time being his cheerleader and coach, only to have him turn surly and negative about his job prospects.

Jonathan did have his good qualities, however. He was great at housekeeping, a fabulous cook, and, Nicole admitted, a fantastic lover. Every time she suggested that he make alternative living arrangements while job hunting, he promised that he'd do his best, and then showered her with appreciative comments and compliments. Yet weeks later, here he was, still unemployed, still in her apartment, and Nicole didn't know what to do.

She sighed as she told me that this was far from the first time she'd gotten involved with a guy who had serious problems functioning, but this was the worst position she'd ever been in, and she was desperate to find a way out that wouldn't hurt or upset him. While Jonathan was clearly taking advantage of her, her focus was on his need to feel good, not hers—a perspective that is very typical of the Compassionate Rescuer.

Nicole's Backstory: The Origins of the Compassionate Rescuer

Inevitably, the Compassionate Rescuer comes from a family where she was thrown into playing the role of caretaker for a parent in need and as an adult, she still feels responsible for that parent's happiness and well-being. She had to care for her parent emotionally, encouraging her mother or father and listening to them complain about their lives. She usually had to care for them practically, as well, making sure dinner was in the oven and that the checkbook was balanced because Mom or Dad wasn't capable of doing it and for whatever reason, the other spouse couldn't play that role. Sometimes, the parent was simply suffering from an illness or was physically disabled in some way. Often, however, there was something going on that the family didn't want to talk about or deal with because there was such stigma attached: mental illness, alcoholism, abuse, or cheating. Rather than acknowledging the unfairness of putting adult burdens on a child, talking with her about her feelings about being put in this position and trying to come up with a better solution to the family problems, everyone pretended that Nicole's caretaking was completely normal and acceptable.

In Nicole's family, her father was in charge yet helpless at the same time, because his wife was a quiet drinker who couldn't seem to handle the demands of adult life or parenting and behaved unpredictably. Nicole's older sister, Charise, always seemed to be off somewhere, while her younger sister, Jeannie, was rebellious and fought any responsibilities, but Nicole was by nature an easygoing and cooperative child, so she picked up the slack for her mother. She cooked and cleaned, made amends to the neighbors and shopkeepers that she feared her mother might have offended when inebriated, and was careful not to bring any friends home from school, so they wouldn't see her mother passed out on the living room couch.

Nicole didn't resent having so many responsibilities. In fact, she was proud of her grown-up behavior and self-reliance, and her father gave her a lot of praise for being his dependable child. While she hated her mother's drinking and her behavior when drunk, she admired her mom for being a warm, funny, creative, and free-thinking person. Before her mother's drinking became a problem, she was an amazing painter whose works had won awards and hung in some celebrities' homes. Nicole wished she had her mother's talent and creativity, and secretly wished that her mother would stop drinking and be inspired to paint again instead of always making excuses and isolating herself.

Like Nicole, many Compassionate Rescuers have mixed feelings about their parents, because they blame the illness or addiction for the worst of the behavior and have some very happy memories of when the parent was at her best. Often, the Compassionate Rescuer is defensive about her childhood, minimizing the impact of the parent's problem out of a sense of loyalty as well as a sense of shame. I will often hear excuses like, "At least my father never hit me," or "People didn't understand my mother's artistic temperament," but none of that changes the fact that the parent's dysfunctional behavior placed the Compassionate Rescuer in a position that was very inappropriate for a child and which deeply affected her—and her relationship patterns.

Hidden Beliefs

"WITHOUT ME, MY PARENT WON'T SURVIVE. WITHOUT ME, MY BOYFRIEND WON'T SURVIVE."

As a child, and often even as an adult, the Compassionate Rescuer believes she is her parent's life support. Without her, they can't survive. If her parents have died or she has pulled away from them, she doesn't get rid of this feeling; she transfers it to the troubled men she gets involved with. Nicole couldn't imagine how Jonathan would survive if she threw him out of her apartment. We had to talk through all the what-ifs—what if he had no place to spend the night, and no access to his possessions? What if she simply changed the locks and put his stuff in the hallway? In the end, she decided to do that, because it was nonconfrontational: She put everything in the hallway, changed the locks, informed the super, and took off for a four-day weekend. She was a nervous wreck, but when she returned, Jonathan was gone, and there wasn't even a message on her voice mail. A few weeks later, he left her a sarcastic message and accused her of acting superior and judging him. It upset her, but I helped her to see that this was coming from his own defensiveness. It's common for men who are constantly on the receiving end of the Compassionate Rescuer's help to turn resentful, and accuse her of being controlling or arrogant in order to avoid dealing with their own feelings of shame. To Nicole's relief, she never heard from Jonathan again.

Sometimes this feeling that the parent or boyfriend can't survive is based in a very real set of circumstances. One Compassionate Rescuer I met took in a boyfriend who was on antidepressants and had attempted suicide; she'd been the one to find him and bring him to the emergency room, and she truly believed that if she sent him packing, he would end his life. Another Compassionate Rescuer was the only child of a single mother, and her mother made it clear that she expected her daughter to make sure Mom woke up in the morning in time to go to work. Then the mother would go out drinking, which was very dangerous because she was diabetic. One morning, the daughter almost didn't check in on her mother because she was so resentful about being put in that position, and when she did, she discovered her mom was in a diabetic coma from her binge the night before. Had she not been there to call the paramedics, her mom probably would have died.

If you're a Compassionate Rescuer, with a parent or boyfriend who is this dependent on you, it can be extremely difficult to set boundaries and pull away from the caretaking role. You may have to work with a therapist to set up a specific plan to create a safety net for this person if you were to leave, and deal with the frightening thought that even so, your loved one might die without you. When addiction is at the core of the parent's or boyfriend's dysfunction, an intervention can be extremely helpful. A trained counselor will work with concerned friends, relatives, and coworkers to confront the addicted person about the effect his behavior is having on them, and they will ask him to enter rehabilitation.

An intervention like this should only be undertaken with the knowledge that it may not work and the addicted person may become very angry or go deeper into denial. Yet if you make this serious effort to get professional help for your partner or parent, even if your efforts are in vain, it can change the way you relate to that person and absolve you of any sense of responsibility for what he (or she) does in the future. Gina, another Compassionate Rescuer, confronted her father about his drinking and then suffered his verbal abuse for staging an intervention. Her dad didn't speak to her for a long time. A couple of years later, Gina made the choice to move across the country for her career, leaving her aging father alone and dependent on his extended family and social services for help, and she did not feel guilty about it. Gina felt she had done what she could for him and was entitled to move on with her life.

"MY VALUE LIES IN WHAT I CAN DO FOR OTHERS. I AM NOT WORTHY OF LOVE UNLESS I'M TAKING CARE OF SOMEONE."

Because she spent so much time acting like an adult when she was a child, the Compassionate Rescuer became hyper-responsible, and her identity is wrapped up in being a rescuer. She is attracted to the helping professions, gives too much in all aspects of her life, and is drawn to men who can't seem to survive without her. She easily assumes the responsibility for her lover's happiness and livelihood. In her relationships, she always has a ready excuse for her man's inability to be an independent adult, and for her enabling him—that is, taking on his responsibilities and protecting him from the consequences of his actions. The Compassionate Rescuer often feels that life is being drained out of her, but just as when she was a child, she doesn't set boundaries and gives everything of herself to "save" the one she loves.

When the Compassionate Rescuer is careful about how much she gives, and to whom, she can experience rewards and appreciation. Knowing that she has a pattern of giving too much for too long to people who aren't capable of reciprocating, she can start to be more vigilant about the men she gets involved with, as well as the friends, family, and coworkers she feels drawn to help.

Tough Love

As a Compassionate Rescuer, you face the challenge of recognizing when you're being overburdened and unappreciated, and mastering the ability to say no firmly, and stick to it. It's easiest to practice being assertive in situations where the rejection and resentment you might receive won't cut so deeply. People enjoy being pampered, and dysfunctional people often have a false sense of entitlement to being taken care of, so you should expect to receive some flak for standing up for yourself and refusing to take care of certain people in your life.

Gina worked on getting over her intimidation by taking baby steps. First, she told an annoying coworker that she would not be able to help him figure out how to do something on the computer, so he should call the company's computer expert instead. Then she told her sister that she would not pick her up from the airport because it was too difficult to fit into her schedule, and was relieved when her sister reassured her that she was fine with Gina's decision. Only after a lot of practice with these low-risk confrontations, and tolerating the discomfort of having people irritated with her, could Gina start confronting her very demanding father about the boundaries she wanted to set with him.

Often, the reason it feels so hard to say no is that you fear the other person will get angry and start arguing with you, and you will have to be mentally quick enough to win the argument in the face of their wrath. If that is the case, remember, you do not have to defend your decision. Give your reason and then just keep repeating: "No. I'm sorry, I just can't." That's what being assertive is. If you stick to your *no* and refuse to get into a discussion of why you're disagreeing, eventually, the other person will give up. It may feel artificial to repeat yourself like a tape loop, but you'd be surprised how effective this behavior can be.

Correcting Distorted Thinking

The Compassionate Rescuer is not used to asserting her own needs, but she's great at advocating for others. She can paint the most flattering picture of her boyfriend because she is a master at minimizing his flaws. She learned to do this in her childhood, when her parents acted as if the debilitated parent's problem was no big deal. They simply accepted it and worked around it, never addressing it. As an adult, the Compassionate Rescuer has a very high tolerance for her partner's dysfunctional behavior (and for that matter, anyone's dysfunctional behavior). She will tell herself that his drinking is not a problem, because he's not doing it alone or he's only drinking beer, or she'll insist that that since she didn't have to pay *all* of his bills this month, just *some* of them, there's no need to confront him about his financial irresponsibility. In her mind, she shrinks all his problems down to a manageable size.

At the same time, the Compassionate Rescuer will try to normalize her experience by engaging in black-and-white thinking: "All men gamble," "You can't find any guy who doesn't have a lot of emotional baggage," "Everyone flips out and starts screaming obscenities at their mate once in a while," "Everyone drinks until they get drunk, it's just part of bar culture around here," "No one understands my boyfriend the way I do," and so on.

She also falls into the trap of believing that external circumstances drive relationships and tells herself that one change in the situation will make everything better, whether it's him getting a job or a lucky break at last, or him following through on his promise not to smoke marijuana for a month because they're both convinced that that will break his addiction for good. In reality, those changes may well help, but there are underlying behavior patterns that won't get magically fixed overnight. Focusing on the future is a great way for her to avoid thinking about her current circumstances. She will look at her mate's potential, or even reminisce about his past behavior, before he developed his problem, rather than be honest about where he is and what he is doing right now.

If you're a Compassionate Rescuer, you might find it especially helpful to use journaling to stay on top of your distorted thinking and your feelings. Looking back at the record of ultimatums you issued, promises that were broken, and excuses you made for him can be painful, but very enlightening.

The Rescuer Takes a Vacation

For the Compassionate Rescuer, taking care of her partner's or her parents' every need requires a lot of time, focus, energy, and money, and it distracts her from her own feelings and needs. Many of those feelings run deep and are very painful, such as fear of what might happen in the future or the feeling that she is unworthy of love. To keep those awful feelings locked up, the Compassionate Rescuer will keep herself busy. Nicole, for example, was the go-to girl at work, going way beyond the call of duty to solve any problem that a coworker was having, partly because it made her feel good about herself, but partly because it kept her so busy that she didn't have to think about her unhappiness.

If her relationship with a man ends, the Compassionate

Rescuer will try to find someone else to take care of right away. It may be a friend in need, or even a cause that she can devote herself to. After Jonathan left, Nicole had to struggle not to become a workaholic again, troubleshooting for other teachers and spending far too much time listening to them complain about workplace politics or their personal problems. The void she felt post-Jonathan needed to be filled by nurturing herself, not falling back into the pattern of rescuing others.

Again, we all benefit from the generous nature of the Compassionate Rescuer, so I don't want to imply that if you are this style of dissatisfied single, you shouldn't give of yourself to others, but it's very important to strike a balance between what you give to others and what you receive for yourself. Constantly focusing on others' needs while neglecting your own is not healthy, and will not help you reach your goal of creating a lasting love of your own.

If you're not able to be a caretaker and be in charge of a situation, you may become very anxious. You're probably not the type to put your feet up and let someone take care of you, because it doesn't feel right to receive. You may get antsy when you have unstructured, open time, because that is when difficult feelings tend to surface.

It's time to take a look at why you're so uncomfortable with taking a break from caring for others, and accept that you must start doing this in order to achieve balance in your life and break away from the pattern of continually sacrificing. You must begin figuring out what your own needs are and attending to them, and letting others help you for a change.

Getting in touch with your needs and wishes can be a real challenge. It requires being more observant of your moods and feelings. What makes you happy? What stresses you out or makes you feel sad or frustrated? When you recognize that you need time away from people to regroup and rejuvenate, or that you experience joy when you engage in a hobby, you need to honor that and schedule it into your life—and keep your commitment to yourself. There will always be demands on your time, and it's too easy to push aside the plans you made for yourself with thoughts like, *But this person really needs me, and I can read that new novel by my favorite author any time,* or *I don't really need to meditate every day; I could get into the office earlier and get some work done if I skip it this morning.* You don't have to tell other people that the important engagement you have Wednesday night that can't be canceled is an appointment with yourself to sketch, paint, practice the piano, watch a movie, or do anything else that gives you pleasure.

Remember, you don't need other people's approval for your choices, and sometimes it's easier not to get into the discussion of what you're doing and why. When it comes to letting others help you out, think of a favor you can ask of a friend, relative, or coworker—something you could do by yourself, but which you are willing to delegate to someone else. If they agree to help you out, allow them to do so without dictating exactly how they should go about the task. For example, if your brother-in-law is going to assemble your new computer, don't hover over him and give him directions. Draw a deep breath when you feel yourself tempted to take charge, and let the other person help you in his own way. Controlling situations and taking complete responsibility for solving problems and getting things done is a long-standing pattern. You will need a lot of practice at being on the receiving end of someone's generosity before it feels comfortable for you.

Keep in mind, too, that when you allow other people to help you, you're giving them an opportunity to feel good about themselves. Why should you be the only one who has a sense of being needed and competent? Share the gift of being able to give to others—allow yourself to receive.

New Beliefs, New You

As a Compassionate Rescuer, you will probably resist letting go of your belief that you have to give to others in order to be loved, because giving comes so easily for you, and caretaking is at the core of your identity. If you aren't giving, who are you, and what is your value?

As you start giving up your need to be in charge, you will probably find yourself confused about who you are, and insecure about your worth. Recognize that this is because of your unhealthy hidden beliefs, which you are going to consciously discard and replace with new beliefs, such as "I am lovable and wonderful just as I am, even when I'm receiving instead of giving." Start taking a look at the people in your life who really love you and express it to you. Do they express their love and admiration to you only when you are giving to them? Or are you forgetting about how much they love your sense of humor, or your enthusiasm, or some other quality?

As you start embracing the you that has been there all along, it will become much easier to express those beautiful qualities you have that you've been overlooking for far too long, and to let go of your identity as the wonder worker who can and will solve any problem. You will stop attracting the men who are looking for a mother, because they will sense that you have strong boundaries and will not let them continually take from you. You'll stop feeling the urge to rescue every wounded man you find and fix his life. Instead, you'll be attracted to strong men who can give to you, and you'll be able to receive their love, affection, and admiration without any ambivalence, creating a healthy balance of give and take.

8.

The Wanderer

The Wanderer is an exciting woman, fully engaged by life. She knows how to get along with a variety of people, and her friends, family, and coworkers think she's a warm and kind person. They probably think they know her very well. However, the reality is that the Wanderer keeps her real self safely hidden away, letting in only a select few people.

The Wanderer is an intense and competitive person, but is able to hide it from those around her. She competes quietly because no matter what she achieves, it's never enough to fulfill her. This intensity and competitiveness can be seen in the way she tends to overindulge in whatever she enjoys; for instance, she's the one who can't just do yoga—she has to do hot yoga and hold the pose longer each time. Yet at the same time, she may overeat, feel guilty, and then overexercise. Her need to fill an inner void is so strong that it drives her to compete with herself, and sometimes with others, giving her all to whatever activity she thinks might fulfill her.

Sometimes her friends deeply admire her zest for living, but other times they wonder why she seems insecure and discontent despite all she's achieved. No matter what her accomplishments, it seems she can't quite get enough reassurance that she's successful, talented, skilled, and beautiful.

She works hard at her career, although her fear of taking risks may hold her back. In romantic relationships, the Wanderer gets an A for effort, because she really does try to make a go of things. She always has a boyfriend, but despite her best intentions, the Wanderer has a wandering eye. Inevitably, she ends up being unfaithful, emotionally or physically. She has no intention of getting involved with another man, but that's exactly what she does, whether or not she actually sleeps with him. She gets involved with a lover on the side even though she feels emotionally committed to the man she's already with, and that makes her feel ashamed and out of control. She's not aware that it isn't an isolated incident but rather part of a behavior pattern. Each time she engages in infidelity, she is confused and embarrassed, and honestly doesn't know why or how she got herself into the situation.

The Wanderer is not collecting men to boost her ego. She's not coldly manipulative or deliberately cruel. In fact, she's often a wonderful, loyal friend, daughter, sister, or employee. Those who know and love her would never guess that she has this big secret. If they ever found out, they would be stunned, because it seems so out of character.

The Wanderer's reason for being unfaithful is not what you'd expect. Her current lover may be attentive and affectionate, but the Wanderer has a very deep sense of neediness that she's not able to fully address. She truly wants just one man, for life, but no man can ever fill the void inside her. She always feels she needs more love, more reassurance, more validation that she's a beautiful, lovable, worthwhile person, and to get that, she finds a second man. However, this behavior never gets her what she wants. She remains anxious and feeling like a bottomless pit of need. Because she's being untrue to her lover, she also feels guilty and awful about herself.

Are You a Wanderer?

1. Do you find it hard to stay faithful (physically, emotionally, or both) in a relationship, even if you truly love your partner?

2. Do you go from one relationship right into the next without any (or little) time in between?

3. Do you get anxious when you're not in a relationship, and yet feel anxious when you are in one with a man who wants to deepen his emotional connection to you?

4. Do you tend to overindulge in things you enjoy, such as shopping, going to clubs, exercising, or eating, and secretly wonder why you can't seem to get "enough" to make you content?

5. Do you feel bad about yourself and look for constant reassurance from others about decisions you make?

6. Do you feel that you were missing emotional nurturing from one or both of your parents?

(Continued)

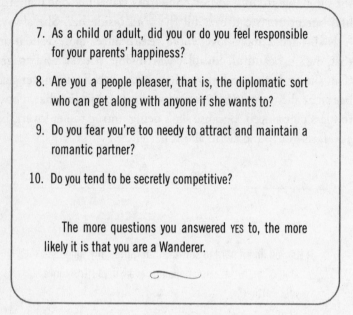

7. As a child or adult, did you or do you feel responsible for your parents' happiness?

8. Are you a people pleaser, that is, the diplomatic sort who can get along with anyone if she wants to?

9. Do you fear you're too needy to attract and maintain a romantic partner?

10. Do you tend to be secretly competitive?

The more questions you answered YES to, the more likely it is that you are a Wanderer.

Looking to Fill the Void

The Wanderer grew up in a home where she didn't get the nurturing she needed, so she has been programmed to seek out that love and attention. She spends her life seeking to fill the emptiness that only a caring parent could fill—and didn't. The Wanderer can't get enough of what she wants, and believes she's unworthy and unlovable, so she's convinced that the only way she can find contentment is if she acquires more and achieves more, and earns the love of other people. As a result, she becomes an overachiever as well as a people pleaser.

The Wanderer is so used to playing the diplomat with people, using her head to solve problems and make sure everyone is content, that she loses track of what is really important to her. Too often, she concerns herself with what other people—particularly her parents—will think and falls out of touch with what she wants. She has a difficult time feeling at peace with herself. Unbeknownst to her, that is the underlying emotional reason for why she can't remain faithful and committed to one man.

Torn Between Two Lovers

Thirty-year-old Amy's ready smile and job as a publicist make it easy for her to find boyfriends, because she is always meeting interesting people and easily strikes up conversations. Currently, she is dating Brian, a journalist, and says she's madly in love with him, but she has a dark secret: She is unfaithful to him. Amy feels horribly guilty, hates her behavior, and is utterly baffled by it—but says she can't help herself. She is terrified she will get caught and Brian will leave her, but has been unable to stop herself from getting together with Steve, her lover.

Amy had a hard time talking about what was going on with her two lovers, and often didn't meet my eye when speaking to me. It was clear she felt ashamed of her behavior, but she explained that whenever she was with Steve, she felt attractive and desirable. When I asked her how she felt with Brian, Amy waffled, explaining that he, too, made her feel attractive and desirable, and that their sex life was great, but the longer she stayed faithful to him, the more anxious and uncomfortable she became. It wasn't that she was looking for a second lover; it's just that she and Steve had hit it off instantaneously and she had "no willpower" when it came to ending the relationship with him.

Often, people assume that a woman who takes a second lover does it because she's sexually insatiable, but that is not the case with the Wanderer. In Amy's case, she found Steve attractive, but not exceptionally so. Sometimes the Wanderer isn't physically unfaithful, but forms an emotional bond with another man. One of the Wanderers I worked with formed a strong bond with a man she began corresponding with on the Internet. Though he lived a thousand miles away from her and they'd never met, or even had a phone conversation, she felt more connected to him than she did to her fiancé.

If the Wanderer is able to be objective about what she wants in a relationship, often, it will be clear which man is more suited to her. Amy felt that Brian was clearly the better boyfriend for her, because they both loved cooking, throwing parties, and going on long bike rides upstate, and they got along beautifully, even when both of them were under stress. What's more, they had both agreed how they might manage having children and yet maintain their careers, working together as a team. Amy couldn't figure out why she felt compelled to be involved with Steve when Brian seemed so "right."

Amy admitted that this wasn't the first time she'd been in this kind of situation, having been drawn into a love triangle in high school, and then again in college. She recognized that this pattern might be causing her to sabotage a relationship that could lead to her achieving her dream of a happy marriage.

I believed Amy when she said her attraction to her lovers on the side wasn't due to lust or selfishness. I could see that she was a Wanderer, searching far and wide for the nurturing she didn't get as a child.

Amy's Backstory: The Origins of the Wanderer

Amy came from a family that seemed, on the surface, to be close-knit. Her father, Philip, was a successful businessman who was known and respected in the community, and her mother, Lucinda, was a homemaker with the sweetest disposition—or, at least that's what everyone said. The inside story was quite different. Amy's father was emotionally distant and in control of everything in the home. And her mother, although sweet, was deferential to her husband in the extreme. She never stood up to him: Amy remembered that she was never allowed to go to sleepovers like the other fourth and fifth graders, and though her mother agreed that her father was being unfair, she wouldn't speak up on Amy's behalf.

Lucinda was distracted by her need to please her husband as well as her own needs. She had immigrated from Eastern Europe and was resentful that she didn't fit into American life and never mastered the language. Moreover, Lucinda missed her family and friends. She relied on Amy to smooth the way for her, translating when she didn't understand, and helping her to deal with the unfamiliar culture.

Amy often wished her father would step in and talk to the landlord about why her mother kept hanging laundry on a clothesline, or to the school about why she and her siblings didn't bring in notes from their parents after absences. Her father was running a restaurant with his brother and worked long hours, so by the time he came home, he just wanted peace and quiet. He didn't want to hear about anyone's problems, and became gruff if Amy tried to explain that she didn't want to have to take on her mother's burdens. Her father would say, "We all have to pitch in and be a team," but he wouldn't be the team's leader and guide, and as a result, his children took on a lot of adult responsibilities. When he was home, he would often retreat into his newspaper or watch baseball and basketball games on TV, making himself unavailable to his family.

Amy and her older brother and younger sister were left to figure out a lot of things on their own, and they weren't always very good at navigating their lives, particularly in adolescence. Her brother, Donnie, started drinking and got in trouble with the law, and her father's response was to ship him off to an out-of-state uncle who he thought could straighten out the boy. When Amy's mother offended the neighbors with her prickly insistence on doing things the way she wanted to do them, Amy and her sister, Cheryl, would cringe in embarrassment, and resent the position their parents put them in. They felt responsible not just for placating annoyed neighbors and taking care of household responsibilities, but also for making both of their parents happy.

I could see that Amy was defensive about her upbringing, because talking about what really happened instead of painting an idealized picture of it for me was helping her to recognize her long-buried anger and resentment, and that was making her feel bad about herself. She had compassion for both her parents, but struggled to square that with the fact that they hadn't been the affectionate, guiding forces she needed them to be. She couldn't remember either of her parents telling her they loved her, although she insists that they must have, and that was a painful realization for her.

The Wanderer feels she not only didn't get her parents' loving attention, but she also couldn't get their approval no matter how hard she tried. Denise grew up in a family where she was constantly playing the diplomat between her mother and father, who had difficulty communicating directly with each other. On top of having to handle the emotional burden of managing her parents' relationship, Denise was also expected to be a model daughter, caring for her younger brothers, cooking, and cleaning so that her mother would be free to do what she felt was important work in the community. Denise's parents and brothers would often ridicule her cooking, or criticize her for not making sure all the laundry was done. They were not particularly harsh people, Denise said, but she was a very sensitive child, and she took their remarks very personally.

Hidden Beliefs

"I'm not worthy of love unless I work for it."

The Wanderer instinctively knows it wasn't right that her parents put her in the position of being overly responsible for the family's needs, but in her childhood, she grudgingly accepted that her parents demanded her practical help with the household. She did not get the nurturing she needed, and whatever love and approval her parents expressed to her was always contingent on what she did for them. As a result, she is constantly looking outside herself for assurance that she really is special, wonderful, and deserving of love.

Because deep down she feels she has to earn the right to be loved, the Wanderer unconsciously pushes herself to be the best and prove that she really is worthy of love. Her overachieving streak can manifest in a lot of different ways, but no matter what she achieves for herself, even if she is wealthier than anyone she knows, more successful, and more acclaimed, she will still hold her dysfunctional hidden belief until she recognizes it and actively decides to reject it. Too often, the Wanderer ends up trying to excel at everything and burns out, or continues to feel empty inside because she's not dealing with her low self-esteem that's causing her to feel she's got to prove herself again and again. While Amy excelled at her job, Denise was an overachiever socially, always remembering everyone's birthday, entertaining, and volunteering to help. In fact, she often clashed with a cousin of hers, Shania, who like Denise would plan family gatherings. Denise was very threatened by Shania encroaching on her territory, because deep down, Denise was afraid that she wouldn't be as good a hostess as Shania was.

With a romantic partner, the Wanderer is fully aware that she's not being a good girlfriend to him because she's unfaithful, and she feels terrible about it. To make up for her infidelity, she may bend over backwards to be the best girlfriend she can possibly be otherwise, and vow to cut off the affair—but she continues to find herself drawn to that other man. The cycle of self-loathing, trying to be a better partner, and unconsciously slipping into emotional or physical infidelity just keeps repeating, whether in this relationship or the next one.

"I AM TOO NEEDY FOR ANY MAN TO STAY WITH ME FOR LONG. I DON'T DESERVE TO BE DEEPLY LOVED BY A MAN."

When the Wanderer is unfaithful, she feels terribly guilty and struggles to figure out why she's behaving that way. She suspects it's because one man isn't enough to make her feel good—that she must be extraordinarily needy—but the thought is so uncomfortable that she quickly pushes it out of her mind. Certain that she's a bottomless pit of need, she fears no one man will be able to fill the void inside her.

Meanwhile, she's afraid that if she is honest with her partner about how much reassurance she needs, she'll be rejected, so she does her best to stay silent and not think about how needy she feels, hoping that the feeling will magically go away—but it never does.

Because she has this emptiness inside her and she feels unworthy of a committed, romantic relationship, true intimacy frightens the Wanderer. When the emotional connection between her and a man is building, she begins feeling unsure about being in the relationship. She starts looking around for an escape—she'll start having an affair, or will line up another lover (although she may not realize she's doing this). Then she'll invent excuses for why the man she is with doesn't measure up, ranging from "He's too into me and I feel smothered" to "I just don't think I can get serious about a man who isn't a vegetarian, like I am."

In those rare moments when she is not involved with a partner, the Wanderer feels especially uneasy and unsettled. She tells herself that the reason she hasn't found a lasting, committed relationship yet is that she doesn't quite know what she wants in a guy. What's really going on is that she is afraid of a deep, emotional connection, and she believes she's not deserving of it, so she finds many ways to avoid creating it with someone.

Valued for Her Role

The Wanderer feels she has to earn the right to be loved and cherished, because nothing she ever did as a child seemed to be enough to make her parents happy. Amy's parents were too caught up in their own responsibilities to nurture her and assure her that she was worthy of being cherished, while Denise got the impression that her family valued her only for what she could do for them. As a result, the Wanderer is very good at being flexible with other people, figuring out what they need, and conforming to their wishes.

In a romantic partnership, however, she soon starts to resent how much work she has to do to make her boyfriend happy. Her relationships can be quite stormy: She strives to be the perfect girlfriend, builds up resentment, quarrels with her man, stomps out, feels regret, and tries to get back together with him again.

Having spent so much energy keeping her parents happy, the Wanderer didn't get to focus much on what her own needs were, so she's genuinely confused about what she really wants. She has some ideas, but the man she is drawn to most is one she can very much influence. She wants to be the special girl he'll never forget, the one who is more exciting than any woman he's ever been with, the one who he'll think of as the most faithful and loving. Yet if he gives her the opportunity to be the most self-sacrificing and wonderful girlfriend ever, she'll be that, but she'll resent it.

Nurture Yourself

Your suspicion that no man can reassure you enough to make you feel good about yourself is based in truth: There is no man, no matter how devoted and wonderful, who can make any woman feel lovable if she doesn't believe that about herself. Your challenge as a Wanderer is to take care of yourself, becoming for yourself the nurturing parent you didn't have.

For Amy to do this, she felt she needed to explore why she had been so emotionally neglected as a child. I encouraged Amy to talk to her mother to try to determine why she had treated

Amy the way she had. Amy asked Lucinda about her experiences in Eastern Europe, and how it felt to come to the United States. In response, Lucinda was defensive and cold, saying, "Why would you want to know about the past?" Undeterred, Amy spoke at length with one of the neighbors who was from "the old country." Her answers to Amy's questions about the immigrant experience gave her some insight into why Lucinda might have suppressed her feelings about being uprooted, deferred to the husband she was dependent on, and been so resentful about her situation. Amy could see why Lucinda shut off her memories and emotions rather than let the anger rise to the surface.

Amy also learned that Lucinda's mother and father had pressured her into marrying Philip—and she even inferred from this neighbor's hints that Philip had affairs throughout the marriage. With that new knowledge, Amy started to realize that her mother had shut her out because she didn't know how to be in touch with her emotions without getting in touch with her anger and resentment, expressing them, and possibly destroying the security of her marriage. Amy felt more compassionate toward her mother, and was able to begin to forgive her for having been so emotionally unavailable to her.

As Amy learned, when you can see your parents and your childhood through the eyes of an adult, it's much easier to let go of the old belief that your parents' emotional rejection of you meant there was something wrong with you.

If you are still looking for the nurturing you never received from Mom and Dad, you will not find it outside of yourself. No romantic partner will fill that void of emptiness, and no great success or accomplishment will fill it either. The only way to stop feeling empty and needy is to nurture yourself by respecting your needs, fulfilling them, and genuinely loving and caring for yourself.

Correcting Distorted Thinking

As you examine your distorted thinking, it will be easier to heal. You'll recognize that your parents' behavior was not caused by you being inadequate, but by them simply being incapable of nurturing you, for reasons that had nothing to do with who you are or your value as a person. You may be minimizing the evidence that your parents have trouble nurturing anyone. Amy, for instance, was so focused on her own experience of her parents that she overlooked the fact that her siblings, too, were neglected emotionally, which was evidence that there wasn't something about Amy that made her less lovable or more needy than anyone else.

Because she had felt unloved as a child and continued to feel that her parents didn't care all that much about her and her needs, she developed a deep hidden belief that her parents had never really loved her. As she came to recognize the other reasons for their behavior, she saw that this was a form of emotional reasoning—assuming her emotional experience was the larger reality.

Given her background of having non-nurturing parents, the Wanderer is quick to personalize, as well. If something goes wrong, it's her fault. Of course, because she is usually being unfaithful to her boyfriend, she will quickly take the entire blame for the relationship not working. She will do this even if he is cheating, too or if he doesn't find out about her affair but ends the relationship for other reasons, because her infidelity is rooted in low self-worth.

The Wanderer does have confidence in one thing, and that's her ability to manage situations and placate people. It serves her well when she has to hide her affairs, but it also causes her to spend an enormous amount of energy thinking through all the possibilities for disaster in the hope that she can avert it. Worrying makes her feel stressed out and on edge, and whether or not she's in denial of her stress, she usually copes with it by trying to quell her anxiety with more sex, more food, more pricey shoes, more exercise, and so on. Those behaviors soothe her nerves in the moment, but they can cause their own stress, as she overspends or gains weight or increases the risk of destroying her primary relationship. The original stress resurfaces, the new stress of her inadequate coping mechanisms piles on top of it, and the vicious cycle of trying to cover up her anxiety continues, unless she makes a conscious decision to get off the merry-go-round and start dealing with her issues.

Stay Faithful and Tolerate the Anxiety

If you are with someone right now, and you're having an affair, you need to end it now, and brace yourself for some difficult feelings to emerge and demand your attention. Your lover on the side is distracting you from the work you have to do on yourself in order to be capable of a lasting committed relationship. You have a relationship already; now you just have to practice being in it without running out to get some backup. Regardless of your discomfort, you must *act as if* you were monogamous and stay faithful no matter what. Remember, as you work on yourself, this healthier behavior will feel more natural to you.

Amy made a point of breaking it off with Steve and not returning his calls. This decision was extremely anxiety provoking, because she feared he would contact Brian, but he never did. Although I reassured her that she had done the right thing for herself, and the danger of Brian finding out about the affair had blown over, she was still feeling anxious. Being committed to a relationship with an available man was making her feel needy and insecure about herself, and it was important for her not to run away from that but to face those feelings and work through them.

When you do break it off with a man, break it off cleanly. Don't attempt to "remain friends," because that will simply muddy the waters and pull you right back into the same place, where you are emotionally involved with another man instead of building intimacy with the romantic partner you've already committed to. Refusing to stay connected doesn't make you a coldhearted person; it makes you someone willing to admit to her weakness and prevent herself from giving in to it.

If you are agonizing over whether to confess about the other man, ask yourself, Would you be coming clean in order to be fair to your romantic partner, or to alleviate your own guilt? Will admitting to the affair (whether or not you were physically unfaithful) help you to create a closer bond with your romantic partner, or will it push him away? If you genuinely want to improve your relationship with your current partner, don't let your subconscious rule, sabotaging your relationship so that you're free to pursue partner number two. If you do, you'll simply reach the same point eventually with partner number two.

I also suggest that to keep to your vow of remaining faithful to the man you're already committed to building a relationship with, you be very careful about drinking. When you consume alcohol, your inhibitions are lowered, and it will be easier to flirt with other men, or to call partner number two, get together, and have sex.

When you are feeling empty and needy, put down your credit card or your slice of double-cheese pizza and ask yourself, Am I indulging in order to avoid dealing with some difficult thought or feeling? You may be in a great place in your relationship but starting to feel anxious, as if there's something wrong and you can't put your finger on it. Your usual pattern is to quell that feeling by overindulging in something in the hope that it will fill the void inside you. Now, however, you are going to face your anxiety and explore your difficult thoughts and feelings.

There is a very good chance that what you're experiencing is discomfort with the intimacy you've created with your partner. Did he just press for a commitment? Did he suggest that you go on vacation together, or meet his family, or move in together? Did he start a light conversation about baby names the two of you like? There may well have been a trigger to your anxiety and your feeling that you have to turn away from him. Stick with the discomfort, work through it, and do not let yourself avoid it. This is your chance to bring yourself further along the road to your goal of a lasting, committed, and deeply intimate relationship, so seize it.

Be careful not to fall into the trap of *believing that external circumstances drive relationships*, assuming that if you just stop sleeping with lover number two, you wouldn't have any problems. It's extremely important that you deal with the underlying reasons why you're so uncomfortable being faithful to one lover. When you take the time to look more objectively at your childhood, reclaim your self-worth, and nurture yourself, you will stop feeling the need to find another partner to achieve a sense of emotional security.

Flying Solo

Of course, sometimes the men that the Wanderer is dating or has waiting in the wings are not right for her. In that case, the challenge is to learn to tolerate the discomfort of being unattached.

If you are not involved with a man right now, it may feel unnatural and scary. That's okay. Allow yourself to be on the lookout for a romantic partner if you don't have one now. Don't let your guilt or shame about your past infidelities convince you that you don't deserve to find a loving man who can commit to you, or that you're too damaged to make it work with him.

If you are rarely without a relationship and are in the trap of believing you need a man in order to be happy, you need to reject the idea that you will be miserable flying solo for a while. You also need to let go of the belief that if you take some time away from men, you'll end up alone forever.

Try to spend more time with yourself, getting to know what you really enjoy and value. Chances are, you're very out of touch with what that might be. After all, as a child, you were so busy trying to placate your parents that you didn't get a lot of encouragement to explore what would give you joy. When you are without a romantic prospect, keep yourself as busy as possible. Try something new, and follow up on an interest you've been neglecting. Join a club, call up an old friend and get together, sign up for a class, or start a new exercise program. In addition to helping you discover what energizes and excites you, keeping busy with these types of activities will help ease some of the anxiety you are feeling.

New Beliefs, New You

If you are holding on to the old belief that you are too needy to find a man who can love you, try to let go of the word *too*. We

are all needy, and the more you focus on meeting your needs instead of worrying about whether they are too great, the less
needy you'll be. Beware of the trap of thinking that worrying is
productive. Obsessing just causes you to get more stressed out,
and you have a pattern of dealing with that stress in an unhealthy way. Fill your needs by increasing your intimacy with
your current boyfriend, and trust that he will be able to meet
your needs.

Yes, it's possible that he will find you too needy—that's always a risk. But you are who you are, and you will be doing
your best to meet your needs in healthy ways and build up your
self-esteem, filling that void inside you. Trust in this process,
because it's a crucial one. I promise you that even if your current relationship doesn't work out, making these efforts will
give your relationship its best chance. If it doesn't work, your
next relationship will be better, because you will be starting
from a more positive place.

If you are constantly trying to achieve more and more as a
way to bolster your low self-image, such as pushing yourself to
be the only one in yoga class who can do ten perfect sun saluta-
tions regardless of whether your muscles and ligaments are
primed for this challenge, you may injure yourself. Even if you
achieve your goal of "beating" yourself (or your opponent) at
something, accomplishing more than you ever have before,
your elated feeling may be short lived, and you may come
crashing down when you realize that once again, you've failed
to erase that larger feeling of not measuring up.

A much better way of addressing this feeling is to internalize the belief that your parents' lack of nurturing wasn't due to
your being inadequate in some way. That will take work. You'll
have to catch yourself when you're making cognitive distortions, and take a closer look at your family dynamics. As you

begin to recognize that you deserve to have your needs met, you'll see that they are not so overwhelming that no one individual could possibly fill you up.

When you reach out to others for nurturing, and you nurture yourself, you will feel more empowered. If your romantic partner isn't constantly reassuring you that you are beautiful, wonderful, and special, you'll be okay, because you'll know you are all those things and more. It will become easier for you to stay faithful to him, and you'll find an inner peace that has escaped you for too many years.

9.

The Uptown Girl

The Uptown Girl doesn't just look good; she looks terrific whenever she's seen in public. She pays attention to every detail from head to toe because she believes so strongly in presenting one's most beautiful self.

Though she may seem superficial—because she's so aware of money and what the upper class is interested in this year, whether it's a particular furniture designer or a vacation spot— the Uptown Girl is a great friend, a loving person, and a compassionate member of the community. She is often the first person to open up her Thanksgiving table to a coworker who would otherwise be alone for the holiday, or a neighbor she truly wants to embrace with kindness.

The Uptown Girl has a job or goes to school, and she does

her best work, but her heart may not be in it. She has been taught that while a career is fine for a woman, what she really ought to be passionate about is having a certain upscale lifestyle and being married with children. She may be simply "marking time" until she gets the chance to achieve the lifestyle she thinks is supposed to make her feel fulfilled. If she does pursue a career that she wants, she will be excited about her work, but over time will probably feel anxious or depressed because she still hasn't got the rich husband, the kids, and the perfect house in the right neighborhood.

In fact, the Uptown Girl has been taught that social class is extremely important because it will provide her with security and happiness. She rarely questions whether or not there may be another path to happiness for her, given her unique talents and desires. So, while she's quick to befriend someone of a different social class, she feels pressured to surround herself with wealthy people who are in the social register, to dress in designer clothes, and be seen in the "right" places. The Uptown Girl will remain loyal to her friends who are not of a higher social class, but feel sad that her two types of friends don't quite mesh, and wish that there weren't divisions between the people she cares about.

When it comes to considering a romantic relationship with a man who doesn't have a lot of money or status, the Uptown Girl may agonize over whether or not to be his partner. She works hard at being beautiful and gracious, because she's been taught that those are crucial attributes for a woman, and in return, she feels a man must bring to the relationship enough money to provide economic security, and enough status to win the approval of her parents and, to a lesser extent, her friends. His assets might include wealth, a family name, good looks, a prestigious job, fame, or influence. The Uptown Girl has internalized the belief that romance is supposed to be a simple equation—but it's one that she can never seem to make work. She also doesn't realize that this simple equation may not add up to happiness.

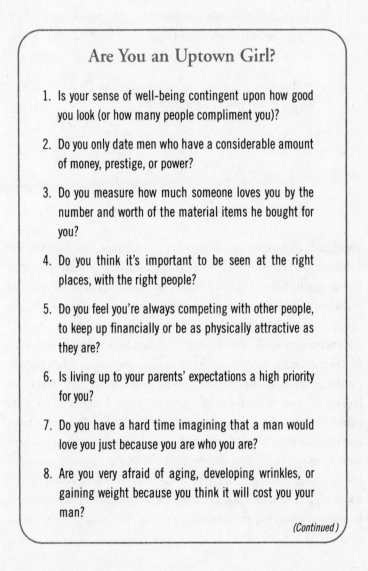

Are You an Uptown Girl?

1. Is your sense of well-being contingent upon how good you look (or how many people compliment you)?

2. Do you only date men who have a considerable amount of money, prestige, or power?

3. Do you measure how much someone loves you by the number and worth of the material items he bought for you?

4. Do you think it's important to be seen at the right places, with the right people?

5. Do you feel you're always competing with other people, to keep up financially or be as physically attractive as they are?

6. Is living up to your parents' expectations a high priority for you?

7. Do you have a hard time imagining that a man would love you just because you are who you are?

8. Are you very afraid of aging, developing wrinkles, or gaining weight because you think it will cost you your man?

(Continued)

9. Have you experienced rejection by a man, or rejected a man, because one of you didn't have enough money, beauty, or prestige?

10. Do you tend to cater to your man, playing a subordinate role in order to protect his ego?

The more questions you answered YES to, the more likely it is that you are an Uptown Girl.

The Status Equation

Despite her careful attention to her appearance, deep down, the Uptown Girl feels unworthy of love. This is a woman who may be naturally beautiful, and that's what she has been validated for all her life—and she enhances her appearance by buying the "right" accessories. She always looks pulled together. If she isn't naturally beautiful, she will work at her looks, and invest a lot of time making sure her makeup is done just so and buying expensive and flattering clothing—in short, doing whatever she feels will raise her value. She goes to great lengths to be gorgeous because she thinks the only thing she has to offer a man is external, and is unaware of the many qualities she possesses that a wonderful man might find far more appealing than a lovely complexion and a flair for fashion. If she is aware of her more substantial qualities, such as her compassion or sense of humor or integrity, she doesn't value them enough.

The Uptown Girl feels that aside from her looks, what she has to offer a man is deference. She is well trained to put her partner's or potential partner's needs ahead of her own, and to cater to his ego. She might be an assertive wisecracker with her girlfriends, but when a man enters the room, she'll snap into her most feminine self, smile at him, and turn the conversation around so that he is at the center of it. She's mastered this skill because from childhood she's been taught that male–female relationships require each partner to play a very specific role, and she knows what hers is supposed to be.

The Uptown Girl says she desires a deep and lasting love with a man who not only takes care of her, but who thinks she is special, too. Unfortunately, she may never settle down with "the one," because she won't consider dating a man who can't bring to the table some sort of status that would validate her external worth. If she has a family name, he has to have the money she lacks. If she is wealthy, he needs to be extremely handsome and powerful. If he can't offer status to her, she will reject him, embracing red herrings such as, "His net worth wasn't what it should be," and, "I wouldn't feel comfortable always having to be careful about my spending."

It's easier to buy into those excuses than admit to herself that she really rejected him because she was certain that ultimately, he'd discover how unworthy she is and leave her. Sadly, deep down, she feels she is nothing—a crippling hidden belief that causes her to avoid connecting emotionally with men. Instead, she unconsciously picks a man with whom she can have limited intimacy, going for a partner who can create a "beautiful couple" with her, regardless of whether he really loves her for who she is.

A Misplaced Sense of Self

The Uptown Girl's dating strategy may work for her, and her friends may be very impressed by the men she has had on her arm. However, she always seems to leave her mate or be left.

She is insecure in whatever relationship she's in, because there's always the chance that her external assets could slip away. Eventually, crow's-feet appear, her waist begins to thicken, and she is racing against time to connect with a man who meets her standards before her beauty fades. She may be very jealous, demanding, and controlling, because she is extremely anxious about losing her man, and she thinks that if she's hyperfocused on him and their relationship, working very hard at it and making sure there are no signs that it is in trouble, she'll be safe. She may insist that her partner prove his love again and again.

One Uptown Girl I worked with needed her man to buy her increasingly expensive gifts. The diamond-and-sapphire cocktail ring had to be topped by an even bigger and more expensive piece of jewelry—something she could show off to her friends and family. If she didn't receive these gifts that validated her external worth, she felt genuinely hurt and disrespected.

The Uptown Girl is especially eager to win her parents' approval for her latest beau. For her, Mom and Dad are the ultimate judge of whether she has achieved enough in terms of wealth and status. She very much worries that her partner won't be "good enough" for her parents.

Unfortunately, the Uptown Girl's anxious behavior can't ensure her happiness or security in a relationship.

Rigid Expectations

The Uptown Girl's rigid expectations of herself and her partner can result in a match that looks just right, but that is an emotional disaster for both of them. They have not been taught to value the really important aspects of a romantic relationship: common dreams, admiration for each other, emotional intimacy, and the like. Instead, they have been taught to focus on the externals, such as money, power, and position, all of which can quickly fade, and in any case, do not contribute to the emotional connection between a man and a woman.

Lucy, thirty-five, came into my office with a shopping bag from Barneys clutched in her hand and Manolo Blahnik shoes on her feet. She practically glowed with good health and looked absolutely stunning. She had been referred to me by another client, and was eager for my advice and insight on what to do about her current romantic dilemma.

Lucy told me that she was very much in love with her boyfriend, Michael, a great fellow she had met at a charity auction. He was from a wealthy family of Beacon Hill Bostonians. Michael, she explained, was the head of his own consulting firm, and was a "great catch." When I asked what she loved about him, she told me that he treated her like a queen, showering her with gifts. He had begun to talk about getting married, and Lucy felt he would pop the question any day. Her parents were all for the match, but recently, Lucy had learned that Michael, while wealthy, was not quite so wealthy as she'd thought he was.

Lucy explained that her father was a proud, self-made multimillionaire who owned an import business and her mother was a fashionable Upper East Side matron whose life revolved around children, husbands, charitable functions, planning vacations, and redecorating their several homes. She said she knew her parents would be shocked and dismayed to learn that Michael's portfolio and salary weren't anywhere near what they would expect of a son-in-law. Lucy herself genuinely wondered if she could be happy with him, when all her friends seemed to be with men who had much more to offer financially. But, she had put a lot into this relationship for three years, she was getting older, and she wondered if she could really get back into the dating scene and, as she put it, "compete with all those doe-eyed twenty-two-year-olds."

I asked Lucy what she did for a living, and she told me she worked for her father. She had attended a prep school and an Ivy League university, and earned a master's degree in fine arts as a sculptor—and yet she was helping market her father's import business and managing his Web site. She told me that after she got married, she planned to phase out her job working for her dad, because she would try to get pregnant right away and have at least three kids and live in a nice house down the street from her two best friends. She had it all planned out, and Michael seemed perfect for the role of husband and father—until she made the discovery about his net worth.

Lucy's Backstory: The Origins of the Uptown Girl

Lucy came from a home where the traditional ideas of men and women's roles prevailed. Her mother, Paola, came from a poor family in Italy, and was very young and beautiful when she married her Lucy's father, Vincent, who was eighteen years older than his wife and who had come to America from Sicily with a small amount of money and built a business empire for himself in America.

As a child, Lucy quickly figured out that in order to get what she wanted from her father—praise, a new doll, candy, and so on—she had to act feminine and coquettish. He liked his daughter to be his little princess, and though Lucy preferred play clothes, she thrived on the attention she got when she wore her frilly pink and yellow party dresses. She also caught on to the fact that her mother was always put together, and always the best looking woman at any party. When an event involved Vincent's business associates, finding the most expensive and elaborate dress to wear was a major undertaking, and Lucy followed her mother from boutique to boutique, and learned that a wife's job is to be a beautiful, elegant reflection of her husband's glory. She remembered her father once getting very angry when her mother had chosen a dress that he felt was too sexy for a particular function, and he angrily demanded that Paola find a substitute outfit immediately. Paola scrambled to find an acceptable replacement, for she knew that her husband would be furious and withdrawn for days if she didn't.

When I asked Lucy about her mother, she told me that Paola had an extraordinary soprano voice and sang in the church choir, and that she had hoped to sing publicly at a charity event once, but her husband insisted that he didn't want his wife "acting like a vulgar cabaret singer." Lucy seemed sad that her mother's voice was literally shouted down, but she explained that in her father's house, they lived by what he called the Golden Rule—"He who makes the gold, makes the rules."

The Uptown Girl gets the clear message in her family home that a woman's value lies in her beauty and poise. She is not given much positive reinforcement and encouragement for her academic, sports, or music achievements, and she's rarely praised for being creative, kind, or clever. If she does not live up to her parents' standards of presentation and behavior, her parents abandon her emotionally. One Uptown Girl, Gillian, was very jealous of her sisters when they were children, because Gillian couldn't seem to master the social graces of being a little lady as adeptly as they could, and her mother and father always seemed to be disappointed in her. One of her strongest memories is of how her mother took her sisters to the wedding of a good friend out of state, but left teenage Gillian at home for the night, ostensibly to hold down the fort and have plenty of time to work on a paper for school. Gillian, who was rather introverted, felt certain that the real reason she was left behind had more to do with her inability to "mingle" properly and impress this "old money" family that her mother wanted to put on a show for. It was a turning point for Gillian who, full of adolescent insecurity, decided to fully embrace her parents' values in order to win them over. Her mother and father were very pleased that she "grew out of her ugly duckling phase," as they put it, but Gillian never got over her sense of inadequacy.

Hidden Beliefs

"INSIDE, I AM NOTHING. THE ONLY THING I HAVE TO OFFER SOMEONE IS WHAT IS ON THE OUTSIDE."

Gillian, Lucy, and other Uptown Girls internalize their parents' values and do their best to meet the standards that have been set for them. Because they know that these external trappings can always be taken away from them, their security in their beauty, wealth, and reputation doesn't run very deep. Moreover, on some level, they know that who they really are has nothing to do with what's on the outside, and they believe that whatever their internal qualities are, they don't matter to anyone. From this, Uptown Girls deduce that *they* don't really matter to anyone.

When I started talking to Lucy about what had originally drawn her to sculpting, she gave me an eloquent and moving explanation of how this art form moved her. She remembered seeing a Rodin sculpture in New York's Metropolitan Museum of Art as a child and crying over the emotional scene it conveyed, and she vowed that she wanted to express her deepest feelings through sculptures that would touch other people the way that sculpture had touched her. I asked her why she hadn't pursued a career in the arts, or at least continued sculpting as a hobby. Her answer was that fine arts didn't pay well and besides, she needed to help out her father with his business and focus her energies on making friends among the "right sort" of people and caring for her romantic partner. She'd had plenty of boyfriends over the years, and they had kept her busy. From what she described, they sounded quite self-absorbed and demanding, like her father.

I urged Lucy to start sculpting again, whether in a studio or her own home. She made excuses for why she didn't have the time, or the space in her apartment, but I gave her the homework of doing some form of sculpting a few hours a week, every week. She went along with my plan, and reported to me that she had been very taken aback by how much joy she experienced reconnecting with her love of working with clay. She had completely forgotten how much it meant to her. I told her that while she was working through the difficult emotions that were coming to the surface as she faced the issues in her relationship with Michael, it was more important than ever that she take the time to sculpt. It would relieve stress and also focus her attention on herself and her feelings instead of on her parents and their opinions and feelings, and on Michael and his needs.

When a child gets the message over and over again that her emotions and desires don't have value, she can lose sight of what they are. If you focus most of your attention on other people—a romantic partner you have built your life around, relatives, friends, and others you are trying to impress—it's important to start turning inward and reconnecting with yourself, your needs, your passions, and your qualities that deserve to be brought out and honored. You may be overlooking many wonderful personal characteristics you have, and once you start discarding the old belief that the external trappings are what matter, you'll start recognizing what an incredible person you are, and how much you have to offer.

"I WILL BE ABANDONED BY THOSE I LOVE."

Because her parents did not provide her with unconditional love and emotionally abandoned her whenever she didn't behave the way they wanted her to, the Uptown Girl developed the hidden belief that those she loves will inevitably abandon her. In fact, strange as it may seem, even when the Uptown Girl is the one to leave her boyfriend rather than vice versa, she experiences a feeling of abandonment. She can't see her role in the relationship: that she was drawn to and pursued a relationship with a man who couldn't give her what she wants (intimacy and acceptance of who she really is behind the pretty face), and she chose to leave him.

Of course, when her partner is the one to leave, it validates her belief that she will always be abandoned by those she loves. Because she believes her value is in her looks and deferential behavior, she convinces herself that the reason her partner left her is that she doesn't have the right "look" for him, or she didn't dress the right way, or wasn't thin enough—or that she was too opinionated. She'll obsess about these perceived flaws rather than subject herself to the pain of looking deep inside to find the real reason the relationship ended: She chose a man who couldn't really be intimate with her, and one way or another, the relationship was bound to end, because it was always going to fall short.

Rediscover Your Inner Beauty

As an Uptown Girl, you need to start rejecting the materialistic values that are preventing you from finding the intimate, loving relationship you want. To start, you'll have to work on being comfortable when you're not looking your best and to look at men with a new eye, going out with a man without bringing the mental calculator to assess his net worth, and truly trying to find a deeper connection.

If you are spending a lot of time around other Uptown Girls—and Uptown Boys, for that matter—it's going to be difficult to remember how unimportant looks and money really are. You may have a hard time letting go of the makeup, the designer clothes, and the mirrors. A great way to help break yourself of the habit of focusing too much on your appearance is to spend more time around people who are not so concerned with beauty, who value you for your other qualities.

Lucy had an especially hard time letting go of her need to work out at the gym obsessively. She told me that her previous relationship was with a man she thought she might marry, but her dreams of a romantic proposal were dashed when her boyfriend admitted he was leaving her for another woman he'd just met, a woman who was "his physical type." This man had criticized Lucy's athletic, solid body, and she'd felt very insecure about it, to the point where she'd seriously considered getting

breast implants to please him, only to have him end their romance. Ever since then, she'd been trying to sculpt her body
into a more feminine one, hiring a personal trainer to help her
achieve the "right" look.

It was painful for Lucy to remember that breakup, and the
excuses she had to come up with to explain it to her friends and
family. What's more, she still worried that her new partner,
Michael, secretly felt that her figure was too boyish, despite the
fact that he'd often complimented her and expressed admiration for how strong and beautiful she looked. I told Lucy she
didn't have to stop working out altogether; she just had to let go
of her obsessive attitude toward it, and her need for constant reassurance that she was lovely just as she was, and that Michael
found her attractive.

Another way to let go of your overemphasis on physical
beauty is to engage in activities that don't require you to dress up.
Getting out into nature is a great way to enjoy yourself while
barefaced and dressed in jeans, and to reconnect with more important things than appearances. Walking in the woods or on the
beach, swimming in a beautiful, cool lake, or meditating under a
shady tree can put you back in touch with your spirituality and
with the cycle of life. Whether your mascara is clumping or the
man next to you thinks your legs are short just doesn't enter your
mind when you're watching the sun sink below the horizon, or
smelling the morning dew as you walk on the grass, listening to
the wind rustling the leaves and the birds calling to each other.

Correcting Distorted Thinking

A fundamental mistake that the Uptown Girl makes is to engage in black-and-white thinking and tell herself, *The only men*

worth having are wealthy and powerful ones. This restriction eliminates a huge number of men, any one of whom might be a soul mate for her. As Lucy began to recognize how destructive her value system was, she started to see Michael in a new light. She began to realize that it really didn't matter if he wasn't the richest of the rich, and she really didn't need to compete materially with her friends. As her sense of self got stronger, she didn't need to play that game of one-upmanship anymore.

The Uptown Girl often overlooks potential partners because she's engaging in shoulding or musting, convincing herself that a man "should" make a certain amount of money, or that he "must" fit into her social class. I want you to notice when you find yourself saying, "He's *got to* make *X* amount of money," "I can't get serious about a man who is a nobody/doesn't mix with my social class/etc." Locking yourself into these standards may very well lock you out of a relationship with a man who is just right for you. If you think you have to look or act a certain way in order to be loved, again, you are engaging in shoulding or musting.

Because she's been taught to play a certain role, and that there are rigid rules about male and female behavior, it's especially easy for the Uptown Girl to fall into the trap of insisting on being in control at all times. Frequently, the Uptown Girls I see are extremely anxious about being abandoned, so in an attempt to prevent their man from leaving, they become jealous, demanding, and controlling. Often, they'll try to use what some would call "feminine wiles" to manipulate a man, and manage his perception of her. While that behavior can provide some illusion of control over a romantic partnership, I'm afraid it doesn't work out very well. Even the most adept and subtle attempts at controlling another person can backfire badly, leading to the very abandonment you fear. It's far better to let go of your anxious need to be in control and be honest with your romantic partner about your needs and his. Lessening control will allow you to start creating intimacy with your partner, intimacy you crave and that you've been missing for far too long.

Interact with Men on a New Level

It's important, too, to break the habit of measuring men according to their looks, money, and status. You probably do this unconsciously and may bristle at the idea that that's all you're looking for in a man. It's perfectly fine to put attractiveness and financial stability on your list of "must have" qualities in a mate. It's when you give those qualities far too much weight that you run into problems. I've seen Uptown Girls who have talked themselves into being with men who don't treat them with kindness and respect, men who don't have a good character and may be involved in shady business dealings, or who have very little in common with them, simply because they have looks or wealth. When it comes to a loving, long-term, permanent relationship, you can't overlook those things just because a man can offer you a certain lifestyle.

When you are getting to know a potential partner, ask him what he likes and doesn't like, and why. You might be surprised at what his answers are. He might like to vacation in Martha's Vineyard or the Hamptons, or some other well-known hot spot, because he absolutely loves biking and Boogie boarding. If he says he loves these places because everyone who is anyone goes there, he is probably out of touch with what he really enjoys. Notice when his eyes light up about something—traveling, cooking, spending time in nature—and consider whether those are interests you have, too. There are some wonderful, wealthy men who have a lot to offer a woman, but when you're honest about what makes *you* happy, you might well realize that they're Mr. Right for Someone Else.

As you make discoveries about him, pay attention to whether he's equally interested in discovering who you are. Don't let your insecurities get the better of you and be grateful just because he's taking you to an expensive restaurant and complimenting you on your looks. When you talk about what matters to you, does he look into your eyes and encourage you to tell him more, or does he nod and change the subject quickly when you're finished speaking? Does he interrupt you a lot? Does he remember important things you told him about yourself, such as that you are a morning person and hate late-night phone calls, or does he call you at 11:30 p.m. on a weeknight and launch into a monologue about himself? If you're an Uptown Girl, I know you've spent a lot of time squelching your deepest desires to focus on playing your role properly. Now it's time to switch your focus, and start really paying attention to what matters to you, and whether the man you are with can give you what you want and honor who you are.

Notice Your Overlooked Qualities

The other aspect of letting go of materialist values is to discover what your many gifts are. Taking up a new hobby, developing a new skill, taking a class, or even changing careers may help you rediscover your talents and personality traits that you've forgotten about or never knew existed. Maybe you have a college degree that you never did anything with, or a secret passion for gardening, public speaking, or playing the piano. Explore your interests. Devote time, energy, attention, and money to them. If you think you don't have the resources to spend on this exercise in self-discovery, consider how much effort you put into looking your best, socializing with people you don't necessarily like all that much, or fussing over your boyfriend.

I also highly recommend that you try doing some charitable work that is hands-on, rather than just participating in fundraising. One Uptown Girl realized that she'd devoted many hours to a charity benefiting children with terminal illnesses and never got to know any of the children that she actually helped, except for seeing them at photo ops. Actually rolling up your sleeves and working in a soup kitchen, volunteering to deliver meals to the elderly or sick, being an assistant scout leader, or helping at the Boys & Girls Clubs are very different experiences than hosting fetes that attract socialites. Fund-raising is important, but it's easy for the Uptown Girl to get caught up in the social politics and glamour and remain distant from the real meaning of what she is doing.

When you start spending more time in nonmaterial pursuits, and focusing less of your attention on your physical appearance, you will feel a little awkward at first, but that feeling will be balanced out by the confidence that comes from recognizing that you have a lot more to offer than your attractiveness and your ability to defer to men.

Let Go of Your Need for Your Parents' Approval

For the Uptown Girl, Mom and Dad's opinion about her choices in life matters tremendously. Even if you've distanced yourself somewhat from your parents, you have probably internalized their values and voices and you find yourself thinking,

"Mother would not think much of this man," and "Dad would not be impressed by him." As you let go of the values your parents instilled in you concerning money, power, and status, you have to let go of your need for their approval at the same time, because while your values may change, theirs may not.

Because you didn't receive unconditional love from your parents, it may feel that they love you only when you're meeting with their approval. That is very rarely the case. Parents may feel hurt and angry, but they will often come around when they see that you are genuinely happy in a relationship with a good man who has a good heart. If they do not, it will be difficult to accept that they can't be happy for you. Remember, their inability to fully embrace who you are is a result of their own inadequacy, not yours.

Lucy's parents eventually did warm up to Michael, despite their fears that he wouldn't be able to take care of their little girl "properly." In fact, Michael had qualities they had overlooked, like compassion and humor. He would listen attentively to Lucy's father's complaints about his business partner, and would lighten up tense family situations with his clever, self-effacing comments and absurd observations. Lucy began to realize that she had truly fallen in love with Michael for all the right reasons—he was the kind of man she could love, admire, and respect, even if he didn't have a great deal of money.

New Beliefs, New You

When you stop focusing on the superficial and start connecting with other people over interests and your new, deeper values, you will have relationships that are of a better quality. You'll stop attracting men who are more interested in the Dow Jones

Industrial Average than what really makes you laugh. You'll stop being attracted to men who expect you to fit into a restrictive, subordinate role and start eyeing the men who are interested in a relationship that's based on the way you and he operate as unique individuals. You'll stop feeling so insecure in your romantic relationships and getting jealous and demanding. You'll let go of your obsessions with aging or weight gain.

Freed from the endless struggle to stay at the top of the heap of eligible women, you'll relax into your new self. You'll be motivated to spend more time getting to know who you really are, instead of spending so much energy trying to conform to others' expectations. You'll also redefine your other relationships. Inevitably, some of those in your circle will fall away, because you no longer feel a kinship with them, but new people who are more in sync with you and your values will come into your life. You can feel confident that the right man is out there for you, a man whom you might have overlooked before, but who now will mirror the more confident, more self-aware person you have become.

10.

The Runaway Bride

Like Julia Roberts in the movie of the same name, the Runaway Bride is capable of developing terrific relationships that seem to make her happy, until the moment comes when the man wants to take it to the next level of intimacy, and then she suddenly and inexplicably looks for a way to get out of the relationship. Sometimes the Runaway Bride makes it all the way to the altar before getting cold feet, but more often, the moment of panic sets in when he asks her to marry him, to meet his family, or to reveal her deepest self to him. In fact, when he begins asking questions about her childhood or her deepest feelings, in order to get to know her better, she perceives him as being nosy, and her feelings of needing to end the relationship begin to stir. The Runaway Bride may become irritable and difficult, or have an affair, as a way of unconsciously chasing away her romantic partner.

The Runaway Bride's sudden departure hurts and confuses her partner and even herself. It seems so out of character for her. In other areas of her life, she is warm, nurturing, stable, and reliable. All her friends think of her as level-headed and able to make good decisions after carefully weighing her options. For instance, she will commit to a college major, a career, or a cross-country move, and make any number of major life choices, and yet when it comes to romantic relationships, she will suddenly leave them, giving an explanation that doesn't ring true. She might say that her man turned out to be "too clingy," or "too stuffy," or blame the breakup on his being a smoker, a nonsmoker, not a Catholic, too Catholic, a homebody, or an adventurer, and yet whatever she pinpoints as his fatal flaw, inevitably it is something she knew about him all along. Those who care about her are left scratching their heads, because it just doesn't make sense that she decided one day that she couldn't be with him for this reason.

The Runaway Bride might be very smart and insightful about other people, but when it comes to who she is and why she does what she does, it's as if she's a stranger to herself. In the movie *Runaway Bride*, the Julia Roberts character, a classic example of this style of dissatisfied single, genuinely didn't know what way she preferred her eggs to be cooked, so she ordered them to be prepared whatever way her current boyfriend preferred them. In real life, Runaway Brides are just as clueless about what they enjoy, or what makes them unhappy or sad. The Runaway Bride may have no strong preferences about anything, which makes her very flexible, but not very self-aware. She may be out of touch with her deepest dreams and her unresolved grief. She may be attracted to a wide variety of men, and talk herself into any number of lifestyle choices in order to build a life with a man she loves, but she really has no idea whether she'll be happy living in an apartment in the heart of the city or an old farmhouse in a rural area. It all sounds good to her, until she feels the pressure to take the relationship to the next level of commitment. Then her deep fear that she will be unhappy with this man kicks in.

Sometimes the Runaway Bride will unconsciously choose a man who mirrors her issues, who will leave her abruptly when he feels the pressure to commit to greater intimacy, whether she's creating this pressure or he's creating it for himself. She will feel victimized, betrayed, and perplexed when he leaves, and yet the clues that he was incapable of commitment were there all along. The sad reality is that unknown to herself, the Runaway Bride chose this man because of those signs, because deep down she knew it was likely that he wouldn't push her to a level of intimacy that would frighten her.

Are You a Runaway Bride?

1. Do you move from one relationship to the next fairly quickly?

2. Do you find romantic partners easily, but always question whether they are really the right one for you?

3. Do you become increasingly critical of your guy as he pushes for more of a commitment?

4. Do you get anxious and nervous when your man starts asking questions about your deepest feelings, worst traumas, and secret dreams?

(Continued)

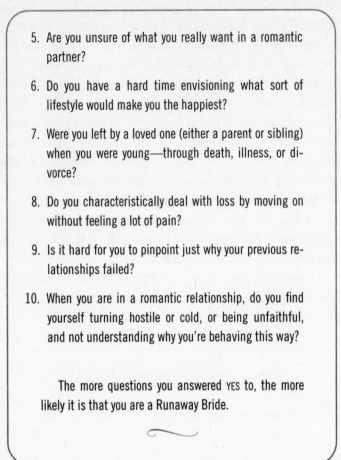

5. Are you unsure of what you really want in a romantic partner?

6. Do you have a hard time envisioning what sort of lifestyle would make you the happiest?

7. Were you left by a loved one (either a parent or sibling) when you were young—through death, illness, or divorce?

8. Do you characteristically deal with loss by moving on without feeling a lot of pain?

9. Is it hard for you to pinpoint just why your previous relationships failed?

10. When you are in a romantic relationship, do you find yourself turning hostile or cold, or being unfaithful, and not understanding why you're behaving this way?

The more questions you answered YES to, the more likely it is that you are a Runaway Bride.

Anticipating the Worst

While all dissatisfied singles have difficulty achieving intimacy, the Runaway Bride has the most dramatic response to her fear of getting to close: She escapes, ending the relationship suddenly and seemingly for no reason. This happens again and again, and unfortunately, the Runaway Bride keeps telling herself that while she isn't exactly sure why she keeps running, it must be because "He wasn't the one for me." That red herring blinds her to a behavior pattern that will prevent her from having a truly intimate connection with any man.

At the root of the Runaway Bride's habit of fleeing from a relationship just as it is getting to the point she says she wants it to get to is a deep fear that if she becomes too close to someone and really opens her heart up, she will be abandoned. She experienced that pain before, in her childhood, when she lost a loved one, and she doesn't want to feel such agony ever again. Although she is an adult, the mere thought that someone will leave her sends her into a panic, as if she will become a helpless, orphaned creature should the relationship end. It's irrational, but her fear is very real—and very much unexamined.

A Sudden Exit

For the Runaway Bride, the urge to leave a relationship just as it's about to become more intimate is a primal one. She has no idea what it's about—why she feels she ought to end it. She may come up with any number of excuses to prevent herself from looking at the hidden beliefs that lead her to her sudden exit.

Elizabeth, age twenty-eight, had just left her boyfriend, and she came to therapy to figure out why she couldn't seem to make relationships work. She had moved in with Pete two months after they met and had lived with him for a year. Pete hadn't proposed, but he had started to bring up the subject of marriage, talking about serious issues like having children, managing their money, and whether they might someday move to another area of the country.

That had caused Elizabeth to churn in emotional turmoil

for two weeks, thinking about what Pete was suggesting. Finally, one day, she called a moving company, had them pack her belongings and put them in storage, and moved in with her sister, Maria—all before Pete got home from a short out-of-town business trip. Elizabeth was dodging Pete's phone calls because she didn't know what to say to him. She explained to me that she didn't feel he was completely right for her—just like the three boyfriends she'd had previously.

Elizabeth never had a problem finding a romantic partner. She'd broken up with her high school boyfriend while they were away at different colleges, not because she was in love with someone else, but because she was uncomfortable with the long distance relationship and his talk of marriage. She felt she was too young to be married. When she was in college, she had a serious boyfriend and after graduation, when he started talking about how he felt he didn't know the "real" Elizabeth and that he wanted to feel closer to her, to know all about her past and her dreams for the future, Elizabeth felt he was getting too clingy. She ended that relationship, too.

In both cases, as is typical of the Runaway Bride, Elizabeth made a quick decision and did not look back. She was very uncomfortable exploring the reasons for the split, even years later, when it was clear she had a well-established pattern of leaving good men with whom she'd had wonderful relationships. Elizabeth wanted to believe that there was simply something wrong with each particular man, but she sensed that after so many quick departures from serious relationships, she was making the same mistake with Pete. She feared she might never find the right man for her—a man she could feel sure about.

Elizabeth's Backstory: The Origins of the Runaway Bride

Elizabeth swore that she wanted to get married and have children, that she greatly valued family and wanted one of her own as soon as possible. She had grown up in the South Bronx, where she'd lived happily with her younger sister, Maria, and her father and mother until she was six years old. That was the year that Elizabeth's mother was diagnosed with breast cancer. Elizabeth was terrified of losing her mother, and was greatly relieved when her mom was pronounced clear of cancer. Unfortunately, though her mother won her battle, she lost the war. The breast cancer came back, twice, and for the next six years she fought valiantly, only to die two days before Elizabeth's twelfth birthday.

Devastated by the loss, and the failure of her childhood prayers to keep her mother alive, Elizabeth withdrew into herself. She had never been very close to her father, who eventually remarried, but she was close to her younger sister. Elizabeth was always very obedient and never gave her father or stepmother any trouble, but she became a more serious child, abandoning the playfulness that had characterized her as a little girl. She was determined to go to college and make something of herself, to honor her mother's wish that she become the first in her family to graduate from college. Elizabeth reached that goal, and became employed as an advertising copywriter, designing ads for the Latino market. She was attractive, mature, and reliable, and everyone spoke of what a good heart she had, but when it came to men, Elizabeth just couldn't seem to put that final piece of her plan into place.

When I asked her about her mother's struggle with cancer and her death, trying to elicit her feelings about the experience,

Elizabeth continually resorted to platitudes about what was meant to be, God's will, and the like. She said she liked to focus on the positive, and the wonderful relationship she'd had with her mother. In fact, she said she sometimes still talked to her mother and said she believed her mom was listening. Her assessment of why she became such a serious child after her mother's death was simply that she had realized that she was a young lady and she had to stop acting like a child.

The loss of Elizabeth's mother coincided with a pivotal time in her life when she was on the brink of womanhood. It made her even more quick to repress the raw emotions of grief and abandonment she was experiencing and talk herself into putting the past, and her childhood, behind her. Other Runaway Brides I have worked with made less dramatic but equally profound decisions to avoid their grief over the death or departure of a parent or sibling. Because they were mere children when the traumatic losses happened, they experienced abandonment, although the loved one who left may have done so for reasons beyond his or her control.

When she was a child, Cora had a very ill brother. Her mother was so caught up in caring for her son, who was born with cystic fibrosis, that she could not be there emotionally or practically for her daughter. Cora felt that there must be something wrong with her that her mother had so little time for her. She couldn't help resenting her brother, and feeling angry at her mom for not being nurturing and attentive to her. When she was ten, her brother died, and she felt very guilty for having had such negative feelings about him and her mother. Her guilt exacerbated her already low self-esteem. As an adult in therapy, she was able to examine her childhood experiences, and the emotions and beliefs they created in her, with a new awareness. She was able to see that these feelings were only natural for a child in her situation, and she forgave herself and let go of her guilt about her emotions.

Of course, getting to that point took time, and a lot of painful exploration. Even as an adult, she discovered she was still harboring resentment toward her mother for not attending her fourth grade play because she was at the emergency room with her brother. Those emotions were so deeply buried that she was quite surprised, and even shaken up, to discover them.

In fact, Cora came to realize that as a result of her childhood experiences, she also had fears she had never explored—fears of hospitals and doctors, for example. Her grief at her loss had been so overwhelming that she'd allowed herself to feel only a fraction of it and she'd had no idea how sad she still felt. Because she was afraid of being abandoned and experiencing that horrendous pain of loss again, she had developed the pattern of leaving her lover before he could leave her.

Hidden Beliefs

"I WAS ABANDONED BECAUSE I AM UNLOVABLE."

As a child, the Runaway Bride was too young to be able to make sense of why her beloved parent (or sibling) left, and in her innocence, she thinks she drove them away by being unlovable. Cora became convinced as a five-year-old that her protests about going to kindergarten were somehow the cause of her father divorcing her mother that fall. Her father never contacted her again, and when she began to explore her feelings about this as an adult in therapy, she began to see how she'd turned the emotional reality of the situation around to blame herself for his abandonment. In actuality, her fear of going to school was rooted in the fact that she was picking up on the tension between her parents, and feeling deeply insecure that something terrible might happen while she was away from home during the day.

To make matters worse, the Runaway Bride still believes she is unlovable, and thinks she will always be abandoned by those she loves. When she's able to get to the root of why her parent actually left, she will stop blaming herself, and fearing that she drives people away. Sometimes, of course, the Runaway Bride can't know the truth. If her father abandoned the family with no explanation, she may never learn why he walked away. Some men can't handle the pressures of their lives and so they'll leave with no explanation, but that's not the fault of their wives and children. Some men will leave because they are deeply troubled, or in constant conflict with their wives, and have convinced themselves that their families will be better off without them.

"MY NEEDS ARE FAR TOO GREAT FOR ANY MAN TO HANDLE."

As a child, the Runaway Bride does not have her emotional needs met—and sometimes, her practical needs are also neglected. For example, with her mother so busy attending to her ill brother, Cora fended for herself a lot. Though she was supervised by an elderly neighbor after school, she often had to prepare her own simple dinners, opening cans of soup and making macaroni and cheese, because the neighbor didn't know how to cook or was unwilling to.

Cora believed that the reason her needs weren't met was that they were too great—that she was already enough of a burden on her mother. It didn't occur to her that she might be entitled to eating home-cooked meals and having a parent get involved in her interests and help her with her homework. She grew up feeling that her emotional and practical needs were too great for her mother or anyone else to deal with. Ashamed, she hid her needs, and pretended that she was perfectly fine with the neglect.

When the adult Runaway Bride begins to feel needy, she doesn't express this to the people who care about her, and she doesn't trust that her level of need is valid. Instead, she feels embarrassed and bad about herself, so she covers up her needs and denies them. That is why often her friends have no idea that she is experiencing difficulties, or needs love and support. They see her as very self-reliant, and don't realize that the reason she rarely comes to them—or to anyone—for reassurance, practical support, or advice is that she doesn't feel she deserves those gifts.

"IF I DON'T WANT TO SUFFER, I HAVE TO LEAVE MY LOVED ONE BEFORE HE, INEVITABLY, LEAVES ME. AND HE DEFINITELY WILL LEAVE, BECAUSE I'M UNLOVABLE."

The Runaway Bride is utterly convinced that she is unlovable and as a result, she will eventually drive away anyone she loves. Because she so greatly fears the pain of abandonment, she will abandon her lover when she feels that he is starting to get too close and on the verge of discovering her dark secret: that she is not worthy of love. That irrational fear of abandonment, and the pattern of leaving others before they can leave her, plays out in all areas of her life. If she deeply offends a friend, she will fire off an e-mail or leave a message on her friend's voice mail telling her that it's best that they part ways. She can't bear to face the conflict and listen to her friend express anger, so she divorces herself from the friendship rather than subject herself to what she knows will be an accusatory speech about how unworthy and awful she is. She will find herself shaking with nervousness while walking to her boss's office, sure that the private conference with her he's called for is going to result in him firing her—and then discover that he called her in to promote her, or tell her that he's leaving the company. In short, any time there is a conflict that requires her to trust that the other person will not cut her off but instead focus on solving their differences and reconnecting, the Runaway Bride assumes the worst and wants to flee immediately.

Face Your Fears

Rather than go with your instincts, which tell you to play it safe and get out of a relationship before you get hurt or abandoned, you need to master the difficult task of trusting your loved ones enough to stick with them. You may have heard that it's important to listen to your heart, not your head, when it comes to romance and relationships, but when you think you're listening to your heart you may actually be listening to your subconscious, which is very frightened of abandonment. This is why you might feel compelled to leave a romantic partner even when you can't pinpoint the reasons you want to break up with him. Your challenge is to stop tempering your difficult emotions and quickly repressing them, and instead tolerate the discomfort of experiencing them so you can work through them.

Elizabeth was so out of touch with her grief, anger, and fear of abandonment that she was genuinely shocked when those feelings began to surface during therapy. I asked her to watch the movie *The Joy Luck Club* and come to our next session ready to talk about the emotions the film stirred up in her. If you haven't seen the movie, it's about four Chinese-American daughters who are frustrated with their mysterious mothers, who keep many secrets from their children and reserve their love and approval. For example, Ming-Na plays June, a woman who felt she could never please her demanding mom, Suyuan. Just before she died, Suyuan angrily told June that she had two other daughters she had abandoned in China during World War II who were far more worthy daughters than June is. Struggling with that painful revelation, June travels to China to meet her half sisters, fearing that they, too, will disapprove of her and abandon her. Meanwhile, the other daughters in the movie struggle to connect with their mothers, and each mother eventually reveals that it is her personal pain, not her daughter's unworthiness, that makes it so difficult for her to express her love to her child.

Elizabeth found herself weeping profusely several times during the movie, because she was connecting with the pain and fear her mother must have felt during her battle with cancer, knowing that she might leave her daughters behind. She identified with June, and finally allowed herself to remember that her beloved mother had been very harsh with her and her sister at times—a memory so painful that she had repressed it. She didn't know why her mother had been so unable to nurture her daughters, but the movie made her realize that it probably wasn't because Elizabeth was lacking in some way.

For the first time in years, Elizabeth was able to recognize that she had buried many very difficult emotions surrounding her mother and her mother's death. Those feelings came as a total surprise to her. With the emotions now surfacing, she was able to process them, using her adult insights, and work through them rather than allow them to continue to foster her irrational fear of abandonment.

Correcting Distorted Thinking

The most common type of distorted thought the Runaway Bride embraces is that because she has been abandoned, she must be unlovable. It's a form of black-and-white thinking: lovable people are never abandoned; people who are abandoned are always unlovable. From that belief, she forms another belief, which is an example of fortune-telling: "Because I was abandoned by a loved one in the past, I will be abandoned by loved ones in the future."

Some of the Runaway Bride's distorted thoughts are the result of her anxiety about her current relationships. She will minimize her romantic partner's good points and maximize his flaws in order to come up with an excuse that justifies her leaving him, because that prevents her from having to look at her painful hidden beliefs about her self-worth. One of my clients was considering leaving her boyfriend of six months because, she said, "He's not intellectual enough; he doesn't even read the newspaper," and "He doesn't appreciate classical music, and I could never marry someone like that." I urged her to consider that the real reason she wanted to leave was that he had started talking about their future together, and made it clear that he wanted to move forward with their relationship.

Cora also engaged in emotional reasoning. Because she was anxious and uncomfortable in the relationship, she convinced herself that it meant the relationship wasn't working. I asked her to write down a list of what was working and what wasn't, and then compare lists. Not only was the list of what was working much longer than the other list, the entries had more weight. Looking at her thoughts written in black-and-white, she could laugh at how "he doesn't like the same kinds of foods I do" was downright trivial compared with an entry like "he expresses his admiration for me and genuinely gets excited about my accomplishments."

Being Honest about Your Feelings

It's very painful to think that you might have left your relationships not because they had no future, but because you were terrified of intimacy. I hope you can understand that this fear runs very deep, and has been inside you for so long that you can't possibly blame yourself for reacting to it. Now that you know better, you will do better. When you feel the extreme anxiety that comes when he starts asking about the experiences in your life that really matter, or about the difficulties you two are having, you will recognize it for what it is—a very primitive fear that needs to be managed so that you can talk honestly with him instead of finding a way to escape the conversation, and even the relationship.

Humor can be a great help. Come up with a funny name for the butterflies of anxiety you feel, a name that expresses what they really are—the result of a totally irrational, emotional response that will naturally change once you start using your tools of breaking through your distorted thinking, working through your emotions, and connecting with your spiritual self in order to gain perspective.

Be honest with your romantic partner about how difficult it is for you to have intimate discussions about your relationship. Again, you can joke about how you, unlike the woman who wants to take the emotional temperature of a relationship every other day, would prefer to believe it's at perfect room temperature at all times so that you don't have to experience a moment's anxiety. Reveal your fears to your partner and allow him to reassure you. It's natural for a relationship to experience bumps and conflicts, and being reminded of your exquisite sensitivity to criticism can help him to remember to talk to you in a way that is less likely to put you on the defensive and make you want to run out the door.

As you learn to *act as if* you aren't terrified of your deepest emotions, thoughts, and memories, it will be easier to explore them. For Cora, whose father had abandoned her family when she began kindergarten, bringing to the surface her anger, fear, and guilt over what had happened allowed her to recognize how irrational her guilt was. She began to talk to her mother about this painful episode in their past, and to her surprise, learned that her father had been abandoned by his own father, and had a serious drinking problem. In fact, her mother believed that her husband had left because he couldn't handle his son's illness and he felt the family would be better off without him. She was able to reassure Cora that her father had loved her, but clearly had been overwhelmed by his life (and, in fact, had died just two years later from cirrhosis of the liver). Cora and her mother were able to establish a new level of communication in their relationship, and it gave her the confidence to be more honest in her relationship with her romantic partner.

New Beliefs, New You

For Elizabeth, Cora, and all Runaway Brides, the biggest challenge of all is to know what you want. If you're a Runaway Bride, chances are that beginning with your loss in childhood, you've been ignoring your deepest feelings—and not just your difficult feelings, but your positive ones, too. When you cut yourself off from your painful emotions, you ultimately end up blocking all your emotions, positive and negative. You prevent yourself from feeling the full force of your joy, your amusement, and your excitement. It's as if your emotions are a stream of water that are barely leaking through a faucet that's been turned off.

When you find the courage to face your painful emotions of the past, and explore everything that happened, good and bad, in your childhood, it will actually free up your emotional flow. You will have a better sense of what makes you happy, sad, or angry today. You won't find yourself so confused about what you really want in a man or in a relationship, and when you find the right guy, it will be so much clearer that he's the one you've been looking for. That upsetting ambivalence will start to disappear.

Your past may hold good surprises as well as bad ones, and the insights it will provide you will help you to stop engaging in the distorted thoughts that are holding you back, and will help you to build your self-worth. Connect with your past, and with your present emotions, and you can set a course for the future and feel confident that you will achieve your dream of a lasting relationship with the right person for you.

PART III

Change Your Behavior
and Your Life

11.

Learn New Dance Steps: Understanding and Changing the Family Dynamics That Influence You

Once you have a much clearer idea of what type of dissatisfied single you are, it's important to start breaking away from your old way of thinking and behaving that is not serving you. To start, you'll need to understand how your family's overall dynamic and your role in it continues to influence your choices and behaviors in relationships, and start refashioning your role.

Every family has its own dance of interaction, and a central myth that captures the essence of what they believe about themselves. When each member buys into that myth and follows the steps she is expected to follow, the family dance can continue uninterrupted. Everyone feels secure knowing that nothing has changed and interactions between members are predictable. Unfortunately, by continually playing your role in the family dance, you are engaging in a behavior pattern that's carrying over to your romantic life. Embracing that role is causing you to unconsciously avoid intimacy and to sabotage your relationships. Although it can be difficult to change your role, you have to do it so that you can find and create a lasting love.

Some of you may no longer be close to your families, or your parents may be deceased. You may have decided that you would prefer not to interact with your family at all. Even so, the role you stepped into as a child in your family is one you now play in other areas of your life, so you must recognize it, understand it, and begin to change it if you are going to be able to break your self-sabotaging patterns in relationships.

Letting Go of the Need for Approval

Whatever your type, whether you are conscious of it or not, you are seeking the approval of your parents or siblings (or both). Whether you are close to your family or not, you hope they will applaud your choices and be proud of you.

The reality is that you have no control over whether or not your family will support you and your decisions. If you make changes in your life that are healthy and beneficial for you, and that will bring you closer to achieving what you want—in this case, a committed and intimate relationship—your family may be uncomfortable, hurt, or even angry with you. They most likely are unaware that you need to change in order to get what you desire (and what they say they desire for you). Their lack of understanding and approval can cause you a lot of pain, but it's important to recognize that while your parents, brothers, and sisters may genuinely want you to be happy, there is also a part of them that clings desperately to the status quo, their own comfort zone. The unknown is frightening, so when you start changing the family dance, they can become very upset.

How the Dance Works

As with any group of people, each family member's behavior influences the rest of the family and contributes to the dynamic. If one member changes her behavior, the entire dynamic shifts. For example, when Elizabeth, the Runaway Bride, first began to talk to her sister, Maria, about what they experienced as children when their mother was dying of cancer, that was not part of the family's choreography. Until that point, everyone had agreed not to talk about or examine that painful time in their lives. Maria was very resistant and even a little hostile toward her sister, saying, "Why do you want to live in the past? It's over. Mami is gone." Elizabeth was very hurt by this rejection and needed a lot of encouragement from me to approach her sister again and ask her to consider revisiting their past and discussing their feelings about it. I knew it was important for Elizabeth to get more information about what happened in her family when she was younger, and to connect with them over her unresolved grief so that she could stop cutting herself off from her feelings and avoiding emotional intimacy with a man.

Sometimes, the dance is so unhealthy for all the members that it's extremely helpful for one person to change the dance, even in the smallest way. Other times, the results of the new choreography aren't clear at first. It may seem as if one of the followers has stepped on the toes of the leader, and yet in time it becomes clear that the dance works better for everyone when more than one person is leading it. For example, Lucy, the Uptown Girl, had been raised to be just a little afraid of her father,

Vincent, who expected to be the undisputed leader of the family. Her mother, brothers, and sister were afraid of changing their dance and incurring Vincent's wrath. Lucy suspected that Vincent's need to be in charge at all times stemmed from a deep-rooted fear that he might one day lose everything—his money, his social position, and the respect of his community— and end up penniless, as he had been as a child in Italy.

Knowing that, Lucy believed it would actually be healthy for her father to let go of some of his need for control, and so she felt even more confident about changing her role, and by extension, the family dynamic. She began dressing more casually when she went to family dinners and gently expressed her opinion that looks, money, and social position weren't any guarantee of happiness. Her mother and siblings, encouraged by her rebellions, began to follow suit and take a little control away from Vincent. Because they were basically a very close and loving family, Vincent actually handled the eroding of his authority much better than Lucy had expected, and everyone was a little happier.

Who's the Original Choreographer?

Your parents decided what your family dance would be when your immediate family first began to form. Before they had children, they created their own dynamic, influenced by their personalities, their desires, the larger culture, and also by their experiences in their own families. Then they had a child, or children, and that inevitably affected their interactions with each other as well as with their children, and caused them to create a new family dance. As the adults, they had virtually all the power to determine how the dance would be carried out.

Of course, children need structure and to be guided by people who can take care of them. But although your parents love you and may really have done their best, they may not have been meeting your needs, because they didn't recognize them, they just had no idea what to do for you or how to do it, or unbeknownst to them, their own issues got in the way. Then, as you learned in reading the backstories of the various types of dissatisfied singles, you were left to interpret why things were the way they were.

As a child, you had to go along with what your parents' rules were because it would have been far too scary to stand up for yourself and not participate in the family system. Even as a teenager, when you had more insight and were more articulate and independent than you were as a younger child, you probably understood that you really couldn't survive without Mom and Dad. So while you may have bristled at their rules, you basically went along with them—or at least did your best to hide the evidence when you didn't! Some of you may have grumbled, and rebelled in a way that gave you some sense of independence and control without damaging your parents' opinion of you, but the truth is you never really did achieve the emotional freedom you were striving for. In the end, you did what you could to please the people you were dependent on, or whose anger you feared. You became dependent on their approval.

The Same Old Dance

Conforming to the dynamic your parents set up worked for you when you were growing up in your household. Even children who grow up in very dysfunctional and abusive families can find extraordinary ways to adapt to the situation, out of a sense of self-preservation.

The problem is that after we become adults, even when everything around us changes, we tend to remain in the emotional world of our childhood, because our adaptive behaviors and the old rules feel so familiar—they're a part of our core selves. If you grew up in a chaotic, unstructured home where you never knew when dinner would be served or what your father's mood would be like, you may wish for a calm, peaceful life, and yet you find yourself inexplicably drawn to situations that in some way mirror your life as a child, because they just feel "right" to you.

What's more, one of the biggest unconscious motivators of your behavior as a dissatisfied single is your fear of losing your parents' love and approval. That fear is what is holding you back from changing the family dance and from creating the love you desire. However, you are most likely underestimating your parents' capability and willingness to change with you and help you achieve your dreams. If your fear *is* realized and you feel you have to meet your parents' expectations in order to connect with them, you have to decide if you want to go along with your parents, who expect you to sacrifice your own needs and your chance at love in order to satisfy their desire to keep you in your childhood role. But what is the cost of compromising yourself to that degree?

You may also fear that your romantic partner will reject you if you stop working so hard to please him. If you, like the Runaway Bride, have a strong fear of abandonment, the fear of losing the man you love can be blown out of proportion. The thought of losing him is terrifying, because it taps into your old feelings of abandonment and low self-worth.

It's scary to contemplate being rejected by those you love,

and especially so if you have very little emotional independence from your family. Even if you are no longer close to your family, you may look to someone else in your life to give you approval—someone you care a lot about or whose authority you fear. You might be very concerned that your siblings, friends, and bosses wholeheartedly agree with your actions and decisions. And yet, you're probably unaware of this. Your task is to look more closely at your relationships with other people and to consider whether or not you're carrying out your childhood role with them, and casting them in the role of your parents, hoping they will give you the approval your parents didn't give you.

The Dance with a Romantic Partner

When you don't feel free to be an individual who operates without her loved ones' approval, you continue to behave the way you always have, and you choose a romantic partner who mirrors your issues. He may manifest his fear of abandonment in a different way than you do, or he may express his need for control differently than you do, but he has the same issues, and comes from a family that was emotionally similar to your own.

Rachel (an Old Faithful), who was overly dependent on her parents' approval and was her father's emotional confidante, got involved with Adam, who was overly dependent on his mother's approval and was his mom's emotional confidant—they were mirrors of each other. A Runaway Bride may choose a Runaway Groom, who, like her, runs when the intimacy in a relationship becomes too scary and he feels pressured to commit. A Compassionate Rescuer is likely to choose a man who feels compelled to rescue others (although he might be trying to rescue someone else, not the Compassionate Rescuer), or a partner who is still acting out his childhood role of being the troubled child, testing his loved ones to see if they will rescue him from danger. Meanwhile, the Compassionate Rescuer plays out her childhood role of being the good girl or the hero, the one who rescued her troubled sibling or parent from the consequences of his actions. Again, while all these singles are causing themselves a lot of pain by recreating the traumas of their childhood, the familiarity of the dynamic is so comforting and the fear of the unknown (that is, what it would be like if they changed the dynamic) is so great that they unconsciously choose to stick with the familiar.

Looking back on your past, you may feel it's unlikely that you'll ever stop choosing partners who mirror your issues. The fact is that you probably always will choose a partner who is your emotional reflection or your emotional twin on some level. The difference is that this new man will be able to commit to you even as you are working on your own fear of intimacy. You'll be much more likely to get involved with a man who can laugh with you about your mutual foibles and bad habits, deal with them honestly, and work through them with you.

Your Family's Central Myth

Changing your part in your family's dance begins with recognizing what that dance is. What is your family's central myth that determines how everyone will interact? These myths play out differently from one family to the next, but they are essential to the backstories of the eight styles of dissatisfied singles.

Does your family embrace one or more of the five following myths?

"We're one big, happy family."
"Our men are *real* men and our women are
real women."
"In our family, we're the perpetual victims of
bad luck."
"We are a special, superior family. We never
have problems or fall apart."
"We can only trust each other because
everyone else is dangerous and
untrustworthy."

What behaviors would contradict your family's central myth and break the rules of your family's particular dance? What would be the consequences if you were to deny their myth and break those rules? As you contemplate the answers to these questions, you might want to discuss your answers with a therapist, a close friend, or a family member, or you might want to work through your thoughts on paper in a journal.

"WE'RE ONE BIG, HAPPY FAMILY."

The most common of the family myths, this false belief is held by the majority of families of dissatisfied singles because it's a basic form of denial. Whatever problems crop up, the family tells itself, "We can handle this because we're always happy and united in perfect harmony." Everyone loves each other every minute of the day and gets along beautifully at all times—or so they want to believe. If there is a blowup and harsh words are exchanged, the next day everyone pretends it was no big deal and there are no hard feelings (although there most definitely are).

It's impossible for such a level of harmony to exist all the time, but many families refuse to acknowledge disagreements because they are terrified of conflict. They hold back their thoughts and emotions from other members, and themselves, and put on a happy face. Real emotions will emerge somehow, usually through passive-aggressive behaviors. The family will cheerfully agree to meet at Grandmother's house for Thanksgiving at 1 p.m. and then start a string of hurt and angry phone calls to their siblings complaining about how Mom pressured them into agreeing to an early dinner when they really wanted to arrive in the late afternoon. Conflicts are never played out in the open, but anger is expressed indirectly in the hope that the other person will read between the lines of the stiff smiles and respond to the subtle, hidden disapproval.

The myth of the perpetually happy and harmonious family helps everyone ignore any serious problems that are creating emotional difficulties for the children. For example, in the Runaway Bride's family, everyone denies how much pain one parent's death or abandonment causes the children. In the Wanderer's family, everyone denies that the child is not being emotionally nurtured and feels burdened by taking on adult responsibilities. They also ignore the fact that she feels very sad or angry (or both at once) because she has to shoulder the burden if she's to receive any love and approval. And in the Forbidden Fruit Hunter's family, the myth is that they are a wonderfully close family, but really what's going on is that the child is too intimately involved with one parent, having to take on the responsibilities that are not hers to take on.

When your family embraces the myth that they have no problems, it can lead to your engaging in emotional reasoning when you're an adult. You are so used to dismissing problems or glossing them over that you may feel you're in a terrific relationship, and experience shock when it becomes undeniably clear that your relationship isn't so terrific after all—it's just that you've been engaging in wishful thinking and denying very real problems.

You may also develop the habit of repressing your difficult feelings and expressing your anger and fear indirectly rather than confronting them and opening yourself up to the risk that your partner will end the relationship. The fear of bringing your problems out into the light of day makes you pretend everything is just fine, and remain in a relationship that isn't working. You may feel you have to say, "I love you" and kiss and make up quickly, even after you have been deeply hurt.

"OUR MEN ARE *REAL* MEN AND OUR WOMEN ARE *REAL* WOMEN."

In some families, everyone buys into the myth that men are one way and women are another, and that these gender differences are rooted in nature and are not to be questioned— despite evidence to the contrary. Of course, if you look at men on the whole and women on the whole, you will find some differences, but there are always individual variations. In the family that embraces this myth, a girl who is naturally assertive and competitive will feel pressured to stifle those characteristics, feel bad about herself whenever she's in touch with her "unfeminine" desires, and will likely express them in an unhealthy way as a result (for instance, being very competitive with her sisters, to the point that it damages her relationship with her siblings). At the same time, if she has a brother who is by nature shy, introspective, and artistic, he will feel his family's disapproval of these characteristics and be strongly directed to act like a "real" man, which they probably define as a competitive, aggressive person who makes good money and has a "killer instinct" that plays out in sports and business.

This myth about "real" men and "real" women is always embraced by the family of the Uptown Girl. However, families of other dissatisfied singles may embrace it, too. I often see this myth in the backstory of Whirlwind Daters, who are so caught up in their parents' ideas of how they "should" be that they fall out of touch with who they really are. Carole, for instance, got the message from her parents that she was not supposed to "waste time" enjoying and appreciating nature, even though she was drawn to spending time in the woods. She spent so much effort conforming to her parents' many expectations that as an adult, she was very unhappy and confused until she rediscovered the aspects of herself that she had repressed. No wonder she had difficulty letting a romantic partner get to know the real Carole—even *she* didn't know the real Carole anymore.

The belief that you must fulfill a certain role and get married to a man who plays the complementary role leads to the trap of believing you need a man to be happy. After all, without him, you feel like an incomplete person.

"In our family, we're the perpetual victims of bad luck."

The family that believes this myth suffers from the "poor me" syndrome. They truly believe they are victims of what's called Murphy's Law—"Everything that can go wrong, will go wrong." They're convinced that a black cloud hangs over them, and this allows them to avoid taking responsibility for anything that happens to them, or acknowledging their role in creating their own circumstances. If the breadwinner loses his job, it's through no fault of his own. If they are evicted for not paying the rent, it's because the landlord is an unfair jerk who should cut them slack because they have fallen on hard times (even though they are always experiencing hard times). If one of their children gets in trouble at school and starts taking drugs, the parents will blame it on their son's or daughter's "no good friends" and peer pressure rather than look at how they might have contributed to their child's behavior.

The family that buys into this myth is in denial about each member's contribution to the dance, and they are usually very resistant to anyone criticizing them, or even making comments or behaving in ways that cause them to feel criticized. They are extremely defensive, because on some level they know that they bear a certain amount of responsibility for their so-called bad luck.

The Compassionate Rescuer's family usually embraces this myth, because it's less painful to blame someone else or the fates for their misfortune than admit that they are creating it by not dealing with their very real problems, such as alcoholism, mental illness, depression, and the like. However, many of the families of other styles also embrace this myth in order to ignore each member's responsibility for creating their family's problems. Alyssa, the Forbidden Fruit Hunter, bought into her mother's victimhood for years until she began looking more objectively at what had happened in their home. For instance, while her mother claimed that she'd had no choice about staying with her husband, who had been abusive to her and to her children when Alyssa was young, JoAnn actually could have ended the relationship long before Alyssa's father died in a car crash when Alyssa was a teenager. In fact, Alyssa's mom, JoAnn, carried over her "poor me" attitude to all areas of her life, claiming to be the victim of unfair workplace politics at the jobs she'd held, the victim of uncaring sons who, unlike Alyssa, didn't call her every day, and so on. Alyssa started to see that like her mother, she had unconsciously gotten into the habit of not taking responsibility for her choices—notably, more than once she had told herself she couldn't help getting involved with a married man, that it was just bad luck that she'd fallen for someone who was unavailable and she'd had no choice but to pursue the relationship.

"WE ARE A SPECIAL, SUPERIOR FAMILY. WE NEVER HAVE PROBLEMS OR FALL APART."

Some families embrace the myth that they are better than others. They may feel superior because of their social class or family pedigree, or because they think their members are smarter, more creative, more self-sacrificing, or more psychologically functional than the members of other families. While some may perceive them as snobbish or self-righteous, they genuinely feel bad for people who are not like them and guilty because they have so much more money, prestige, intelligence, talent, or psychological insight. They wish that everyone could be like them, but because that's not the case, they feel they are something special.

They also feel entitled to protect that specialness by snubbing would-be in-laws who do not meet their standards. They seemingly look down on people who aren't like them, but secretly, they feel very threatened by them. When they see that someone is happy and well-adjusted, and yet doesn't share their gift of prestige, class, and so on, it shakes them up. They start to wonder if they really are special after all, and if they're not, then what is their value?

This belief system also allows the members to believe in the most common family myth—that they have no difficult emotions or problems to deal with—because they feel they're above any problem or conflict. Of course, that isn't actually the case, and they are very unsettled when traumatic events occur, but they continue to buy into the myth that their specialness and superiority form a barrier between them and hardship. Denial rules, as each member brushes aside the evidence that just like any other family, they have troubles and weaknesses. They react with hostility to any suggestion that they have any flaws, or that they aren't all that special. Any member who is ambivalent or unsure, vulnerable or weak, is expected to buck up and put on a strong front so that everyone can feel secure in the belief that the family and its members are above having any real problems. This is a family that can be anti-therapy, very much threatened by any display of vulnerability, or they may be pro-therapy, as long as it allows them to buy into the illusion that they're addressing their dysfunction while not actually allowing any changes in the choreography of their dance.

The pressure to maintain appearances is extraordinarily tough on the members of families that embrace this myth, and they respond in different ways. Some completely close themselves off emotionally. Others feel the need to flee the family, or to avoid them, rather than have to suffer the pain of hiding who they are and how they feel.

The Wanderer's family, which holds such high behavioral standards for its children, often embraces this myth. The children anxiously work to get their parents' approval, and their parents, anxious about the community's approval (and perhaps their own parents' approval), tell themselves that they are a special family that doesn't have problems like other families do. When it's clear that there's a problem, they'll usually overreact— just like Carole the Wanderer's parents overreacted to her minor teenage rebellions—because they have such an intense need to believe they are a perfect family.

In the Standstill's family, the attitude is "We are especially strong and we're overachievers. We aren't vulnerable and we don't compromise." Finding common ground, opening yourself up to emotional intimacy, and the like are not valued. Similarly, the Runaway Bride's family equates emotions with weakness and takes pride in their family being unemotional, never showing vulnerability.

Sometimes, the Compassionate Rescuer's family will buy

into this myth of superiority, believing they're better than other people because they are so self-sacrificing. This allows them to overlook the dysfunction of being self-sacrificing to an extreme instead of being in more balanced relationships with people. This family creates the myth that one must continually give to others to the detriment of one's self, and they do this to perpetuate the myth that they are more noble than others.

"WE CAN ONLY TRUST EACH OTHER, BECAUSE EVERYONE ELSE IS DANGEROUS AND UNTRUSTWORTHY."

In the family that embraces this myth, everyone is mistrustful of outsiders. This family may have gone through terrible traumas together, or the parents may have suffered tremendously as children, and this affected the parents' ability to have faith that when push comes to shove, people outside of the family really will be there for you. Often, they fall into the trap of insisting on being in control at all times, and they control the information about the family that outsiders might hear about. They have plenty of family secrets that no one outside of them is privy to—they may even keep these secrets from members who marry into the family. The secret might be that one of the members is mentally ill, or that someone is having an extramarital affair, or that they are not who they claim to be (for instance, they might pretend to be wealthier than they are). Everyone is worried that these secrets will be revealed, so they collude to keep outsiders at a distance.

This fear of outsiders makes it very difficult for any family member to trust enough to create deep intimacy with a romantic partner. If a family member does marry, the new spouse may be treated warily for years until he proves himself trustworthy.

This myth often overlaps with the myth about being special, because this family believes that their members are trustworthy while everyone else isn't. You'll also see this myth held by families who believe the myth that they suffer from bad luck. They will insist that as long as they don't extend trust to outsiders, they'll be safe.

In the Compassionate Rescuer's family, there is often suspicion of outsiders who bring "bad luck" and who aren't as self-sacrificing as the family perceives themselves to be. In the Forbidden Fruit Hunter's family, because one parent abandoned the family, everyone has a fear of abandonment that makes it hard for them to extend trust. Alyssa, who was extremely close to her single mom, bought into the myth that their mother–daughter relationship was something special, and no man could be trusted to enter their tiny circle, because he would bring heartache. That shut out Alyssa's brothers to a certain extent, and prevented both Alyssa and her mom from forming intimate relationships with romantic partners. Their dance could well be called "you and me against the world."

Being overly involved with your family can prevent you from bringing new people into your life and forming intimate relationships with them. It can also create resentments, anger, and guilt, because the boundaries between you and your family members have been blurred.

Everyone Participates in the Dance

Embracing their family myths, the family of the dissatisfied single carries out their dance, with each member dutifully following his or her choreography. In the Compassionate Rescuer's family, the mother might be clingy and dependent and expect her child to be her caretaker while the other members of the household help maintain this dynamic. In the Old Faithful's family, the father abdicates his role as his wife's confidant, and the child's siblings recognize that their sister has a "special" relationship with mom. They may complain about their mother favoring their sister, but basically, they accept the situation. In the Standstill's and the Runaway Bride's families, one child might be cast in the role of the "good girl," the one who never causes anyone a moment's heartache, which puts enormous pressure on her to be perfect, yet no one questions these unreasonable standards of behavior. In creating and perpetuating these roles, the family disregards who the child is and what her needs are as a vulnerable young person who is in the process of learning life skills and who will naturally make mistakes.

Because the family is choreographing its dance quite unconsciously, it is influenced by distorted thinking, and it's hard for family members to recognize that their dance isn't working for their child—and probably not for them, either. As the children grow up, they continue to behave the way they always have, just as their parents and siblings do, taking comfort in the familiarity of the dance, not questioning if there's a better way to interact that will make all of them happier. The family dance continues to preserve everyone's emotional unity long after the children leave home and are no longer physically dependent on their parents.

Learning New Dance Steps

Rarely does a family consider the upside of changing the dance steps. Instead, we continually talk ourselves into sticking with the old ones, no matter how uncomfortable we are. For example, you might subconsciously think, *Mom will always love me because she depends on me so much. If I call her every day, which is what she insists I do, then she'll continue to love me.* A thought like this provides a false sense of security, which keeps you in the same old choreography. But what if you did change the dance? What would happen if you didn't call every day? Would Mom stop loving you? Would she fall apart, because she couldn't depend on you? Would you experience the pain of her anger and rejection? If you're calling her out of a fear that rechoreographing the dance in a way that makes you happier will result in disaster, examine your hidden beliefs and distorted thoughts.

The old way of doing things has not been working for you. If you have the courage to debunk your family's central myth, think through the changes you would like to make, confront your loved ones with your decision, and stick to your vow to change the choreography, you will break out of the old behavior patterns that have prevented you from achieving your dream of lasting love.

12.

Build Boundaries and Bridges: Forging Healthier Relationships with Family, Friends, and Lovers

Because of your experiences as a child, and what your style, backstory, family dance, and myths are, you either need to start creating boundaries in your family and in your life, or building bridges toward greater honesty and intimacy. In this chapter, you will learn practical ways in which you can achieve those goals. By maintaining these boundaries and bridges you will create, you'll be capable of having a romantic relationship that is long-lasting, committed, and as fulfilling as you've always dreamed a relationship could be. You'll also have better friendships, get along better with your family, and perhaps most important, feel secure, loved, and worthy of love.

Meeting Resistance

While the boundaries and bridges you forge will lead to much better relationships, more often than not, the changes you propose will be met with resistance. Your parent or sibling may not be happy with your refusing to compromise your own needs to accommodate their wishes. When you draw a boundary, they may say, "You're really upsetting everyone with your behavior. I just want things to go back to the way they used to be, when everybody was happy." Your lover might say, "I don't get it. Why are you suddenly so uptight about me wanting to crash at your place?" or "I don't want to have some long, drawn-out conversation about 'us.' Why do we have to analyze what's going on between us?"

Because those you care about may not react positively when you reveal that you want to change your behavior with them, I encourage you to start small, by building boundaries and bridges in situations at work or with neighbors or friends. For example, you may ask your neighbor to turn down his television's volume late at night. If you encounter defensiveness or anger, it will be easier to handle because the stakes aren't so high, and you'll get practice at speaking up for yourself. When you have built up a little more confidence, you can start making small changes with your loved ones, and graduate to bigger ones.

Whether or not you explicitly say that you want to do things differently, the people you care about will most likely interpret your desire to change as a criticism of the way they operate. They may sense that something about their dynamic is not functional but be afraid of facing the truth about your relationship with them. It's natural for them to get defensive and go into denial, become angry or hurt, and try to convince you to maintain the status quo. Try to communicate openly and honestly, considering your words carefully and paying attention to their level of discomfort. If you push too hard, you can get hurt, and so can they, so remember to begin with small changes. Carefully consider your needs and theirs, and what your priorities are. You want to make changes that will be good for everyone—even if they don't realize it!

It takes a lot of courage to change how you interact with your family, friends, and romantic partner. Remember, people are resistant to change because they assume that change is most likely to be negative. Change that leads to a better situation can be very uncomfortable, but it is necessary. Try to have patience when they dig in their heels, and reassure them again and again that the new way of doing things is going to be okay.

Confronting Your Loved Ones

Confrontation can be very scary because we tend to anticipate the worst-case scenario: that the person we confront will be so angry or hurt that he will utterly reject us, leaving us alone and unloved. Even if you know that your thinking is distorted, it's still hard to gather your courage to start the conversation. Here are some ways to open the dialogue while limiting the risk that you will be rebuffed and hurt:

- *Write a letter.* Some people find it easier to communicate their difficult feelings in writing. When writing to a loved one, you can take your time creating several drafts, allowing yourself to express the brunt of your emotions and, as you rewrite, tem-

pering your words so that they will be less painful
for him or her to read. You don't even have to show
your letter to your loved one. I always recom-
mended waiting at least several days before sending
a confrontational letter, if not longer. You want to
express your feelings in a way that won't immediately put the other person on the defensive.

- *Start on a positive note.* If you do choose to talk to a
  loved one—perhaps after working out your feelings on paper, or with a therapist or friend—start
  the conversation by reassuring him how much you
  care about him. Remind him that you value his
  good qualities and the things he's done for you.
  This will make it much easier for him to hear the
  next part of what you have to say, which he may
  find painful.

- *Use "I" language.* If what you are confronting this
  person about is an action she took or something she
  said in a given situation, present your experience of
  that situation, using "I" language. In other words,
  rather than saying, "Mom, when you told me last
  time we got together that I always attract losers,
  you really hurt my feelings," express it as, "When
  you told me last time we got together that I always
  attract losers, I really felt hurt." This gives the other
  person the chance to save face, and express that
  she's sorry you took her comments badly. Even if
  what she said was really ugly, and you were furious
  about it, approaching the conversation in this way
  is far more productive than angrily accusing her of

behaving badly. While you may think that she should have known how much pain she was inflicting, she may have been completely unaware of it. Or, she may have been so caught up in her own pain, anger, or disappointment that she was unable to consider your feelings at the time. Give her a chance to explain herself and apologize. If your loved one becomes defensive, again, using "I" language, reassure her of your love, and your willingness to believe that she meant no harm, and remind her of how painful her behavior was for you. I know this can be hard to do because this person's behavior really upset you, but keep in mind that most people, rightly or wrongly, will automatically try to defend themselves when accused.

- *Be patient.* It is possible that your loved one will not be able to admit to his behavior or apologize for it, no matter how gentle and loving your confrontation is. You may feel hurt because here you are, opening up and being vulnerable, and he is not reassuring you—or worse, he's compounding the pain by continuing to invalidate your feelings and experiences. If this should happen, back off for now. Recognize that this process takes time and you may have to approach him several times before he becomes willing to consider changing. Give yourself credit for taking care of yourself emotionally, and for doing a lot of work on yourself to get to the point where you can start expressing your true feelings and opinions to the people you love most. This person is probably unaware of your decision to start changing your behavior patterns, does not know the steps you have taken to get to this point, and may think your new behavior is coming from out of the blue. He may be totally unprepared for what you are telling him and quick to get defensive. However, when he's had time to take in the fact that you are changing, he may apologize for his initial reaction.

- *Manage your own stress response and anger.* If you feel anxious or furious at this person's response to you, there are a number of things you can do to temper your reaction. (1) If you feel your heart pounding and your breathing becoming fast and shallow, try lifting your tongue and pressing it to the roof of your mouth to slow down your breathing. (It may sound like you are on the verge of snoring when you do this, because you're restricting the air flow.) This will actually help your body to feel less tense and calm you down. (2) You may need to take a short break to do some breathing exercises or collect your thoughts before continuing the conversation and trying to find another way of being heard and understood; (3) You may have to walk away and continue the discussion later. If so, don't be too hard on yourself or feel that you've failed in some way, because you walked away for a little while. Rejection by those you love can be deeply upsetting. Be proud of having had the courage to initiate the conversation, and try again at another time, or in another way (for instance, writing to him instead of talking to him).

- *Be willing to experience some discomfort and risk being hurt.* There's no way to change your role in any relationship without stepping on some toes, or having yours stepped on. You will have to confront people, tell them the changes you'd like to make, and be prepared for them to react with stony silence, defensiveness and protests, accusations, sarcasm, or invalidation of your feelings, values, and perceptions. Even if they nod their heads and agree to go along with your new rules, such as not asking you for details about your romantic relationships, don't be surprised if they respond differently when you actually follow through with your commitment to change your behavior and responses to them. If your loved ones have a great fear of confrontation, it's highly probable that they will automatically say yes to whatever you propose rather than admit aloud that they feel uncomfortable and reluctant to change. They may even quickly switch the subject.

Over time, the new dynamic of your relationship will begin to take hold because you're going to insist on it. This will not feel natural or comfortable, and at times you may feel scared of losing the other person's love, furious with them for resisting the changes, or frustrated that this process is taking so long. Frankly, your loved one may never totally embrace the changes you've introduced, and that can be hard to accept. Know that by breaking with your old behavior patterns, you've maximized your ability to meet your goals in life, such as creating a lasting and committed romantic relationship. This awareness can help offset your sadness, frustration, or anger that those you care about aren't easily able to change along with you.

Setting Boundaries

If you are overly close to your family, too caught up in your need for their approval, and you are maintaining an intense emotional intimacy with them at the expense of creating emotional intimacy with a romantic partner, you need to set stronger boundaries between you and your parents. Similarly, if you are prone to adapting yourself so fully to a romantic partner that you allow him to ignore your needs or disrespect you, you need to learn how to set good, strong boundaries to protect yourself from being hurt, and to allow the real you to blossom in a relationship.

Knowing that you can have some privacy and still be loved and accepted will give you a stronger sense of emotional security than you have now. It's not healthy to be completely dependent on someone else for approval and advice on how to live your life. The goal is to have such a strong sense of self-worth that while you value the approval of others and appreciate their suggestions when you're feeling stuck or confused, you aren't dependent on them for validation or guidance.

To start creating better boundaries, determine what rules you'd like to set up before starting the conversation about making some changes in the relationship between you and the other person. Of course, you should care what they want, and you will have to negotiate the rules with them—at least somewhat. However, if your habit is to let other people dictate the boundaries between you and them, it's best to have a clear idea of what you want first, and then ask them what they want. Besides, if you are overly involved with someone—perhaps you're an Old Faithful who is her parent's confidante, or you are a Compassionate Rescuer whose boyfriend expects you to run interference for him when he gets into trouble—that person will probably not be eager to help you find ways to create distance from him. Start the process by getting in touch with what makes you most uncomfortable in your relationship with him, and approaching him about making one small change in that area. Over time, you can push for more changes, and eventually you will significantly alter that aspect of your relationship.

- *Does your loved one criticize you bluntly, without regard to whether or not you need or want to hear this criticism?* Maybe your mother constantly criticizes your relationships, your friendships, your career, how you dress or conduct yourself, or your life decisions. Maybe your romantic partner feels free to give you unsolicited advice, using a parental, judgmental tone of voice. What areas of your life are you willing to let them advise you on? Can you tolerate hearing their advice without feeling that you absolutely must follow it? Do you have to defend yourself to them?

- *Does your loved one pry into what you feel should be personal matters, giving you advice and causing you to feel too vulnerable?* Maybe your father gets too involved in your career and financial decisions, or your romantic partner is always trying to tell you what you ought to do in every area of your life. Feeling that you can't have any secrets, that you can't take the time to mull something over before laying it on the table for dissection by someone else, can make you feel powerless. Is this other person's behavior making you feel judged or bullied?

- *Does your loved one expect you to always give your relationship with them priority over your relationship with others, or your personal priorities?* For example, your parents may insist that you call them every day, spend the entire day with them every holiday, and eat dinner with them every Sunday night regardless of what else you might want to do. Your romantic partner might demand that you put him first, neglecting your friendships and giving up your personal time to cater to him and his needs and desires. Are you sacrificing your time to another's needs?

- *Does your loved one put you in the middle of every crisis, relying on you too much and expecting you to fix everything?* Sharing hard times is part of intimacy, but it's not fair for those you love to expect you to become completely emotionally engaged in their every crisis and fix all their problems. Families will often designate one member to be the go-to girl that they call immediately when there's a crisis. Your romantic partner may insist that you deal with his depression, his career crisis, and his problems with his family to the point that you neglect your own needs. Are you continually giving while the other is continually taking?

- *Does your loved one confide in you more than you'd like him to?* Whether they want you to fix their problems or just offer emotional support, your family members may come to you with every single problem as soon as it arises, no matter how minor or how personal, even if it makes more sense to approach someone else. A romantic partner may feel that he has to unburden himself of all his secrets, including the intimate details of his past sex life, his sexual fantasies, and every doubt he has about his relationship with you, but this might place a tremendous emotional burden on you.

Think about the times when your family or loved one has made you feel angry, mistreated, or taken advantage of. What boundary did they cross? Do you want to strengthen that boundary? I suggest you start your boundary settings by choosing the one boundary that is most important to you rather than putting up a lot of barriers right away, in order to prevent an extremely defensive reaction from your loved ones.

Boundary Problems for Each Style of Dissatisfied Single

Depending on your style and your behavior patterns, you will set different boundaries. The Old Faithful has to firmly insist to her parent and ex-boyfriend that she will no longer play the emotional confidante for them. The Wanderer has to set her boundaries and stop doing the work for both of her parents, leaving the two of them to communicate and negotiate with each other, without her as their go-between. She also has to be clear with her romantic partner about her likes and dislikes, rather than conforming to his preferences, then building up resentment toward him. The Forbidden Fruit Hunter has to break away from the parent she is overly involved with and allow her mother or father to fend for themselves. She also has to set up clear rules about the availability of the men she dates, steering clear of any partner who is married or involved with another woman.

The Compassionate Rescuer may still be sacrificing too much in order to take care of her parent emotionally or practically, and this has to stop. For the Uptown Girl, the challenge is to insist on having her values respected. She has to cease being deferential and speak up for herself and her feelings and opinions. Of course, when an Uptown Girl begins insisting that she be valued for who she is, she is likely to meet resistance from the type of men she usually dates, or from her current partner. She may have to set boundaries like not allowing him to criticize her looks or treat her with disrespect just because she doesn't defer to him.

Practical Ways to Set Boundaries

Once you've recognized your boundary issues with your loved ones, you'll have to think of some ways in which you can create healthier boundaries. Here are some concrete suggestions that the dissatisfied singles I've worked with have found helpful:

- *Choose which functions you are willing to attend and what you are willing to do, or not do, for your loved one.* Your mother's idea of what constitutes spending the holidays with the family might be that you show up a day before the event, help her to clean, shop, and cook, stay for the entire event and keep a smile on your face even when other family members are behaving badly toward you, clean up afterward, and not breathe a word of your unhappiness

over what took place. If you know that this is what
she considers a terrific holiday, and the very
thought of it angers, frustrates, or depresses you,
put some thought into what you're willing to do or
not do. Question family traditions and consider in-
venting new ones. Decide what you can contribute
to your family without your feeling resentful. If
taking an hour out of your day to pick up a relative
from the airport because she doesn't like cab rides
is going to make you feel angry and taken advantage of, then make the decision not to do that, tell
your family, and remind them that there are other
options.

Similarly, you have to decide how much you
are willing to do for your romantic partner. Does
he want you to give up some activity that is important to you? Does he insist that you attend certain
functions with him? Maybe he expects you to
spend every night with him, neglecting your girlfriends, family, and self. Or, perhaps he expects
you to act like his mother and make sure that every
morning he has a clean, pressed white shirt, even
though he's perfectly capable of handling this responsibility himself.

- *Choose to make some subjects taboo.* You do not have
  to discuss all subjects with your parents, or even
  your lover. For instance, some dissatisfied singles
  are extremely open with their parents about everything from their finances to their sexual lives, not
  because they want to be, but because they feel that
  they would be hurting their parents by not being
  completely honest with them about everything at

all times. You may want to close the discussion on sex, relationships, money, and religious beliefs, or any subject that you find often leads to your family saying things or behaving in ways that make you feel judged, criticized, and invalidated.

With a romantic partner, of course you want intimate communication, but you also want to respect each other's feelings and values. He may have very different religious beliefs from yours, but once you've established that, it's really not necessary for him to grill you about your beliefs every time you set off to a religious service. You may not want to know the details of his sexual past, or want him to know the details of yours. In your desire to create intimacy, don't rush to tell each other everything without regard to how it will be received by the other person, or how you feel about revealing this secret.

- *Choose to make certain language, expressions, and forms of humor taboo.* Your loved ones may be in the habit of labeling, calling people hurtful names when they are angry or feeling defensive. You have a right to insist that they refrain from putting a negative label on you or your behavior.

  Your family or romantic partner may also use humor in a passive-aggressive way. Sarcastic remarks about you being overly emotional or unattractive may seem funny to them while you find them painful. What makes a comment like that passive-aggressive is that behind the sarcasm you will find hostility or judgment, but when you point that out to the person who is joking, he or she will hide behind the excuse, "It was only a joke," and insist that you're being too sensitive or reading too much into their remark.

I can't emphasize enough that if someone's words make you feel bad, you don't have to defend your response. You are entitled to your level of sensitivity, and you're entitled to have others respect that sensitivity. When you are upset by a sarcastic comment, express your feelings and expectations clearly using "I" language—"When you joke about my being too emotional, I feel judged and ridiculed so I want you to stop doing that." The speaker may argue that it wasn't his intent to make you feel that way, but he needs to accept that his words had that effect on you, and if he cares about your feelings, he needs to watch what he says.

- *Decide how often you would like to communicate.* Is it really necessary to call your loved ones as often as you do, or as little as you do? Perhaps you call your parents every week and they become angry if you don't call for two weeks, insisting that not calling means you're being disrespectful. It's important to try to find a middle ground so that when you do call, you aren't doing it out of resentment but because you genuinely want to talk to them. Talk to them about whether you are comfortable committing to calling them a certain number of times a month, reassure them that you do love them, but explain that you want to call them for the right reasons, not because you feel pressured to do so. Similarly, you may not want to talk to your romantic partner eight times a day via phone, text messaging, or instant messaging. If the amount of communication he wants to have with you makes you uncomfortable, speak up.

- *Make the most of communication technology.* Using e-mail for communication can give both you and your family a sense of control over the amount of the communication. After all, no one has to feel pressured to stop what they are doing and respond immediately, nor do they need to feel pressured to limit how long the communication is, because the other party can read the e-mail at her leisure. It also is an excellent device for slowing down your communication, allowing you to edit your words and temper the expression of your anger before hitting SEND. You might also consider using a caller ID service to screen your phone calls.

- *Set up rules regarding your loved ones advising you and you advising your loved ones.* You may feel that the people you care most about are too quick to give you advice, or maybe you resent that when they advise you, they use a judgmental, condescending tone. You may feel that they come to you for advice too quickly, before they've had a chance to think through their options and run them by their spouse or others, placing an emotional burden on you. Keep in mind, too, that some people will seek out advice from others rather than make their own decision because if they are unhappy with the results, they can blame whoever advised them. If you don't want them telling you what to do, you may have to stop confiding in them about your problems, or give them only the gist of what's going on and let them know everything's under control rather than delving into details and opening yourself up to their advice.

- *Walk away from the conversation.* Walking away from a conversation is not selfish or cowardly. I believe that when you truly want to communicate in a loving way with the people you care about, you deserve to feel safe in doing so. If you feel you're being attacked, you are entitled to hang up the phone, leave the room, or walk out of the house to temporarily end the conversation. Later, when you are feeling less vulnerable and more in control of your own emotions, you can try to reopen the conversation.

  I also think it's important to walk away from an argument when you find yourself getting so upset that you fear you will lash out verbally, or even physically. There's nothing wrong with getting angry and having a heated discussion, but there's no reason why you have to continue it when you or someone else is on the verge of being hurt unnecessarily. What you have to say, and what the other person has to say, is always more easily heard when you are both feeling in control of your emotions. If you and your family members or romantic partner are in the habit of engaging in angry fights, talk to them about the new rule you'd like to establish about walking out of fights. Assure them that you believe the conversation will always be much more productive if you're having it when everyone's anger is in check.

• *Choose how you will respond if your boundaries are not respected, and communicate the consequences to those you love.* It's important to tell your loved ones about your new rules, and also to let them know what will happen when they break them. You will most likely have to remind them several times that you are going to follow through on those consequences if your boundaries are not respected. The first few times you actually walk away from them or say, "I'm not answering that question" when they speak disrespectfully to you, they will probably react with disbelief. Calmly remind them of your new boundaries, and follow through, every time, without falling into the temptation to launch into a long defense of why you've chosen these new rules. If your self-worth is a little shaky, you will tend to feel you have to defend all your decisions to anyone who questions them. Don't. If you are consistent in following your new rules, over time, your loved ones will probably give up trying to pull you back into the old way of doing things.

Of course, if you set strong boundaries and stick to them, there is the chance you will be rejected. Your family, with whom you have a long history, is probably far less likely to abandon you than a romantic partner would be. While it is always sad to break up with a partner, it's not worth compromising yourself and your needs to stay in a romantic relationship. You deserve so much better.

Building Bridges

If your parents never gave you the emotional nurturing you needed, revealing what you really feel inside will help you build bridges to your family members and create intimacy with your romantic partner.

It may be very frightening to consider revealing to someone you care about that you have a different opinion, or different feelings, than he does. Keep in mind that it's often easier for others who are resisting intimacy to start getting closer to you if you let them learn a little more about yourself before you begin asking them probing questions. When you expose your doubts, insecurities, and foibles, you make it easier for them to open up about theirs. One dissatisfied single was deeply moved when she revealed to her mother her pain over discovering that she had a learning disability that had affected her ability to succeed in school and on the job, only to have her mother reveal that she had the same disability and it had caused her to feel bad about herself, too. That honest conversation about their mutual insecurity drew the two of them much closer together.

For the Standstill, who has been hiding her unhappiness, fear, sadness, and shame from everyone for years, sharing her vulnerabilities can help her to be much closer with her friends and family. However, because she is so vulnerable, she has to be careful about how she approaches her loved one to build this bridge. Rather than reveal these emotions to her parents and brothers right away, Julie, the Standstill, began by being more honest with her close friends. When they validated her feelings and offered her love, acceptance, and encouragement, she got up the courage to begin revealing her feelings to her family. After she'd had a little practice, she felt secure in her decision to be more open and honest about her feelings with those she loved, so she was able to see that her family's dismissive remarks about her new behavior stemmed from their discomfort and fear. She told them that she identified with "flighty Aunt Tricia," a relative the family had always disparaged for being too emotional. She defended her aunt and herself and to her surprise, her family grew silent, clearly embarrassed about how they'd made fun of both of these women. They actually stopped ridiculing Julie and her aunt after that.

The Runaway Bride and the Wanderer both have a need to confront their parents about the lack of nurturing in their childhood. Opening this conversation can be difficult, and the family may be defensive about their dynamic, but often what happens is that having the conversation and getting some validation, however small, from their parents that Mom and Dad could've been more nurturing is extremely healing. Confronting her parents didn't change matters for Amy, but she reconnected with her sister and her troubled brother, and they were able to bring to the surface the disappointment, anger, and pain produced by their childhood, express these feelings to each other, and have them validated. As a result, the three siblings changed their family dance and began to give each other the nurturing and encouragement they all felt they'd been missing.

The Whirlwind Dater often is afraid of expressing anger and hurt to her parents, which is crucial in an intimate relationship. When Carole's family began to make fun of her for oversalting a side dish she had brought to a holiday gathering, Carole expressed her feelings of hurt and anger to them for the first time, saying, "Mom, Dad, you know, as a kid, when you made me cook for the family, I really felt unfairly burdened with this responsibility, and unappreciated and hurt when everyone in the family joked about how bad a cook I was. I know you were only teasing, but it really, really hurt, and even just now, when you said my macaroni and cheese was too salty and you laughed, I felt like a kid all over again—like I'll never live up to your expectations and get your approval. After what you just said, I can feel myself ready to cry. I'm so angry, and so hurt." Carole had prepared herself for the possibility that they would dismiss her feelings, and indeed, her father began to tell her she was being oversensitive, but her mother jumped in and validated Carole's feelings, apologizing to her for her insensitivity. That evening was the beginning of a new, deeper intimacy with her parents, and while it took much longer for her father to accept the new Carole and change his behavior than it took her mother to adapt, eventually both of them made changes that Carole had never dreamed they'd been able to make.

For the Runaway Bride, who is terrified of being abandoned again as she was in her childhood when her parent left her, the challenge is to build bridges with her family and learn to be comfortable with intimacy. Elizabeth's choice to approach her sister, Maria, and finally talk about the taboo subject of her mother's death was her first step toward establishing a new intimacy.

Here are some ways in which you can foster the relationships you have with your family and your romantic partner, and build bridges of intimacy:

- *Request more frequent communication.* Do you feel you can call your sister only on special occasions, because she always seems distracted and short with you on the phone? It may be simply that you're calling her at inconvenient times, or she doesn't like speaking on the phone instead of in person. Using "I" language, express to her that you love her and would like to talk more often, and then get into the specifics. Would she be comfortable if you called her a few times a month, or if you got together for lunch to catch up every few weeks? Be open to her ideas about how to communicate.

Similarly, be honest with your romantic partner about how often you would like to communicate. If you can't stand not hearing from him for days, let him know. Ask him if he is willing to commit to having conversations more often.

- *Ask your loved one to consider communicating with you about subjects that have been taboo.* Whether the topic that is off-limits is your mother's death or the emotions you are experiencing today, if it's a subject you'd like to talk about, ask your loved ones if they would be willing to discuss the topic. Think about saying something like, "At some point, I'd like to talk to you about Dad getting older and needing more help from us. Do you think we could have a conversation about that sometime soon?" or "I'm feeling the need to talk about what happened when we got together last weekend, so maybe we could do that tonight, or tomorrow?" rather than just diving right into the subject. Give the other person the opportunity to set some boundaries on the conversation—the timing of it, whether anyone else should be involved in the conversation, where it takes place, and so on.

- *Let your loved ones know that you would like to hear them express their love to you verbally.* While it's difficult for some people to say "I love you" or "I really appreciate you," if you approach the people who care about you without accusing them of being unloving or insensitive, you may find them more open to being expressive than you realize. Remember to use "I" language—"I spend a lot of time taking care of Mom, driving her here and there and helping her with doctor's appointments. I know it makes sense for me to do this because you live so far away, and I don't resent it, but sometimes I feel unappreciated because I never hear 'Thanks for taking such good care of Mom.'" Or, you might say to your romantic partner, "When I say, 'I love you,' and you say, 'Back atcha,' I don't feel as reassured as I'd feel if you actually said, 'I love you.'"

Consider, too, whether or not you are as verbally expressive with them as they'd like you to be. If you say "I love you," "I'm so glad you're in my life," and "Thank you," they just might follow your lead and start opening up and saying these things to you more often. On the other hand, do not be hurt or discouraged if they don't, or if they find it difficult to express their emotions. They may have trouble doing this with anyone, not just you. Try to be patient.

- *Bond with your family members at a family reunion.* If you live far away from your family members, reunions can be difficult to arrange, but don't assume they are impossible. One of my clients talked to her sister about getting together with their half siblings several states away, and they realized that there was a ski resort that was about a four-hour drive from each of them where they could rent lodges in the off-season for very little money. If it's important to you to get together with your family member, make it a priority to figure out the logistics. Be sure to let them know what the purpose of the reunion is. If you want to discuss difficult subjects, it may be best to enjoy each others' company in person and agree to not get into any painful or upsetting topics until a later date. You might say, "At some point, I would like to talk to you about how we feel about the pressure our parents put on us to be overachievers, but if you don't want to talk about that now, I'll understand. It's just that I'd like you to think about when we might broach that subject, because I'm trying to work through my feelings about it," giving your family member the freedom to decide whether he or she wants to talk now or later.

- *Make use of modern technology.* Again, sometimes it feels safer to express your deepest feelings by letter or e-mail rather than in person, so consider that avenue of communication. A cell phone can keep you in touch with a romantic partner about the little things. One of my clients is working with her partner on improving their communication, and they've found it very helpful to use their cell phones while they're on the go, calling each other to say, "I felt we parted on a sour note," or "I was in a rush before and I should've acknowledged what you were saying about being scared to meet my family tonight."

- *Use movies and pictures to start a conversation.* If you are trying to create greater intimacy with someone, you might watch a movie together to bring up a difficult subject, or look at old photos together and use them as a springboard to a conversation about your past, present, and future relationship with your loved ones. Elizabeth, the Runaway Bride, showed her sister, Maria, an old photo album from their childhood that she hadn't opened for years, and as they looked at it together, both women began to talk about the circumstances behind each photo, slowly revealing more about what they had experienced when their mother was ill, when she died, and when their father quickly remarried.

- *Engage in activities you both enjoy to help you feel your connection.* When it's difficult to communicate with someone you love and feel a deep emotional connection, you might want to ask them to get together with you and do something you both love. Go with your sister to the arcade you enjoyed as kids and play Skee-Ball together, or go back to the dance floor where you met your partner and laugh about how much the music and crowd has changed; then go home and replay the CDs you listened to when you first met. This can help you to reconnect.

- *Don't automatically end the conversation if the other person says something that hurts your feelings or makes you angry.* Many dissatisfied singles avoid confrontation at all costs, and become silent or change the subject when a difficult topic comes up or the other person says something that makes them feel hurt, scared, or angry. If you do this, I'd like you to start developing the habit of staying in that conversation, trusting that your loved one wants you to feel loved and secure, and see where it takes you. If you don't have disagreements, you can't achieve intimacy. If you don't clear up misunderstandings, you'll build up resentments and begin pulling away from the person you love.

- *Decide ahead of time how you will respond if you are rebuffed.* If you are afraid that your loved one will not be ready to take your relationship to the next level of intimacy, remember that you do have other people you can talk to about those topics. If it's a family member, think about opening up lines of communication with other family members—parents, siblings, aunts, uncles, cousins, and grandparents—and with friends. You can also talk to a therapist, or even people you meet online. You might join an electronic mailing list or online discussion group, where you can talk with others who share your circumstances. (Be sure that you change any identifying details about yourself to protect your privacy, and check the discussion list's policy on making its archives available to the general public through the Internet.) Knowing that there are others out there whom you can form relationships with and can communicate to about difficult feelings will help you set healthy boundaries, build bridges where you can, and accept that your loved one isn't going to change as quickly and dramatically as you might like him to. If it's your romantic partner who is unwilling to let you get closer to him, you may have to accept that he isn't able to give you what you want: a committed, loving relationship.

I think you now know in your heart that some people are just not ready for deep intimacy with you, and that may have nothing to do with how they feel about you. Be proud that you're doing so much work to improve your ability to be intimate, and yet also protecting yourself from feeling taken advantage of or unappreciated. Have faith that there are people who are able to emotionally connect with you. You just have to discover who they are, build those bridges, and maintain those healthy boundaries you've set for yourself.

If the thought of getting closer to the ones you love is a little scary, because you're imagining rejection and abandonment, that's only natural. Continue to *act as if* you weren't scared, and the changes you make in your relationships will result in some much deeper connections. In the meantime, it will be very helpful to learn more about managing the strong emotions that will inevitably arise as you say good-bye to the old habit of repressing your feelings and step into a new, richer emotional life.

13.

Experience All Your Feelings: Recognizing and Processing Your Hidden, Difficult Emotions

Facing the truth about your family dynamic and recognizing that until now, you've been unconsciously behaving in ways that have kept you single and dissatisfied is bound to bring up many difficult emotions. Strong emotions can be scary, because their intensity is unfamiliar. Experiencing them may even make you feel out of control.

In your family when you were growing up, you may have been taught that it is not okay to express sadness, anger, or fear, and as a result, you learned to repress those feelings. If you've developed the habit of squelching your emotions, you probably don't even realize you're doing it. You have a flash of uneasiness, and before you can say, "I'm really angry about this" or "This is frightening to me," that feeling gets pushed down deep inside you, and you revert to the old behaviors that aren't working for you—pretending nothing is wrong, conforming to the expectations of everyone around you, and not exploring why you do the things you do. It's going to take time to break this habit and develop the new habit of bringing difficult emotions to the surface, experiencing them, examining them, and finally, letting go of them.

I don't want you to get stuck feeling bad for a long time, but not allowing yourself to feel bad at all is worse than suffering the temporary discomfort of being sad, angry, or frightened. As you uncover your hidden beliefs and examine and reject the distorted thoughts that have been holding you back from achieving your dream of a lasting love, commit yourself to experiencing the emotions that inevitably surface, no matter how painful they are. Processing your emotions takes time and effort, but it is absolutely necessary, and it does get easier.

If you consider yourself a very emotional person, it might be very frightening to think about feeling the full force of your repressed emotions, but I assure you, it's not as bad as you might imagine. For one thing, the feelings are temporary. For another, every time you allow yourself to experience your feelings without tempering them, you get closer to getting rid of the sadness, anger, and shame you've been holding on to for years. You will still experience difficult emotions at times, but you will move through them more quickly. When a relationship ends, your pattern may be to fall into deep despair and self-loathing, but you can get to the point where your response to a relationship ending is to calmly, sadly, accept that it wasn't meant to be. You can face your painful emotions, stop projecting your issues onto men, and continue to work on eliminating the behavior patterns that are sabotaging your efforts.

There's another reason that experiencing your emotions might not be as painful as you think it is: Acknowledging your feelings for the first time, and letting them flow forth, is incredibly empowering. Knowing that you can handle great sadness, anger, or resentment, for example, makes you realize just how strong you are. If you grew up in a home where experiencing strong emotions was considered a sign of weakness, you may be shocked to discover just how good you will feel about yourself when you experience your emotions at their full intensity and yet still are able to be productive and to think clearly. So often, Standstills and Runaway Brides that I work with are convinced they will become a weepy mess and watch their lives fall apart if they tap into their deepest feelings. What a relief it is for them to discover that they actually feel much stronger and more confident when they stop being afraid of their innermost emotions.

The Core Emotions of Dissatisfied Singles: Shame and Inadequacy

If you're like most dissatisfied singles, when you're asked the question, "So, why are you still single?" you feel uncomfortable, insecure, tense, worthless, foolish, helpless, and weak. All these words describe the feelings of shame and inadequacy: the predominant emotions of being a dissatisfied single. Those feelings are rooted in your childhood, when you mistakenly came to believe that you were unworthy of love. The low self-esteem this distorted hidden belief created got validated again and again by your distorted interpretations of what happened to you over the years. For instance, if a man rejected you, you probably jumped to the conclusion that he did this because you are inadequate in some way. If a relationship didn't work out for you, you probably assumed it was because somehow, you failed.

Experiencing the feelings of shame and speaking them aloud

leads to a release. You will gain freedom from intensely exaggerated feelings of personal failure and responsibility. You can finally let go of those hidden beliefs like, "There is something wrong with me; I'm damaged," and "I will be alone forever."

Shame is also connected to feelings of guilt. You may be in the habit of blaming yourself whenever something goes wrong, so now that you recognize that you've contributed to your unhappiness by behaving in ways that aren't conducive to creating a healthy, loving relationship, you may be tempted to blame yourself. But how can you assign blame when you behaved the way you did unknowingly? Even if you sensed that you were accidentally sabotaging yourself, you didn't have the insight to be able to see what you were doing, so of course you continued in your familiar behavior patterns. Your fear of being rejected by a romantic partner or your family kept you from looking at your behavior patterns and thinking seriously about changing them. It's not fair to blame yourself for things you did unconsciously.

The Four Stages of Processing Your Hidden, Difficult Emotions

Now that you are aware that you're not the victim of bad luck, nor are all of the good ones taken, you're going to start changing your behaviors, and that requires you to work through the emotions you've been repressing for years. This process will unfold in four stages: discovery, regret, mourning, and acceptance.

STAGE ONE, DISCOVERY

The first step is to increase your self-awareness, discovering the emotions that you've hidden inside you. You'll begin to understand what is driving your behavior: your emotions, your

hidden beliefs, your distorted thoughts, and your
family dance. Instead of allowing yourself to beco
of your long-standing behavior patterns, you will st
your own destiny.

This process of learning about yourself can be quite daunt-
ing and painful. The feelings that will surface—such as sadness, shame, and inadequacy—are not going to be easy to deal
with, but using the practical techniques in this chapter will
help.

As you work through stage one, beware of developing a
"poor me" complex. When Amy, the Wanderer, first realized that
she'd been unknowingly contributing to her unhappiness, she
started going back and forth between feeling angry at her parents for their role in creating her behavior patterns, and feeling
sorry for herself for having been stuck in them for so long. She
was very caught up in these emotions for several months and
finally had to recognize that perceiving herself as a victim, and
reinforcing her belief that she was powerless, was keeping her
immobilized.

When you're in this stage, acknowledge your feelings, but
also recognize your power to make different decisions and take
alternative actions. Your behavior yesterday does not determine
your behavior today. Remember that your authentic belief
about yourself is what you will be communicating to the world
and determines what you will be attracting to your life. If you
feel powerless to attract a man who can make a commitment,
you will unconsciously send out the signal that you are unable
to accept and embrace a man who is comfortable with intimacy
and commitment. If you feel unworthy, you will not be able to
attract a man who thinks you are worthy. It's very important
not to fall into distorted thinking and traps that will keep you
believing that you can't have what you want.

Stage Two, Regret

In this stage, "if only" thinking emerges. You start to feel that you've wasted invaluable time unknowingly entangled in a pattern of behavior, and you tend to fall into obsessive thinking: *If only I had . . . If only he had . . .*

When Rachel, the Old Faithful, was in stage two, she realized how much time she had been wasting being stuck on her ex, Adam (and, in the past, being stuck on other boyfriends after she'd broken up with them). Focusing her attention on her previous relationship and allowing herself to constantly think about rekindling it had prevented her from exploring relationships with many other men who had been interested in her along the way. In fact, she became very upset when she realized that one man in particular, whom she hadn't allowed herself to pursue a romance with because she was so emotionally caught up in her past, might have been an excellent partner for her. She found out that this man was now happily married, and Rachel had a hard time forgiving herself for rebuffing him years before.

You may experience a lot of anger at yourself when you're in stage two because you're judging yourself harshly. Keep in mind that judging yourself will also slow your progression or bring you to a halt. Remember Julie, the Standstill, who had been without a partner for years? She was approaching her fortieth birthday, and all her regrets about having put so much effort into her career at the expense of developing a personal life and pursuing romance were hitting her hard. She began labeling herself, saying, "I'm a fool," "I've become nothing more than a robotic superwoman," and so on. Getting stuck in the past and beating herself up for having made choices she regretted was taking its toll on her self-esteem, draining her of energy, and making it very difficult for her to stick to her goal of meeting new men, which was crucial for her progress as a Standstill.

When you are in stage two, be compassionate toward yourself. Learn from your past, but don't waste time and energy obsessing about it. You can't get back lost time and you don't want to sacrifice any more of it. It's easy to become mired in regrets, and then end up having more regrets because you wasted so much time being stuck. You must move on.

STAGE THREE, MOURNING

Mourning the past and what has been lost is crucial if you don't want to get stuck in grief. Often, dissatisfied singles have the habit of cutting short the grieving process. It begins in their childhood, when they are afraid to feel, or at least to express, just how sad and frightened they are that a parent has abandoned them, emotionally or physically. They feel powerless to change the situation, which makes them sad and angry, and at the same time, they blame themselves for it, which makes them feel guilty and ashamed. It's too painful to face all these difficult feelings, so they choose to repress them—and their families may encourage this behavior. As a child, whenever Amy, the Wanderer, tried to tell her father that she was unhappy, overwhelmed, or resentful at having to take on so many adult burdens that belonged to her mother, and that she was in need of some nurturing from her emotionally absent parents, her father got angry and defensive. He did not want to hear any complaints. Moreover, her mother was completely unapproachable. Amy got the clear message that her feelings were unimportant. Rather than try to deal with them herself, she did her best to ignore them. There was no one to validate her feelings or guide her through the process of working through them.

As an adult, you probably don't know how to deal with

strong emotions, so you continue to repress them. However, you can't avoid those feelings forever. You have to mourn what you have lost, whether it's a parent or a romantic partner, and what you were not able to have—a nurturing childhood, guidance on how to process your feelings, and so on. It's important to experience the sadness that comes with knowing that if you'd had more insight into yourself earlier on, you would not have struggled so long with trying to make relationships work, to no avail.

Your emotions may be very raw, and may come up suddenly and unexpectedly—for example, when you experience a small loss, such as discovering that your parent discarded a beloved childhood toy you'd left in the attic of your house, or you hear a news report about some celebrity who died, you might feel your own repressed grief and feelings of abandonment surface in a huge wave. Don't scold yourself for being overly emotional. If this event gets you in touch with your grief about larger losses, it serves a purpose. The pain you experience during this very emotional phase will help you move forward out of being a dissatisfied single.

STAGE FOUR, ACCEPTANCE

In stage four, you recognize that life presents situations beyond your control and you start feeling some peace about the past and about your current situation. You begin to accept that you will have to work harder and feel more pain to attain a relationship than you imagined you would. Instead of obsessing over the past, or feeling immobilized by grief or anger, or worrying about the future, you begin to feel hopeful and at ease with being single for now. This is the stage in which the anxiety seeps away and you are left feeling calm and confident. You become free of shame and are able to move forward and create a new story with an ending that is now unknown.

This transformation does not happen overnight. It is a process that unfolds. Don't be hard on yourself if you fall back into stage three unexpectedly, or if a friend of yours seems to be solidly in stage four while you're struggling to stay there. You'll move forward at your own pace. Keep in the forefront of your mind that all things in life happen just as they should.

Nicole, the Compassionate Rescuer, was without a romantic partner for a long stretch after she had locked her boyfriend, Jonathan, out of her apartment, thereby ending their relationship. While she was proud of herself for not giving in to the temptation of getting involved with yet another man who clearly had problems, she felt somehow cheated, because she'd had the courage to end a bad relationship and work on her own issues, only to have no romance on the horizon. She feared that the only men she would attract were fixer-uppers—men who needed a lot of guidance and help from a woman in order to get their career and personal life on track. It was hard for her to have faith that she could attract a man who wasn't so needy. However, she was determined to be optimistic about her future. By *acting as if* she had complete faith in herself and her romantic fortune, she was able to quell the anxiety that in the past would have led her to settle for dating an immature man she knew wasn't capable of commitment. She made it a habit to reread her old journals and remind herself of how far along she had come in changing her own behavior, and that helped her stay the course.

As you move through the stages, don't rely on others to praise you for your transformation, telling you, "You're so confident and assertive now. That's great!" Regardless of whether you get validation for your growth, know that you have changed for the better. Be proud, and reward yourself for your courage and hard work. While it's very encouraging to hear a friend say, "You just seem to glow with happiness these days!

I know that you're going to find a guy soon," depending on other people to keep you feeling positive and confident is just setting yourself up for failure. You can't control the fact that someone might say something insensitive, like, "You're still not seeing anyone? It's been so long since you broke up with that nice guy—why didn't you marry him?" Know that you are on the right path, and enjoy the encouragement whenever you get it, but don't get caught up in whether or not others believe that you're going to find the love you're seeking.

It's helpful to make a point of noticing the small, subtle changes you are effecting in your life. For example, if you have had a hard time feeling like a sexual woman in the past, and you begin to feel sexy and get noticed by men, that is noteworthy. Don't dismiss it! Linger in that feeling of being attractive. Give yourself credit for your efforts. If you're starting at *A* and the goal is to get to *Z*, it's important to recognize that you've gotten to *B*, then *C*, then *D*, and so on. If you've gotten from *A* to *F*, that's huge! If you are a Whirlwind Dater who has never gone a week without a romantic prospect or a boyfriend, and you've now gone two months without a date, are comfortable enough to really enjoy the swimming class you started taking, and you've befriended a couple of women at the gym, that is worthy of a celebration. Buy yourself something nice, brag about your achievement to someone you care about, take yourself out to a special event—treat yourself in some way. Don't focus on the fact that you don't have a partner on the horizon. If a man who is just right for you shows up tomorrow, you are much more ready for him than you ever were.

Whatever your journey requires—and that depends on what your style is and your underlying behavior patterns—you need to walk it and not keep looking at your watch. If you wait merely for the results (that is, a committed, loving relationship), you will miss the motivating milestones that get you there.

Practical Techniques for Processing Yo Emotions

It's important to experience your strong emotions, but it's also valuable to have at your disposal several techniques for managing your feelings so that you can experience them, analyze them, and let them go. Talking yourself out of your feelings very quickly, or getting stuck in being sad, angry, or ashamed without examining why you're feeling that way, can prevent you from making progress toward processing your emotions in a productive way. These techniques can help you finally release yourself from the grip of painful emotions instead of constantly reexperiencing them.

DECONSTRUCT YOUR THOUGHTS

Emotions are very strong, and they feel very real, and yet what drives them is often a memory or a thought. When you do the work of examining your thoughts to be sure they aren't distorted, and revisiting your own backstory to get a clearer, more rounded view of what happened, you might find that your emotions are not quite so strong, and you can deal with them more easily. Carole, the Whirlwind Dater whose parents had been so hard on her as a child, began revisiting her past and getting in touch with the pain of having her parents make many demands on her and not validating who she was. By talking with me about her past and writing about her feelings in her journal, she came to consciously realize that her parents had been deeply uncomfortable allowing their daughter to explore her own interests—like spending time in nature—because they were extremely anxious. Carole recognized that her parents had always been afraid of what other people would think of them if their daughter didn't embrace a certain set of values

vide them with opportunities to prove to
ey were worthy. Their overreactions when
ble as a teenager provided more evidence
ther were terrified that she would cause
y didn't control her every move.

stopped believing that they'd acted this way because
she was somehow inadequate and began to feel sorry for her
parents. While she experienced the pain of rejection whenever
she got in touch with those memories, the feelings of shame
and self-loathing dissipated. She recognized that her sadness
over being denied the chance to spend time throwing pebbles
into a pond and sitting on a rock basking in the sunlight was really just a part of her grief over not being cherished for who she
was, and not being given freedom to explore herself and her interests.

Now that you know how to examine and reject your distorted thoughts, you need to make a habit of doing so. When
you feel a painful emotion, stop yourself. Recognize the feeling,
name it, and ask yourself, "Where is this coming from?" If
you're dreading a date, catch yourself and say, "Okay, I'm feeling depressed here because I've just told myself that this date
will go badly." Recognize the distortion: "I'm fortune-telling
again." Say to yourself, "I'm feeling self-loathing because I'm
convinced he won't be attracted to me, because my age is starting to show. I'm mind reading—I have no idea what he'll think
of me. And I'm feeling bad about how attractive I am because
I'm minimizing my good points and maximizing my crow's-
feet." Allow yourself to feel your emotions, talk to yourself
about them, and then notice if your feelings aren't a little more
manageable.

Note any evidence that your thoughts were distorted. If the
date goes well, and the man seemed attracted to you, remind
yourself that your initial assumptions were false. You now have

clear evidence that sometimes dates are a lot of fun, and the guy
you go out with thinks you're beautiful and sexy despite the fact
that you sometimes doubt your attractiveness. Whenever you
deliberately point out to yourself the evidence that your negative thoughts were distorted after all, you make progress toward
breaking the long-standing habit of engaging in negative distortions.

KEEP YOUR SENSE OF HUMOR

Humor can be an excellent tool for working through emotions, allowing you to experience empowerment instead of feeling overwhelmed by your pain, anger, or sorrow. The subject of
her mother's drinking had been taboo in the family of Nicole,
the Compassionate Rescuer. Yet Nicole felt that to change her
habit of getting into relationships with troubled men and denying just how severe their problems were, she needed to start acknowledging what had happened in her childhood. She found
that when she began talking about her past with friends, it was
easier if she could joke about it. Laughing about the dysfunction in her family helped her to break free of the denial, and
from there she could begin slowly getting in touch with the
pain, sadness, and anger she'd been repressing, which were
rooted in her childhood.

Humor can also help you get perspective on a situation, and
reaffirm your faith that "this too shall pass" and you will get
through it. Julie, the Standstill, found that cracking jokes about
her fears of getting back into the dating world again after years
of avoiding men made it easier for her to keep that fear from
overwhelming her. She felt less nervous when she was able to
admit to herself that being vulnerable and risking the rejection
of men was something she found scary. She discovered that
when she could find humor in the situation, she was less likely
to engage in distorted thoughts like, "Men think I'm uncom-

fortable and uptight, so I don't know why I'm bothering to go out on a date," or "No man will find me attractive." In fact, men responded positively to her humor, which broke the tension of blind dates.

PRACTICE CINEMATHERAPY

Watching a movie that portrays themes that are playing out in your life can be a great way to get in touch with your repressed feelings. By getting caught up in the story of someone else who is wrestling with her need to define herself differently from how the outside world sees her, or struggling to set boundaries with her family, you can access your hidden, difficult feelings about these experiences. When you watch a movie and have strong emotional reactions to it, allow those feelings to flow, even if it seems strange to be so moved by something that's fictional. After you've gotten in touch with your anger, grief, insecurity, and so on, think about why you had those strong reactions. Did you identify with a particular character in the movie, and if so, why? Did you find yourself getting angry at a character? Why do you think that is? What themes in the movie are playing out in your life? Asking these questions and exploring your answers can be extremely enlightening.

The following are some movies that I think will be especially helpful for you to watch in order to access and process your difficult emotions:

If you're an Old Faithful, you have trouble letting go of relationships and moving on. Take a look at *My Best Friend's Wedding*, with Julia Roberts (1997), a movie about a woman who had rejected her best friend when he tried to take their relationship to a more intimate level, but then becomes attracted to him all over again once he announces he's getting married. And *Gone with the Wind*, with Vivien Leigh and Clark Gable (1939), can help you explore your own difficulties achieving sexual and emotional intimacy with the same man. (It's long, but it's worth viewing to get in touch with this issue in your own life.)

If you are a Whirlwind Dater, you might watch *Under the Tuscan Sun*, with Diane Lane (2003), which will probably bring up feelings about being without a man, on your own, and scared and overwhelmed, and trying to trust that the right man will come at the right time. You might also benefit from watching a movie about failing to meet your family's and society's expectations and yet surviving, finding your own sense of purpose, and being happy and successful—for example, *Erin Brockovich*, with Julia Roberts (2000).

If you are a Standstill, it would be helpful to watch a movie that acknowledges your need for love and romance as valid, and reminds you that you have a feminine, vulnerable side that should be valued. You might watch *Moonstruck*, with Cher (1987), or *The Matchmaker*, with Janeane Garofalo (1997).

If you are a Forbidden Fruit Hunter, try watching the very funny, very honest *Postcards from the Edge*, with Meryl Streep and Shirley MacLaine (1990), about a woman who is struggling to get out from under the shadow of her narcissistic parent, define herself, and create a healthy, intimate relationship with a man. Or take a look at *Muriel's Wedding*, with Toni Collette (1994), a comedy about a young woman who feels she is "nothing" and keeps trying to find her self-worth outside herself, until she finally learns that her value as a person has nothing to do with whether or not she's successful in the eyes of her family or community.

If you are a Compassionate Rescuer, constantly focusing on others' needs to the detriment of your own, watch *Grace of My Heart*, with Illeana Douglas (1996), about a songwriter who learns to stop always giving to others and make a point of nurturing herself. The classic Hitchcock movie *Suspicion*, with

Cary Grant and Joan Fontaine (1941), may help you to get in touch with your own tendency to make excuses for a man you're involved with who is not capable of giving you what you need and deserve.

If you are a Wanderer, a movie featuring a woman who can't decide between two men, such as *Legends of the Fall*, with Brad Pitt and Aidan Quinn (1994), might help shed some light on what you want in a romantic partner, and your issues with commitment and intimacy. *Unfaithful*, with Diane Lane (2002), will probably elicit some strong feelings about your own affairs. (The moralistic ending may be especially wrenching to watch.)

If you are an Uptown Girl, consider watching a movie about a woman who breaks away from her limited ideas about what makes a man a potential romantic partner, such as *Crossing Delancey*, with Amy Irving (1988), or a movie about a woman who utterly rejects her family's ideas about whom she ought to marry, such as *Persuasion*, with Amanda Root (1995), based on a Jane Austen novel.

As a dissatisfied single, you might also want to watch some movies that explore setting boundaries with your family and changing the family dance. Try *Bend It Like Beckham* (2002), with Parminder Nagra, about a teenager in England who has very different ideas about what she wants for herself than her family has; *Hanging Up* (2000), with Meg Ryan and Walter Matthau, about a woman who feels trapped by her obligations to her aging father; and *Tortilla Soup* (2001), with Hector Elizondo, about a father and his three daughters who are ready to change their family traditions and dynamic but are afraid to talk about it.

If you're struggling with facing your fears about dating, consider watching *Edie & Pen* (1996), with Meg Tilly and Stockard Channing, about two recently divorced women regaining the courage to be vulnerable and date again; or *Next Stop Wonderland* (1998), with Hope Davis, a funny and poignant movie about a cynical young woman who starts to regain her faith that she will meet a man who is a true soul mate.

Another way to use movies to work through your emotions is simply to watch films that provoke emotions that you typically repress. If you're afraid or unable to get in touch with grief or sadness, a tearjerker can be great for helping you to unbottle your feelings. You'll start by crying about what's happening in the movie, and then, because the tears are flowing, you'll get in touch with sorrow that you've been hiding from yourself. You might watch *Born Free*, with Virginia McKenna (1966); *Terms of Endearment*, with Shirley MacLaine (1983); *Brian's Song*, with Billie Dee Williams (1971, remade in 2001 with Mekhi Phifer); *Beaches* (1988), with Bette Midler and Barbara Hershey (1988); or *Steel Magnolias* (1989), with Sally Field. After you've cried, you can explore where all your sadness is coming from and whether or not you have grief that you haven't processed.

Great movies about repressing difficult feelings include *Ordinary People* (1980), with Timothy Hutton and Mary Tyler Moore , who play a son and mother who can't talk openly about their grief and anger over losing a family member; and *On Golden Pond* (1981), with Jane Fonda and Henry Fonda as a daughter and father who have been unable to express their love for each other for years. After you've watched these movies, think about how your own family handles sadness and resentment.

Practice Bibliotherapy and Audiotherapy

As with cinematherapy, using books or music to get in touch with your feelings and gain insight into yourself can be really helpful if you are a dissatisfied single. Whether you read a memoir or a novel, the right book can help you to access emotions because it feels less scary to experience anger, sorrow, or fear vicariously. Again, when you find yourself emotionally connecting with a particular character, or reacting strongly to something that happens in a book, consider it an opportunity to explore the emotions and beliefs you've been hiding from yourself. One of my clients was very moved by the novel *My Sister's Keeper*, by Jodi Picoult, which is about a family who decides to have another child solely for the purpose of having a source for bone marrow to help their first child, who suffers from leukemia. This stirred up in her feelings about having her own needs sacrificed for the needs of others in her family. Another client discovered truths about herself and got in touch with her spirituality and sense of purpose after reading a memoir by Jane Goodall, who spent years sitting in the African jungles, intently studying chimpanzees. One client of mine found that *Tuesdays with Morrie,* by Mitch Albom, helped her to see that getting bogged down in her worries of the day wasn't productive, and also kept her full of fear, unable to embrace her life and live it to the fullest. She says it strengthened her commitment to work on her habit of worrying and to spend more time engaging in activities she found joyful and meaningful, regardless of whether her loved ones approved.

While listening to music may in some cases help you to gain insight into yourself and your behavior patterns, my clients mainly use it to access their emotions. Julie the Standstill gets in touch with her grief about lost opportunities, and her fears that she won't find love or that her relationships will turn sour, by listening to Chicago-style blues. The upbeat feel of the music and the sense of humor it often incorporates makes it less frightening for her to experience her grief and fear. Country songs, which often tell stories, can help you to feel less alone in your emotions, and believe that you aren't the only one experiencing the situations and feelings you're struggling with or have struggled with.

Sometimes music can inspire you to feel hopeful about the future, when a romantic relationship is not on the horizon or you've just broken up with a romantic partner. You might find that listening to strong female singers, like India Arie, Aretha Franklin, Natalie Merchant, Sarah McLachlin, Alanis Morissette, and Alicia Keys, who sing self-confident songs, can put you in touch with your own confidence.

Listening to specific music that has emotional meaning for you can also be useful. Rachel, the Old Faithful, listened to the CDs that she enjoyed with her ex-partner, Adam, to reconnect with her grief and work through it by experiencing it, while following through with her vow to not see him for many months. Nicole, the Compassionate Rescuer, made a point of listening to jazz CDs that she'd bought after her painful, ugly breakup with Jonathan, who had been taking advantage of her. She had taken a trip to a jazz festival and deliberately immersed herself in the music the bands were playing and enjoying the festive atmosphere to keep herself from focusing on her anxiety about finding someone new and her feelings of low self-worth that were rooted in her past. Every time she played this music for herself, she got back in touch with that courageous and adventurous trip she took that she'd found so nurturing, and was reminded that she could survive her anxiety and discomfort without falling back into her old pattern of latching on to the first available man in order to boost her esteem.

JOURNAL

Many times, I will ask clients to bring their old diaries from college, high school, or even childhood, to their session, and have them read passages. Much to their surprise, they often discover the root of their behavior patterns with their family, friends, and romantic partners. It can be very enlightening to see how far back your patterns of avoiding conflict, placating others, and hiding anger reach.

If you have journals from your past, I urge you to set aside some time to peruse them and look for the origins of your own behavior patterns. What did you fight with your family about when you were a teenager? What have your boyfriends had in common? How did your romances end?

If you have never used a journal, now would be a great time to start journaling in order to access and work through your hidden, difficult emotions. Here are some hints for getting the most out of using a journal:

- *Make a commitment to taking the time to express your thoughts and feelings in your journal.* It's very self-nurturing to make this commitment to putting your thoughts and beliefs on paper, in a permanent form. You might want to set aside a particular time each day that you write, or decide to fill in a certain number of pages every day or every other day. Some of my clients prefer to use their journal only when they are feeling an urgent need to express themselves or work out their thoughts and emotions through writing, but in general I think it's best to journal regularly. In doing so, you develop the habit of getting in touch with your thoughts and emotions rather than automatically pushing them aside.

- *Value your innermost beliefs and emotions enough to purchase a beautiful journal that you find easy to write in.* This may sound trivial, but the journal you choose is a reflection of your commitment to expressing and valuing what you are thinking and experiencing deep inside. Using a lovely journal and pen is a tangible reminder that what you feel and think is important.

- *Write freely, and don't allow yourself to think about writing for posterity.* You are not writing for publication or aiming to impress anyone with your writing skill, so try not to become self-conscious as you write. A journal is a place not only for thoughtful reflections but for raw emotions. Don't concern yourself with how someone you care about might feel if they read your journal. (In fact, it's always a good idea to keep your diary or journal out of sight, because people can feel tempted to read it.) One of my clients specifically asked a very trusted family member to burn her diaries if she should die, because knowing that no one will ever read anything she writes in them makes her feel free to express her very darkest emotions in her journal pages.

CREATE POEMS, MUSIC, AND ART

If you enjoy writing poems or songs, playing an instrument, singing, dancing, sculpting, painting, or expressing yourself creatively, I encourage you to use these activities to get in touch with your feelings. Don't think that you have to write a brilliant rap song or dance perfectly. When you are using this tool for getting in touch with and working through your emotions, do your best not to think at all about the possibility of having an audience. That can be a challenge if you are a professional artist, or tend toward perfectionism, but it's very important not to lock yourself into trying to make great art at the expense of letting your feelings flow. In fact, there are many creative professionals who have a secondary creative outlet just for this reason (musicians who choose to paint, painters who choose to dance, and so forth). They use their secondary creative outlet to explore and express their emotions without feeling pressured to conform to the professional standards they hold for themselves in their primary creative outlet.

If you choose to write about your life, whether it's in the form of essays, a memoir, or a novel, consider it to be a therapeutic act. Don't edit yourself. If your goal is to discover emotions and beliefs you've kept hidden, simply write, and then take a closer look at what you've written, because how you tell a story from your life can be very revealing. What you leave in and what you leave out and the tone you take (angry, melancholy, quietly reflective, or whatever) say a lot about you and your patterns. For instance, if you use humor to tell your story, leaving out the painful memories, it may be because you're avoiding a deeper layer of emotions and beliefs. Consider dropping the humor and writing about an event that makes you extremely uncomfortable. You might tell the tale as if it happened to someone else. On the other hand, finding the humor in the story, or finding the hopeful or inspirational aspect of it, can be empowering and help you to find the courage to continue exploring your inner world.

At some point, you might want to show the results of your creativity to people you care about. That's a risky prospect, of course, because they might respond negatively. Think carefully about whether you want to expose yourself in this way. You might want to write for your own purposes, choosing not to share what you've written down.

As you learn to manage your emotions, it will be easier to allow the most painful ones to surface, because they won't seem as frightening to you as they used to. You'll know how to handle them, and work through them, and you'll feel an increasing sense of confidence in your ability to let go of the old behavior patterns that haven't served you well. You'll continue to dismantle the distorted thoughts that trick you into being pessimistic about the future.

Even so, there will be times when you feel sad or discouraged. In the next chapter, you'll get guidance on embracing *what is*: adopting a spiritual perspective that will keep you on track as you move forward toward achieving the lasting, committed relationship you deserve.

14.

Embrace *What Is:* Achieving and Maintaining a Spiritual Perspective on Your Singlehood

It's a shame that we can't all just follow some simple steps and *boom,* magically meet a man who is right for us. Even the people who clearly know what they want and have no ambivalence about intimacy don't have this much control over their fate. The reality is there are no guarantees about when you will meet your perfect match. While you are doing the work I've laid out for you in this book, it can be enormously helpful to develop a spiritual attitude about your life, your purpose, and your ability to create the relationship you want. Spiritual beliefs can comfort you, inspire you, and keep you feeling optimistic even when you're not seeing the immediate effects of the positive changes you are making in your life.

I'm sure you have heard many reassuring old adages such as

"Every pot has a cover," "Things happen when you least expect it," and "Love comes when you're not looking for it." While those sayings may seem like platitudes that have no meaning or value, they exist for a reason—because there is truth to them. Many people have amusing and inspiring stories about how they, too, almost gave up on love and became cynical, but one day everything changed for them. There will be times when that is very hard to believe, but I have found that when dissatisfied singles engage in the following nine spiritual practices, they are better able to maintain their positive perspective and maximize their chances of finding the love they long for.

For each of these practices, I've given you a suggestion to make a list or write out your answer to a key question or two. You can do that in a journal or on a piece of paper, but it's a good idea to actually write out your answers rather than keep them in your head, because you're more likely to remain aware of your responses. You might also want to try the meditation exercise under Practice 7 several times, perhaps once a day for a week, to experience its effects more deeply.

On those darkest days when you're feeling depressed or hopeless, I hope you'll come back to this chapter and reread it, and make a conscious effort to change your attitude and engage in these practices. I promise that doing so will make your journey much easier.

Practice 1: View your experiences as opportunities to learn and grow.

We all have a soul, and each soul has a purpose. It's the lessons we learn that help us discover just what that purpose is. Luckily for us, the universe supports our purpose by continually presenting us with opportunities for learning and growth. Unfortunately, the situations we learn the most from are often the ones that cause us the most pain. In our suffering, it's easy to forget that this new knowledge and awareness will serve us in the future. Naturally, we would all like to avoid pain, but when we can't, we can give it meaning by looking at our situation as an opportunity for growth. As Albert Einstein once said, "In the middle of difficulty lies opportunity."

When a relationship doesn't work out, you'll need to grieve the loss, but you also need to examine what happened and learn what you can from the experience. Maybe the lesson of that particular relationship is that you have to work on being true to yourself instead of contorting yourself to fit someone else's expectations. Or maybe your challenge is to develop the habit of speaking up for yourself and your needs instead of letting your partner take advantage of your good nature. Whatever the lesson is, if you don't learn it, the universe will create another opportunity for you to do so. That is why so often you'll find yourself thinking, *This situation feels so familiar. Why do I keep ending up involved with a guy who doesn't appreciate me/wanting to flee a relationship just as it's getting serious/alone again on a Saturday night?* The answer is because you've been avoiding the lesson, and the universe is nudging you to pay attention!

From the moment you are born, you encounter opportunities for growth and learning that will foster your soul's quest. In fact, in some spiritual traditions, it is believed that before we are born, our soul is clear about its purpose in this life, and deliberately chooses a family to be born into that will allow it to learn the lessons it needs to learn. A soul might want to learn the lesson of self-sufficiency and independence, and choose to be born into a family that will place on her many expectations and demands. If a soul wanted to develop compassion, it might choose a parent who is cold and neglectful, someone it's diffi-

cult to feel loving toward. In other spiritual traditions, it's
that God chooses to challenge us so that we will grow and dis
cover our destiny.

Imagine that you've had the unhappy experiences you've
had along the way not because you've suffered from bad luck,
or because you have somehow failed as a person, but because
your purpose is to learn the lessons inherent in these experiences. You might find that your worst experiences have their
own hidden gifts.

Alyssa, the Forbidden Fruit Hunter, began to examine the
painful relationships she'd had with men who were emotionally
unavailable, in which she had tried so hard to conform to their
needs in the hope that doing so would entice them into giving
up the other woman for her. She came to realize that the lesson
she had been avoiding for years was that love does not require
you to give up yourself; it requires you to take care of yourself
and truly care about the well-being of other people. Her
mother, JoAnn, who had been her role model, had given her the
false impression that love means constant sacrifice, and in fact,
she expected Alyssa to devote enormous amounts of time and
attention to her even if it meant Alyssa was neglecting her own
need for a romantic relationship with a man. Once Alyssa realized this, she started recognizing when she was once again mis-
taking love for self-sacrifice. She continued to insist on having
stronger boundaries with her mother than she'd had before, and
she set boundaries with others in her life that she felt she was
giving too much to. When she began dating again, she made a
point of allowing herself to be nurtured without protesting that
she "didn't need fussing over," which is how she used to feel.
Because of her efforts, she was able to let go of any guilt or ambivalence she might feel whenever her partner pampered her.

Whatever your own experiences have been, if you examine
them closely, you will start to see the lessons they have to teach

have integrated this knowledge, it will be much
new and brighter future for yourself.

t three of the most painful things that have
you in your life. What lessons might you learn
from those experiences? Do you feel you've truly learned
those lessons, or do you still come up against them in your
life? What do you think might help you to learn the lesson?

Practice 2: Trust in karma.

Karma is essentially the idea that what goes around comes
around, that whatever you do, good or bad, will be rewarded or
punished accordingly, and that your attitude and behavior influence everything that happens to you. If you trust in karma,
you take responsibility for changing your actions, knowing that
you won't achieve the results you desire unless you do so.

When you trust in karma, you don't assign blame or tell
yourself, "It's my fault I'm still single." Being single is the state
you're in. The relationships you had that didn't work out are
now in the past, and you can't do anything to change them.
However, trusting in karma means you acknowledge that your
thoughts, feelings, and behaviors influence your relationships
and determine the type of men you attract. Up until now,
you've been communicating to the universe your hidden beliefs, not your conscious desires, and it has listened and sent you
exactly what you think you deserve. Now that you are replacing
your hidden beliefs with more positive ones, like "I am lovable,"
and "I deserve a loving and committed relationship," the universe will be able to respond in kind. Gandhi said, "Happiness

is when what you think, what you say, and what you do are in harmony." Your hidden beliefs are no longer contradicting your conscious desires, so you won't be sending out the wrong messages and ending up unhappy and disappointed again and again.

For Julie, the Standstill, the challenge was to trust that if she felt sexy and desirable, men would see her that way, too. Of course, not every man would be attracted to her, but some definitely were. Difficult as it was for her to believe them when they said, "You're incredibly beautiful," she continued her practice of taking long, sensual baths and dressing more attractively to remind herself that compliments like these were warranted. She also noticed that she was quick to make a joke to deflect those kinds of remarks, and worked at developing the habit of responding with a gracious thank-you instead.

Rachel, the Old Faithful, had to accept that she had been sending out signals that she felt unworthy of having emotional intimacy and sexual intimacy in the same package, because she was still too emotionally attached to her father. She realized that until she resolved her inner conflict, she would attract one or the other, but not both at the same time. Nicole, the Compassionate Rescuer, subconsciously believed that her worth was based on fixing others, so she attracted one needy man after another. As these women began to change their hidden beliefs, they began attracting different types of men—and they found they were drawn to men who were unlike the ones they'd been involved with previously. You, too, will find that when you change on the inside, the universe will respond.

Can you think of anything you are doing that might be attracting men who are needy, emotionally unavailable, and drawn to you for the wrong reasons? Are there hidden negative beliefs you are still holding on to? How do they man-

ifest when you are on a date, interacting with your part-
ner, or trying to move to the next level in your relation-
ship?

Practice 3: Exercise your free will.

We all have freedom of choice and free will, but until now,
you've been unconsciously sabotaging your ability to make
choices based on that free will. You've been trapped in behavior
patterns and didn't realize it. Now, however, you can see what
the patterns are and choose to break the old habits and take actions that serve your goal instead of your subconscious desire
for familiarity. You can set and stick to boundaries, behave in
ways your loved ones don't approve of, break out of your behavior patterns that originated in your childhood, and reach
out to create a deeper emotional intimacy with your romantic
partner.

While making these choices may cause you discomfort,
even pain, recognize that it is only temporary. It's wonderful to
have choices and to be aware of that, instead of being on
autopilot, constantly dating the same men who don't really appreciate you for who you are, or being stuck at home, afraid to
make a move to meet a potential romantic partner.

Increasingly, you will become aware that you're at a cross-
roads, and you have a choice between the old behavior and the
new one. Do you agree to the blind date, or do you refuse to
take the chance? When your new romantic partner confesses
that he is still married, do you quickly change the subject and
tell yourself he's surely going to get a divorce, or do you start
asking him hard questions so that you have the information you
need to protect yourself from getting hurt? Be proud of your-

self for recognizing that you have a choice, and make the one that you know will lead you to your happiness, understanding that you can live a rich, joyful life no matter what your romantic situation.

If you're tempted to start dating another man, or at least lining one up as a backup because you're uncomfortable in your current relationship, acknowledge that engaging in this Wanderer behavior will not result in the relationship you want with either man. Exercise your choice to stay in the relationship. Work on building intimacy until you reach a point where you are clear on whether you want to be with him or not. If you start to consider compromising your beliefs or dreams, or hiding an aspect of yourself, in order to maintain a relationship with a man, recognize your choice: You can continue to pretend you are someone you aren't, and never achieve the relationship you want, or you can bravely face the possibility of rejection, and have faith that you will ultimately find a man who loves you for who you are.

Frightening though it may be to make the choice that will cause you discomfort and lead you down the unfamiliar road, away from the old path that you know so well, it's the only way to get to where you want to go. *Act as if* you're brave enough to face the consequences of making a good choice, even if you think you aren't. As Eleanor Roosevelt said, "You must do the thing you think you cannot do."

Over the course of a week, notice every time when you feel you have to make a choice between falling into your old relationship behavior pattern and embracing new, healthier, more productive behaviors. You might jot down a note to yourself in a mini-notebook you carry around, or you might take some time at the end of the day to think back to the choices that came up and write them down. What choice did you make in each case? If you chose to fall into the old pattern, try to identify why you did so. Was it an unconscious choice? Were you feeling fearful for some reason? Pretend that you could rewind time and make the right choice this time. The next time the situation comes up, you can choose the new behavior. Remember, at first, the new behavior will make you uneasy, but each time you make the better choice, it will feel more comfortable.

Practice 4: Accept that life isn't fair.

At times, you may think that everyone but you has found a great guy. I know it can feel that way, but of course, this is a distortion. There are plenty of women—and men—who are still looking for a deeply fulfilling and lasting relationship. Today, you happen to be one of them, but that might not be the case tomorrow.

If you start to compare yourself to someone else, thinking, *How come she found love but I haven't? It's not fair!* here's an experiment to try. Look at that other person's life—her entire life—and ask yourself whether you would be willing to trade places with her if you had to give up everything you have and take on everything she has. Maybe she has a wonderful man, but has health problems, or she doesn't have a good relationship with her family like you do, or she isn't happy in her career while you love your job. When we compare ourselves with others, we pick and choose what details to notice, carefully selecting the ones that will validate our feelings of jealousy and frustration.

We want to believe that if we feel miserable, it must be because we're victims of bad luck. By now, you know that you are capable of making yourself feel awful simply by indulging in distorted thoughts. So, if you find yourself feeling jealous and frustrated, use the tools you have learned about to help you deal with those feelings. Turn inward, and ask yourself why you believe you can't have what that person has—a loving, committed relationship. Don't indulge in comparisons, because they keep you mired in anger, frustration, and envy.

The fact is that life just isn't fair. Parents die, or abandon their children, and while that shouldn't happen to any child, perhaps it happened to you. Every child should feel nurtured and accepted, and yet maybe you never felt that way. You may be a delightful, warm, generous person who approaches relationships with optimism and enthusiasm and yet, for whatever reason, you've had to endure pain and loneliness, while some other woman, who is less giving and loving, seems to be happily married. It may seem unfair that you have so many issues to work through, because you happened to be born into a particular family and as a result developed behavior patterns that are self-defeating.

Remember, life is about learning. Everyone has her unique set of challenges and painful situations to deal with and lessons to learn. When you can let go of the need for fairness, you will free yourself up to focus on learning what you need to learn, changing the behaviors you need to change, and healing yourself.

> *What happened in your life that hasn't been fair? How did you handle it at the time? Knowing what you know now, how would you handle the situation? What lessons can you learn from this situation?*

Practice 5: Be kind and compassionate toward yourself.

In my experience, dissatisfied singles find it easy to be self-deprecating. The challenge is to be nice to yourself, to refuse to give in to feelings of self-loathing, shame, and low self-worth, or talk about yourself negatively—even in jest. Kindness, compassion, and forgiveness are values all religions share. Yet often we forget that we're supposed to be compassionate, forgiving, and kind toward ourselves as well as to others. Being harsh with ourselves serves no purpose, spiritual or practical.

What you feel about yourself is what you express to the world, whether you're aware of it or not. So, if you're expressing that you are unworthy and unlovable, the universe will respond to that message. You will attract to yourself people who treat you as if you were unworthy and unlovable. That is karma. On the other hand, if your message to the universe is that you deserve love, nurturing, and kindness, you will attract all of that. Being hard on yourself, focusing on all your mistakes and the flaws in your behavior, is self-defeating. You need to cultivate self-awareness and begin healing yourself.

When you're tempted to judge yourself harshly, focus on the fact that you have a particular set of behavior patterns you need to change, and you have a choice about whether or not to work at changing them. You can dwell on the negative aspects of your life and the things you have done and the way you operate in the world, or you can choose to think about how you would like to change all of that for the better.

If you can commit to knowing yourself, and accepting yourself as you are right now, you will be setting the foundation for a loving, fulfilling relationship. Look to the future, and work on your behavior patterns, but don't obsess about what isn't working for you today. Acknowledge it, pledge to change it, forgive yourself, and start *acting as if* you were comfortable with the new, healthier behaviors you want to adopt. Over time, those new behaviors will be fully integrated into your life, and you will be able to celebrate the results of your hard work and determination.

Being kind and compassionate also means letting go of resentments toward other people. Staying angry eats up your energy, sours your attitude, and causes you to close yourself off from the possibility of truly trusting other people. You need to be compassionate, forgiving, and loving if you want to achieve true intimacy in a relationship.

Whom are you still angry with? Do you feel anger at your ex or your parents, or can you feel love and compassion for them?

Think of three times when you were very hard on yourself. What did you do? What could you have done or told yourself that would have been kinder and more compassionate?

Now, think of three things you could do for yourself that would make you feel nurtured and cherished. They may be as small as buying yourself flowers or out-of-season fruit you enjoy, or as big as getting control of your finances so that you have the money to take yourself on a dream vacation. What could you do regularly to achieve your goal of being kinder to yourself? (Buy yourself treats, put money away for that vacation and indulge in planning it to the last detail, stop yourself whenever you're being self-critical and think of one of your positive qualities, and so on.)

Practice 6: Trust in timing.

I wish I could promise you that if you change *X*, *Y*, and *Z* by such-and-such a date, you can be sure your Prince Charming will promptly appear. The reality is that even after you've gone through all four stages of self-awareness, discovered your part in it all, examined your hidden beliefs and discarded your red herrings, and made substantial progress in changing your behavior patterns, you still may have to wait for your opportunity for love. The difference is that when it comes knocking, you'll have done the work to be able to receive it this time.

I know it can be difficult to trust that things happen just as they should, on a timetable that you can't orchestrate. One of my clients spent a lot of time in her mid to late twenties feeling sorry for herself because she hadn't found love. She was pessimistic about ever getting married, and felt ashamed that her thirtieth birthday was approaching and she still hadn't created the relationship she wanted. Then, less than three months after she turned thirty, she met the man of her dreams. Their connection was instantaneous; they began talking about marriage within days (although they wisely waited for their relationship to unfold at its own pace), and by age thirty-three, she was married to this wonderful man. However, she deeply regretted that she had been so miserable in her twenties, so certain that she would never achieve the relationship she wanted. She told me, "If I'd only known I'd find him right after I turned thirty, I could have relaxed and really enjoyed my twenties. I wasted so much time feeling bad!"

Unfortunately, no one has a crystal ball to tell you what the future holds. But does it make more sense to be optimistic, and keep putting yourself out there, expressing your self-love in how you walk, talk, and operate in the world, or to be pessimistic, stay home every weekend or stay stuck with a partner who makes you unhappy, and tell yourself that there's no hope for anything better?

One dissatisfied single I worked with was told about a guy she might be interested in, but at the time she was an Uptown Girl, so she let her friend know that she wouldn't want to go out with a man who didn't have a college degree and worked with his hands. (He was an electrician.) After she'd gone through a series of unhappy relationships and done a lot of inner work to break the old behavior patterns, someone at work asked her if she'd be interested in going on a blind date with a friend of his who was an electrician. This time, she was willing to date a man who wasn't a college-educated, white-collar worker, and to her surprise, she discovered by accident that it was the very same man she'd turned down, sight unseen, years before. You guessed it—they ended up together. In retrospect, she realized she wouldn't have appreciated him three years earlier. As it turns out, three years previous, he had been, as he called it, "the walking wounded": he'd ended a painful relationship and was too upset to be emotionally available anyway.

Thinking back, have you ever missed an opportunity to find permanent love? Was there someone who might have been right for you, that you weren't willing to pursue a relationship with at the time? Why? What hidden beliefs do you think were in your way?

Practice 7: Live in the moment.

Buddhists say it is important to practice mindfulness, that is, being fully aware of what you are experiencing right now, in this moment, whether it's eating an orange, sweeping a floor, or feeling sadness. Most of the time we are focused on the past or the future, doing one thing but thinking about another, and as a result, we are unaware of what we are doing. We're upset, but forcing ourselves to think about making some important business calls. We're cooking a meal, and thinking about how much nicer it would be to eat at a restaurant with a handsome man. As a dissatisfied single, with many painful emotions buried deep within, you probably are in the habit of distracting yourself so that those emotions won't surface. But when you do that, you prevent yourself from working through those feelings and releasing them at last.

Being mindful of what is happening in the present instead of getting stuck in the past, or yearning for the future, also allows you to break out of the automatic actions and reactions that you engage in. As you've seen, getting caught up in shame, resentment, blame, and anger do not help you move forward toward your goal. The old, hidden beliefs became ingrained in you because you were not aware that you were constantly reinforcing them with fleeting thoughts like, *I'm such a fool, Of course, he doesn't want to be with me, Uh-oh, I'd better shut up about wanting to see him more often because he seems uncomfortable with that.* When you're mindful, you can catch yourself engaging in distorted thoughts. It's so rewarding when I see a dissatisfied single in my office pause for a moment after saying something, and then say, "Wait a minute. I know what you're going to tell me—I'm mind reading here!" or "Oh boy, there I go, telling myself I'm not good enough." Recognizing and acknowledging those false, negative assumptions allows you to immediately discard them rather than imprinting them on your subconscious.

When you are mindful, you stay in the present. Yes, you

can have dreams and goals, and envisioning the future you would like for yourself can help you to be clear about what you really want, but when you obsess about what's to come, there is a danger that you will fall into the trap of thinking that external circumstances drive relationships. If you convince yourself that you can't be happy until your life changes—until you are married—you will make yourself sad, angry, and frustrated. If you buy into the notion that you can't be happy right now, you will create that reality. Every day you wake up, you'll feel angry and resentful that once again, you are waking up alone. That is not going to lead you to lasting joy, or a lasting relationship.

Accepting that your life is good right now, just as it is, gives you the freedom to really enjoy each day and to continue to feel optimistic about the future. Because you aren't spending your energy obsessing about when you will create the relationship you want, you'll be able to do all the right things to set yourself up to attract the man you would truly love to be with. Be open to what the day brings. As eighteenth-century writer Maria Edgeworth said, "If we take care of the moments, the years will take care of themselves."

Do the following meditation/mindfulness exercise. Find a tree in a quiet spot, sit with your back to it, and close your eyes. Breathe deeply for a few minutes, letting your thoughts come into your mind, but not exploring them. Simply let them float into your mind and dissipate. When they start to distract you, focus on your breathing and the sensation as you draw in breath slowly, and exhale slowly.

Continue this meditation for at least ten minutes. When you open your eyes, be aware of how you feel.

Practice 8: Cultivate gratitude.

One of the ways we distort our thinking is to focus on what we don't have and to ignore the riches we do have. As a dissatisfied single, you probably think a lot about the relationship you wish you had, giving it so much weight that in your darker moments, you forget everything in your life that you truly value. When you are tempted to give in to the loneliness and despair, you can pull yourself back to a more balanced view of your life by taking the time to be thankful.

Cultivating gratitude means looking at the larger picture. You have a unique set of wonderful qualities that make you who you are, but you may not even be aware of them because you're trying so hard to please other people. When you cultivate gratitude, you acknowledge your warmth, your sense of humor, and your responsible nature, you experience the pride of knowing that you are a valuable, lovable person, and you're thankful for all that you are. You have created rewarding friendships, you have influenced other people in a positive way, and you may be excellent at your job and a terrific daughter, friend, and citizen. Yet it's easy to forget how lucky you are when you're focused on the relationship you don't have yet.

You can cultivate gratitude by making a list of things you're grateful for, and adding to it every night as you think back on your day. You may have gotten stuck in a traffic jam, made a huge mistake at work, and come home to the voice mail message from your date that "something has come up" and he's canceling your plans for the evening, but even on a day where everything seems to have gone wrong, there are things you can be grateful for.

The more obvious gifts you have are your health, your intelligence, talents, and skills, your friends and family, and your material wealth (which, while it may not be great, is probably greater than it is for many people in this world). However, there are little things to be grateful for, too. Maybe today you saw the first signs of spring in the buds on the trees, or you bought the first strawberries of the season, on sale, and they were delicious. These may seem like minor, fleeting pleasures, but when you take the time to savor the gifts you've been given, your attitude and your perspective shift.

There's a wonderful story in Rachel Naomi Remen's book *Kitchen Table Wisdom* about a woman who had recently undergone chemotherapy who decided to spend a weekend with her husband in San Francisco. Her oncologist discouraged her, because he knew she was too sick and weak to enjoy the usual sights and tourist attractions, from the restaurants to the trolley car rides. She went anyway, and when she came back, she spoke eloquently of how delicious it had been to spend the weekend with her husband making love in a bed with crisp sheets, dining together, and enjoying fabulous meals in the hotel room instead of eating the hospital food she had grown used to, and gazing out the window at the beauty of the city. Because she had spent so much time deprived of sensory pleasures, she was able to appreciate all of this far more deeply than her doctor could have imagined.

Appreciating all that you are able to experience opens you to more fully embrace the life you have, and to stop fretting about the life you might have if you had a relationship. In fact, if you are in a relationship, cultivating gratitude can help you get perspective on any troubles you may be having with your partner, instead of feeling overwhelmed by anxiety and thinking that every problem that comes up, no matter how small, is a sign that the relationship won't work.

*Choose a day—perhaps New Year's Day or your birthday,
or pick a day once a month or even once a week—to devote
to reflecting on your blessings. Throughout the course of the
day, notice everything in your life that you are grateful for.
For example, each time you sit down to a meal, be aware
of how thankful you are for plenty of healthy food. Appreciate the connections you have with friends and family.
Constantly stop yourself and simply sit with the feeling of
gratitude as you experience your cat purring in your lap or
the beauty of snow falling.*

Practice 9: Stay faithful to your journey.

There will always be potholes along the road of life, and the
goal is to ensure that they don't make you give up on your
dreams. You can do all the right things to heal yourself and
break from your old behavior patterns, but even so, there will
be days when the consequences of those changes cause you a lot
of pain. For the Whirlwind Dater, choosing not to date can be
very anxiety provoking, while for the Standstill, choosing to
date can have the same effect. Setting boundaries with people
can expose you to their anger, contempt, or ridicule. It's not
easy to make changes and endure the emotional ripples and
waves that result.

Other times, it may feel as if the universe is ignoring the
new, positive energy you are sending forth. The phone doesn't
ring, you realize after a date that you and this man are never going to connect, or you fall hard for someone only to have him
unexpectedly give you the brush-off. Those disappointments
could veer you off course, but if you recommit yourself to these

spiritual practices, and continue doing the work you are doing to change on the inside, things will turn around.

Remember that it is far too easy to focus on the negative instead of on the positive in our own lives, and it's only when we focus on the positive that we can make our dreams come true. Most of us have heard of Babe Ruth, and know he is the all-time home run king. But most people don't know that Babe Ruth also held the record for the greatest number of strikeouts. Can you imagine what his career would have been like if every time he struck out, he talked himself out of going up to that plate again and swinging the bat? Babe Ruth was also heavyset and a slow runner, so if he wanted to make it as far as first base—much less home plate—without being thrown out by the fast, agile players on the other team, his only choice was to hit that ball right out of the park—and that's what he did, time and time again, despite long hitless streaks, and fans booing and shouting that he was a wash-up. Your challenge is to find your inner Babe Ruth, stop obsessing over your strikeout record, and step up to the plate every day, confident in your ability to achieve your goal of creating a fulfilling, lasting relationship.

> *List five things that could throw you off course and set you back to operating the way you used to. Think of ways to counteract those setbacks. (For instance, could you call a friend to get a pep talk, watch a movie that will inspire you to have faith in yourself, or indulge in a vigorous workout that reminds you how much you love your body and think you're attractive?)*

As you embrace these spiritual beliefs, I encourage you to explore your own faith more deeply, and to read books on spirituality, such as *Seat of the Soul* by Gary Zukav, *If the Buddha Dated* by Charlotte Kasl, *Going to Pieces Without Falling Apart* by Mark Epstein, *Kitchen Table Wisdom* by Rachel Naomi Remen, *The Four Agreements* by Don Miguel Ruiz, *The Gift of Change* by Marianne Williamson, *The Alchemist* by Paulo Coelho, and *The Road Less Traveled* by M. Scott Peck. You might also consider incorporating regular spiritual practices into your life, from meditating to attending church or synagogue to spending time in nature, appreciating its beauty and its lessons about the cycles of life. Each time you greet a new day, recognize the possibilities it offers you, and reaffirm your commitment to make the most of your opportunities to grow, and to follow through on the changes in your life that you now know you want to make. I am convinced that every day, you're going to do a little better at loving yourself and opening yourself up to the love you deserve.

PART IV

Dissatisfied Single No More

15.

Happily Ever After: Success Stories

In the process of reading this book, you've begun to discover your behavior patterns and think about ways in which you can start changing them. Some of you, particularly Whirlwind Daters, will be eager to forge ahead and start looking for a romantic partner, while others, particularly Standstills, will want to hold back a little, and do some more self-exploration before going out there into the dating world. If you're thinking that merely reading this book will solve enough of your problems to allow you to change your behavior patterns immediately, slow down. Everything I am describing takes work. You cannot put a timetable on how long it will take for you to process your emotions, or get in touch with the aspects of yourself that you've repressed for many years. I want you to start the process of change and be optimistic, but also be realistic about how much time and effort it will take. When you close this book, the real work begins.

If at this point you are feeling that you have a huge amount of work to do on yourself and it would be best to focus on that and avoid relationships for an indefinite amount of time, consider that you might be making excuses for not moving forward, facing your difficult emotions and hidden beliefs, and changing your behavior patterns. I assure you that just having the insights you've gained so far means that you have changed already. With your new awareness, you can start looking for a relationship, knowing that you're far more prepared than you've ever been to make that partnership click.

If you are in a relationship now, and you are doubtful that it's the right one for you, I'm not going to ask you to end it. For one thing, the process of ending a relationship is very emotionally wrenching, and should be thought out carefully. Take your time with your decision, and consider whether or not your partner, who most likely mirrors your own issues, might be ready to grow with you. If you can be honest with yourselves and each other, and work at getting in touch with your true emotions as well as your values, you may discover that you are both able to make the leap into a deeper level of intimacy and commitment.

Success Stories

When a client leaves my office for the last time, I feel a sense of sadness mixed with joy. I know that they've done the hard work they needed to do to create the relationship they want—whether they are involved with a man or not. There's no doubt in my mind that they have changed on the inside, and the universe is going to respond to those changes. They've finally broken free of their past and the behavior patterns that prevented them from finding the relationship that is right for them.

Here is what happened to eight clients I've profiled in this book:

RACHEL, THE OLD FAITHFUL

Rachel made major strides toward creating some breathing room between her and her father, and between her and her ex, Adam. She began dating regularly and had a couple of short-term relationships, but is currently not seeing anyone. Her attitude toward the men she is dating is completely different from what it had been. She no longer compares them to Adam. She also has been able to be sexual with some men whom she felt an emotional connection to. Her breakups were difficult, but she didn't begin to pine for them; she was able to move on. In fact, she was the one who ended one of the relationships. She has talked to one of these men a few times since, but feels no strong need to romanticize what they had together, or stay in close contact. Rachel feels confident that when opportunity knocks, she'll walk through that door without looking back.

CAROLE, THE WHIRLWIND DATER

Carole has now been with her new boyfriend, Eric, a music producer, for six months. This is a record for her, and she's very hopeful about their future together. It is the first emotionally connected relationship she has ever had. As she's begun her own process of self-discovery, she's shared with Eric what she has learned about herself, because she no longer fears that he will abandon her as soon as he knows the real Carole. He's been supportive of her decision to eventually quit her job as an events planner at the museum and become an independent wedding consultant. It is a scary move for her, because she is finally pursuing a dream of her own that her parents don't approve of, but she is thrilled that Eric is in her corner.

JULIE, THE STANDSTILL

In a lot of ways, Julie had further to travel than any of the other dissatisfied singles. She is still single and not in a relationship yet, but she recognizes what tremendous progress she has made getting to the point where she dates regularly. What's more, she is far more comfortable with her femininity than she has ever been. She dresses completely differently, not only on the weekends but on the job, because she has less of a need to prove that she is "one of the guys." She feels secure in herself and her womanhood, and no longer is embarrassed by her vulnerability. She has made a new, close female friend and says she feels she can truly be herself with this woman, and feels no need to impress her. Together, they go to parties and events, and enjoy each others' company when they aren't meeting men.

ALYSSA, THE FORBIDDEN FRUIT HUNTER

Alyssa has made a real effort to redefine her relationship with her mother, JoAnn, and the work has paid off: They are close, but not intimately wrapped up in each others' lives. Alyssa talked her two brothers into helping out their aging mother more often, and that freed up a lot of time for Alyssa to date again. A few months ago, she met a great guy through some friends and has her first completely available boyfriend. Alyssa is not sure he is the one, but she is enjoying being with him, and very encouraged by the fact that she was finally attracted to someone who wasn't secretly married or involved with another woman.

NICOLE, THE COMPASSIONATE RESCUER

Nicole has never heard from Jonathan, and she feels certain that she has closed the book on the chapter of her life in which she would only fall in love with men who had problems. Nicole met a great guy, Chris, through an online dating service, and she feels certain that she and this new romantic partner are headed toward the altar. Like her, he comes from an alcoholic home, but also like her, Chris has put a lot of effort into changing his pattern of dating partners who are too needy. Each of them mirrors the other's new, healthier, more confident self.

AMY, THE WANDERER

Amy still has a lot of work to do on herself, and she is comfortable focusing on her own needs right now, only rarely feeling anxiety about being single. She hasn't made the effort to date, which is a huge change for her. She says she's content to spend her free time getting to know her friends better, reestablishing her relationships with her siblings, Charise and Donnie, and working through the difficult feelings she experienced in her childhood. She has also developed a strong interest in yoga, not just for the body, but for the spirit, and is getting involved with the local yoga community, learning more about the practice and going on yoga retreats. One of her yoga instructors is eager to set up her brother with Amy, and Amy has agreed to go out with him. Having established much more intimate connections with her brother and sister than she has ever had, she feels confident that if she does get into a relationship, she will not feel anxious if she and a partner start developing emotional intimacy.

LUCY, THE UPTOWN GIRL

Lucy stood up to her father and mother and began acting more like herself and less like the "princess daughter" they expected her to be, learned how to manage her own finances so that she didn't have to rely on her father to help her, and made the decision to marry Michael, regardless of her father's initial discomfort with Michael's level of wealth. She is very happy in her marriage, and has found that Michael has embraced the new, more assertive Lucy. She is considering approaching her father about cutting back her hours working for him, not so that she can have a baby (which her family is pressuring her about), but so that she can spend more time just enjoying her life—sculpting, getting to know Michael better, and exploring who she is.

ELIZABETH, THE RUNAWAY BRIDE

Elizabeth had not spoken to her ex-boyfriend, Pete, more than a couple of times since moving out on him and beginning therapy, but she gathered the courage to write him a long letter explaining that she suddenly turned down the heat on their relationship in order to focus on dealing with her own difficult, unresolved emotions about her past. Pete, who had lost his father at an early age, understood the depth of Elizabeth's pain over losing her mother as a child, and he appreciated her need to reconnect with her father and sister. He was able to handle Elizabeth's need to slowly rediscover herself, and what she really wanted. In the process of self-discovery, Elizabeth got clearer about her feelings about Pete, and they began seeing each other again. After many months, she came to realize that she loved him, and that the two of them shared many values and dreams. Their time apart was a positive experience that helped them see that they wanted to spend their lives together. Pete proposed, Elizabeth accepted, and they are now married.

Scripting Your Own Happily Ever After

You can't know how you will meet the romantic partner who is right for you, or when it will happen, but now you know the process for setting the wheels in motion, and you've started that process. You are now aware of your internal monologue. Before, it was a whisper of negative, distorted, unproductive thoughts and feelings about yourself and the people you care about. Now you've turned up the volume and changed the CD to one that is upbeat, that inspires you to feel confident and positive each day as you pursue your dreams.

There will be times when the old thoughts and feelings return, but now you'll recognize them right away and discard them, because you'll recognize what are distorted thoughts and false beliefs. You know how to work through your feelings, and as you do so, you will stop feeling overwhelmed when they come up. Your anger won't feel so frightening, and your vulnerability won't make you feel lost, abandoned, and unloved. Your emotions will not be blown out of proportion by your thoughts.

When someone rejects you, you won't automatically start doubting yourself. You'll see the situation more clearly, and stop taking on the burden of other people's unrealistic expectations of you. You can be honest about your role in your relationships because you're no longer mired in low self-worth, convinced that you are unlovable and unworthy. Now you realize that you, just like everyone else, will make mistakes or behave badly on occasion, and you deserve understanding and forgiveness, because no one is perfect. However, instead of running away from the consequences of your actions, you now have the courage to face them and learn from them. You're growing every day, and the people around you will change with you or fall away.

As you find your voice and speak your truth, some people won't be able to handle it and will reject you. Rest assured that you can and will replace those people in your life. If someone in your family that you dearly love can't accept the new you, wish them well, stay open to the possibility that they may come around eventually, allow yourself to grieve this loss, and then focus on the loving relationships you do have in your life. Whether you are setting boundaries or building bridges, your honesty will ultimately serve you well.

In this book, you've learned a lot of skills that will help you to create the relationship you want, and you've learned to look honestly at yourself—your deepest feelings and fears, and your subconscious behavior patterns. Simply having these insights will change your life in ways you didn't think were possible. Now you can stop operating from a subconscious level and instead, have your thoughts, actions, feelings, and behaviors in sync with your desires. You've begun breaking free of chains you didn't realize were binding your heart, and as you move forward in your life, know that you're on a new path, one that will

---

Signs That You Are No Longer a Dissatisfied Single

1. After agreeing to a date on Friday night, you don't spend the week worrying about it and dreading it.

(Continued)

2. When your date asks if you want Mexican or Thai food, you don't feel you have to let him choose, or pick the one you think he would prefer.

3. When you get back from a date, you don't speed-dial your girlfriend to vent about how awful it was and how hopeless dating is, nor do you go on and on about how absolutely perfect this guy is.

4. You actually enjoy meeting men and find most of the guys you date attractive and likable, but you don't start fantasizing about the wedding you and he will have.

5. A bad date or a relationship that breaks up doesn't send you into a tailspin of self-doubt.

6. If he doesn't call, you don't fall into self-pity or self-loathing; you take it in stride.

7. When you hear the negative chatter in your mind—*I know he won't like me, He probably thought I was fat*—you'll recognize it for the brain blip it is and laugh it off.

8. It's been a really long time since you thought about your ex, and now that he comes to mind, you feel a little winsome and nostalgic about the good times, nothing more.

9. You maintain clear boundaries with your family, friends, coworkers, and lovers, and you don't feel guilty about saying no or asking to have your needs met.

(Continued)

10. You're aware of your feelings, and instead of being scared by their intensity, you allow yourself to experience them fully, knowing that this too shall pass.

11. You walk away from a guy who has problems before you get emotionally involved instead of paying the tab, making excuses for him, and hoping for the best.

12. Your parents do not know as much about your love life as your therapist does, and you have several rehearsed lines for dodging their intrusive questions about your current relationship.

13. You no longer look outside yourself for approval, validation of your feelings, or reassurance that you are a sexy, wonderful, lovable woman.

14. You are comfortable with who you are, and you genuinely like yourself.

take you to the love you deserve.

Index

abandonment, feeling of, 178–79,
    183–84, 186–87, 200, 211
    bridges toward intimacy and,
        240
    death of parent or sibling and, 178,
        182
    mourning and, 248
acceptance, stage of, 248–50
acting as if, 10, 249
advice, giving and taking, 229–30
age, dating and, 15, 28, 157, 160
Albom, Mitch, 258
Alchemist, The (Coelho), 284
alcohol/alcoholism, 37, 84, 150, 207,
    291
all-or-nothing thinking. *See* black-and-
    white thinking
anger management, 219
anxiety, 13, 28, 44, 78, 281
    hidden, 82
    monogamy and, 149–51
    music as therapy and, 259
    ways to ease, 152, 189
    worry and, 40–41
Arie, India, 259
art, as therapy, 261–63

backstories, family
    Compassionate Rescuer, 124–25
    Forbidden Fruit Hunter, 105–7
    Old Faithful, 51–53
    Runaway Bride, 181–83
    Standstill, 85–86
    Uptown Girl, 162–64
    Wanderer, 141–43
    Whirlwind Dater, 67–69
Beaches (movie), 257
beauty, 94–95, 163, 167–68
behavior patterns, 5, 11, 12, 44, 131
    breaking and changing, 219, 220, 287,
        289
    family dynamics and, 196, 213
    fear of rejection and, 244
    free will and, 270
    hidden emotions and, 245
    journal keeping and, 260
    self-defeating, 273
    spiritual practices to overcome, 275
beliefs, hidden, 11, 44, 242
    changing, 9–10, 21
    commonly held, 22–23
    Compassionate Rescuer, 126–28
    Forbidden Fruit Hunter, 109–13, 117

beliefs, hidden (continued)
  karma and, 268–69
  mirror relationships and, 21
  Old Faithful, 48, 53–56
  red herring excuses and, 12, 13
  Runaway Bride, 183–86
  Standstill, 83, 89–90
  Uptown Girl, 159, 164–67
  Wanderer, 143–45
  Whirlwind Dater, 71–72
Bend It Like Beckham (movie), 256
black-and-white thinking, 14, 29–30, 43,
    168–69, 188
blaming, 32–33
blind dates, 27, 77, 270
body image. *See* weight and body issues
books, as therapy, 257–58
Born Free (movie), 257
boundaries, 214, 295
  confronting loved ones, 216–20
  free will and, 270
  practical ways of setting, 225–31
  resistance from loved ones, 215–16
  setting, 221–24
boyfriends
  catering to, 74–76, 223
  cheating on, 7, 148
  fictional, 84, 92
  "fixer-upper," 6
  gay, 30, 56
  with serious problems, 119, 221
  setting boundaries with, 221–24, 226,
      227, 231
  two at once, 139–40
  See also ex-boyfriends
breakups, 32, 295
Brian's Song (movie), 257
bridges, toward intimacy, 214,
    232–40

caller ID, for telephone, 229
careers, busy, 15–16, 24, 80, 84
caretaker role, 132
catastrophizing, 31
childhood experiences, 22, 70–71, 74
  behavior patterns and, 270
  building boundaries and, 214

in dysfunctional or abusive families,
    199–200
  family dance and, 198–99
  mourning and, 247
children, desire for, 156, 162, 181
cinematherapy, 254–57
clothes, 27, 158, 167, 290
  discomfort with femininity and, 82, 85
  flirtation and, 97
  social class and, 156
Coelho, Paulo, 284
comfort zone, breaking out of, 10, 197
commitment, running from, 7
communication, frequency of, 228–29,
    234–35
comparing, 36–37
Compassionate Rescuer, 6, 118–19,
    201–2, 249
  boundary problems and, 225
  caretaking role, 127
  cinematherapy and, 255–56
  correction of distorted thinking by,
      130–31
  family backstory of, 124–25, 207,
      209–10, 211
  focus on needs of others, 121–23
  hidden beliefs of, 126–28, 269
  humor as help, 253
  identifying yourself as, 119–20
  music as therapy, 259
  new beliefs for, 134
  qualities of, 120–21
  success story, 291
  tough love and, 129–30
  vacation from caretaker role, 131–33
control, being in, 37–39
conversation, walking away from, 230
Crossing Delancey (movie), 256

damaged goods, feeling like, 4, 9, 13, 22
dating
  dating guides, 6, 8, 63
  hiatus from, 77–79
  as "numbers game," 8, 63
  online dating services, 291
  rejection and, 96
  success stories, 288–93

discovery, of hidden emotions and beliefs, 244–45
discussion groups, online, 239
distortions, cognitive (distorted thinking), 18, 24, 26, 30, 278
  identifying, 42–44
  maximizing and minimizing, 31
  shoulding or musting, 33
  traps associated with, 37–42, 245
  worry and, 41
divorce, 112, 113, 270

e-mail communication, 229, 237
eating, overindulgence in, 15, 137, 149
Edie & Pen (movie), 256–57
Einstein, Albert, 266
emotions
  artistic expression and, 165
  beliefs and, 9–10
  blocking of, 190–91
  boundaries and, 230
  changing, 10–11
  cinematherapy and, 257
  core, 243–44
  creativity and management of, 261–63
  emotional reasoning, 35–36, 114, 148, 188, 204
  family myths and, 204, 208, 209
  hidden or buried, 81, 183, 241–43
  journal keeping and, 260–61
  living in the moment and, 278
  management of, 41
  mourning and, 247–48
  practical techniques for processing, 251–63
  red herring excuses and, 12
  stages of processing hidden emotions, 244–50
  in written communication, 216–17
enabling behavior, 128
Epstein, Mark, 283
Erin Brockovich (movie), 255
ex-boyfriends, 13, 30
  anger toward, 275
  of Compassionate Rescuer, 120
  letting go of the past, 56–58

  pining for, 49
  stuck on, 246
  See also boyfriends
exercising, overindulgence in, 137, 149
external circumstances, relationships driven by, 39–40, 114, 151

false assumptions
  black-and-white thinking, 29–30
  comparing, 36–37
  emotional reasoning, 35–36
  fortune-telling, 26–28
  labeling (name calling), 34–35
  maximizing and minimizing, 31–32
  mind reading, 28–29
  personalizing (blaming), 32–33
  shoulding and musting, 33–34
family dynamics, 11, 195–96, 241
  approval, need for, 196–97
  central myths of, 202–11
  dance of roles in, 197–202, 211–13
fashion magazines, 94
father, relationship with
  Compassionate Rescuer, 124, 127–28
  idealized view of father, 33–34
  Old Faithful, 51–53, 60
  Runaway Bride, 190
  Standstill, 86–87
  Uptown Girl, 161, 162–63, 197–98
  Wanderer, 141–42
  Whirlwind Dater, 67–68
femininity, 81–82, 83, 290
  discomfort with, 86–88
  getting in touch with, 96
  hidden beliefs about, 90
feminist movement, 8–9
flirtation, 95–97
Forbidden Fruit Hunter, 6, 99–101
  boundary problems and, 224–25, 267
  breaking away from family dynamic, 115–16
  caretaking role of, 107–8
  cinematherapy and, 255
  family backstory of, 105–7, 204, 207, 211
  hidden beliefs of, 109–13, 113–14
  identifying yourself as, 101–2

Forbidden Fruit Hunter (continued)
  key patterns in life of, 102–3
  new beliefs for, 116–17
  success story, 290
  unintentional affairs of, 103–5
fortune-telling, 26–28, 43, 59, 93, 188, 252
Four Agreements, The (Ruiz), 284
Franklin, Aretha, 259
free will, exercising, 270–72
friendships, 8, 214
  best friends, 5, 49
  bridges toward intimacy, 239
  cultivating gratitude and, 280
  neglect of, 223
future, assumptions about, 26–28, 37–39

Gandhi, Mahatma, 268–69
Gift of Change, The (Williamson), 284
girlfriends, men's, 100, 103
girlfriends, women's, 13, 18, 28, 29, 295
  abusive boyfriends and, 123
  cultivating new beliefs and, 61
  emotional disconnection from, 76
Going to Pieces Without Falling Apart (Epstein), 283–84
Gone with the Wind (movie), 254–55
"good girl," 212
Goodall, Jane, 258
Grace of My Heart (movie), 255
gratification, instant and delayed, 41–42
gratitude, cultivating, 280–82
grieving, necessity for, 56, 57, 247–48
guilt, 8, 33
  Compassionate Rescuer and, 119, 121, 122
  family dynamics and, 54
  Forbidden Fruit Hunter and, 113, 117, 267
  Runaway Bride and, 182–83
  shame and, 244
  Wanderer and, 136, 137, 144, 150, 152

hair, 38, 43
Hanging Up (movie), 256
happiness, 40, 198, 271
history, romantic, 7

hobbies, 65
humor, 227–28, 253–54, 258, 280
hypercriticism, 30

"I" language, use of, 217–18, 228, 236
If the Buddha Dated (Kasl), 283
inadequacy, feelings of, 13, 20, 243–44
Internet, 96, 140, 239, 291
intimacy, 6, 18–19, 175, 177
  bridges toward, 214, 232, 237–38
  distancing from, 100
  emotional, 48
  fear of, 20, 21, 28, 81, 145
  hidden discomfort with, 106
  letting go of the past and, 58
  mind reading as obstacle to, 29
  sharing and, 27, 223, 227
  unconscious avoidance of, 196
  vulnerability and, 72

journal, keeping a, 259–61
Joy Luck Club, The (movie), 186–87

karma, 268–70
Kasl, Charlotte, 283
Keys, Alicia, 259
Kitchen Table Wisdom (Remen), 281, 284

labeling (name calling), 34–35, 42, 59, 113–14, 227–28
Legends of the Fall (movie), 256
love, feeling of unworthiness for
  Compassionate Rescuer and, 128
  Forbidden Fruit Hunter and, 110
  Old Faithful and, 54–56
  Runaway Bride and, 185
  Standstill and, 89
  Uptown Girl and, 158
  Wanderer and, 143–44
love, verbal expression of, 235–36

McLachlin, Sarah, 259
makeup, 27, 38, 82, 85, 91, 158
marriage, 140, 276
  compatibility of interests and, 16
  cultural valuation of, 8
  end of, 4

fortune-telling and, 27
happiness and, 40
parents' influence in, 147
previous marriages, 67
troubled, 32–33
upscale lifestyle and, 156
weddings, 14, 17
martyr, role of, 41
Matchmaker, The (movie), 255
maximizing and minimizing, 31–32, 43, 59, 188
men
alcohol and, 37, 84
bisexual, 100
cheaters, 35
commitment and, 15, 18, 30, 63
emotionally unavailable, 4, 6, 35, 100, 101
emotional reasoning and, 114
fathers as, 142
saying no to, 110–13
families abandoned by, 184
family myths and gender roles, 205–6
as Forbidden Fruit Hunters, 112
gay, 106–7
generalizations about, 14, 37
hiatus from dating, 77–79, 151–52
infidelity to, 136, 144
late for dates, 9–10
married, 6, 100, 103, 104, 112–13
mirror relationships and, 20–21, 291
in search of mother figure, 134
with serious problems, 118–19, 121–23, 126–27, 131, 249, 296
sports and, 31
status and social class of, 156, 159, 161–62, 168–69
woman's need for happiness and, 40
Merchant, Natalie, 259
mind reading, 28–29, 43, 75, 76
mirroring, 20–21, 30, 201–2, 291
Moonstruck (movie), 255
Morissette, Alanis, 259
mother, relationship with
Compassionate Rescuer, 124–25, 127
Forbidden Fruit Hunter, 104, 105, 109, 116, 207

Old Faithful, 51–53, 60
Runaway Bride, 181–82
Standstill, 85–86, 88
Uptown Girl, 161–62, 162–64
Wanderer, 141, 147
Whirlwind Dater, 68
mourning, 247–48
Muriel's Wedding (movie), 255
Murphy's Law, 206
music, as therapy, 257, 258–59, 261–62
My Best Friend's Wedding (movie), 254
My Sister's Keeper (Picoult), 258

name calling, 34–35
neediness, 22, 28, 110, 136–37, 144–45, 152
Next Stop Wonderland (movie), 257

Old Faithful, 5, 47–48, 221
boundaries and, 60–61, 224
cinematherapy and, 254–55
correction of distorted thinking by, 59–60
cultivating new beliefs, 61–62
family backstory of, 51–53, 211–12
hidden beliefs of, 48, 53–56, 269
identifying yourself as, 49
letting go of the past, 56–59
mirroring and, 201
music as therapy, 259
regret and, 246
stuck on lost love, 50–51
success story, 289
On Golden Pond (movie), 257
optimism, 276
Ordinary People (movie), 257
overachievers, 144, 209, 237

parents, relationship with, 196, 273, 296
boundaries and, 60–61, 215–16, 221–24, 225–31
bridges toward intimacy, 233
Compassionate Rescuer, 124–25, 126–28
confronting loved ones, 216–20
family reunions, 236–37

parents, relationship with (continued)
Forbidden Fruit Hunter, 101–2, 103, 105–7, 109–10
Runaway Bride, 197
single-parent homes, 101
Standstill, 85–86
Uptown Girl, 157, 160, 161–64, 166, 172–73
Wanderer, 141–43, 152, 247
Whirlwind Dater, 67–69, 76
patience, need for, 218–19
Peck, M. Scott, 284
people pleasers, 138
personal ads, 13, 96, 97, 116
personalizing (blaming), 32–33, 43, 59, 113
Persuasion (movie), 256
pessimism, 26, 38, 42, 276–77
pickiness, excessive, 16, 17
Picoult, Jodi, 258
pleasure, denial of, 79
"poor me" complex, 245
positive thoughts, 43–44
Postcards from the Edge (movie), 255
princess or "special girl," 49, 53, 56, 60, 292
projection, psychological, 18–19
prophecy, self-fulfilling, 27

red herring excuses, 12–18, 24, 25, 63, 101, 276
regret, stage of, 246–47
rejection
bridges toward intimacy and, 240
confronting loved ones and, 219
deconstruction of thoughts and, 252
expectation of sex and, 41
fear of, 244
by mother, 88
as normal part of dating process, 96
self-doubt and, 293
social class and, 158
Remen, Rachel Naomi, 281, 284
Road Less Traveled, The (Peck), 284
Roberts, Julia, 175, 176, 254, 255
Roosevelt, Eleanor, 271
Ruiz, Don Miguel, 284

rules, breaking of, 71, 72–74
Runaway Bride, 7, 175–77, 179–80, 197
bridges toward intimacy, 233, 234, 238
core emotions of, 243
correction of distorted thinking by, 188–89
facing fears, 186–87
family backstory of, 181–83, 204, 209, 212
fear of abandonment and, 178–79, 200
hidden beliefs of, 183–86
honesty about feelings, 189–90
identifying yourself as, 177–78
new beliefs for, 190–91
success story, 292–93
Runaway Bride (movie), 175, 176

Seat of the Soul (Zukav), 283
self-worth, low, 19, 22, 81, 200, 293
childhood experiences and, 243
music as therapy, 259
Runaway Bride and, 182
setting boundaries and, 231
spiritual practices to overcome, 274
Wanderer and, 144, 153
sex, 33, 34, 41
confiding and, 224, 226–27
Forbidden Fruit Hunter and, 104
man's lack of sexual interest, 48
sexual incompatibility, 49
Standstill and, 81, 82, 83
Wanderers and, 139, 140, 149, 150
Whirlwind Dater and, 75–76
shame, 4, 8, 13, 35
as core emotion of dissatisfied singles, 243–44
of Forbidden Fruit Hunter, 104
hidden beliefs behind, 25
overcoming of, 248
of problem men, 126
of Standstill, 82, 90, 91
of Wanderer, 136, 139, 152
shopping, overindulgence in, 137, 149, 150
siblings, 101–2, 103, 196, 233
bridges toward intimacy, 238
of Compassionate Rescuer, 124

family myths and, 204, 205, 212
gay, 106–7
of Runaway Bride, 180, 181, 182, 183, 197, 234
of Uptown Girl, 164
of Wanderer, 142, 143
singles, dissatisfied, 3–5, 11, 195
boundary problems for, 224–25
cinematherapy for, 254–57
core emotions of, 243–44
eight styles of, 5–8
false assumptions of, 26–37
family backstories of, 199, 200
family myths and, 202, 203
no longer dissatisfied, 294–96
red herring excuses of, 12–18
spirituality and, 265
traps for, 37–42
social class, 7, 16, 155, 156, 168–69, 208
spirituality, 11, 12, 41
acceptance of unfairness in life, 272–73
cultivating gratitude, 280–82
free will and, 270–72
karma and, 268–70
kindness and compassion toward yourself, 274–75
learning and growing experiences, 265–68
letting go of the past and, 58–59
living in the moment, 277–79
optimism and, 264–65
staying faithful to the journey, 282–84
timing and, 276–77
Standstill, 6, 80–81, 282
bravado of, 82–83
bridges toward intimacy, 232–33
cinematherapy and, 255
core emotions of, 243
correction of distorted thinking by, 92–94
difficulty of opening up, 83–85
discomfort with femininity, 86–88
family backstory of, 85–86, 209, 212
flirtation and, 95–97
getting in touch with your body, 90–92
hidden beliefs of, 89–90, 269
humor as help, 253–54

identifying yourself as, 81–82
music as therapy, 258
new beliefs for, 97–98
new self-image for, 94–95
princess role denied to, 86–87
regret and, 246–47
stiff upper lip of, 88–89
success story, 290
status, 158–59
Steel Magnolias (movie), 257
stress response, 219
Suspicion (movie), 255–56

taboos, 226–28, 235
technology, communication, 229, 237
Terms of Endearment (movie), 257
therapy, 9, 33, 36
books and music as, 257–59
Compassionate Rescuer and, 122
family myths and, 209
Forbidden Fruit Hunter and, 104, 107
movies as, 254–57
Runaway Bride and, 179, 183, 292
Standstill and, 84
Whirlwind Dater and, 65, 66–67, 69
thoughts, deconstructing, 251–53
tomboys, 87
Tortilla Soup (movie), 256
tough love, 129–30
true love, one chance for, 49
Tuesdays with Morrie (Albom), 258

Under the Tuscan Sun (movie), 255
Unfaithful (movie), 256
Uptown Girl, 7, 155–57, 197–98
boundary problems and, 225
cinematherapy and, 256
correction of distorted thinking by, 168–70
family backstory of, 162–64, 205
hidden beliefs of, 159, 164–67
identifying yourself as, 157–58
interacting with men on new level, 170–71
materialistic values, letting go of, 167–68, 171–72
misplaced sense of self, 160

Uptown Girl (continued)
  new beliefs for, 173–74
  parents' approval, letting go of, 172–73
  rigid expectations of, 161–62
  status equation and, 158–59
  success story, 292
  trusting in timing, 277

virginity, 81, 82

Wanderer, 7, 135–37
  boundary problems and, 224
  bridges toward intimacy, 233
  cinematherapy and, 256
  correction of distorted thinking by, 148–49
  diplomat role of, 138–39, 142
  exercising free will, 271
  family backstory of, 141–43, 204, 209
  flexibility of, 145–46
  hiatus from men, 151–52
  hidden beliefs of, 143–45
  identifying yourself as, 137–38
  love triangles of, 139–40
  monogamy and, 149–51
  mourning process and, 247
  new beliefs for, 152–54
  nurturing of self and, 146–47, 154
  "poor me" complex and, 245
  success story, 291
weight and body issues, 13, 24, 37, 39, 98
  getting in touch with your body, 90–92

Uptown Girl and, 157, 166, 167–68, 174
Whirlwind Dater, 5–6, 63–64, 250
  breaking the rules, 72–74
  bridges toward intimacy, 233–34
  cinematherapy and, 255
  correction of distorted thinking by, 74–76
  cultivating new beliefs, 79
  deconstructing thoughts and, 251–52
  exterior and interior personality of, 67–69
  family backstory of, 67–69, 205–6
  hidden beliefs of, 71–72
  identifying yourself as, 64–65
  self-discovery process of, 69–71, 76–77
  success story, 289–90
  hiatus from men, 77–79, 282
women
  comparing yourself with other women, 36–37, 82, 94–95, 98, 169
  cultural expectations of, 19
  family myths and gender roles, 205–6
  media images of, 94, 97
  "other woman," 102, 113
  overachievers, 47
  strong female singers, 259
  styles of dissatisfied singles, 5–8
workaholics, 24, 131–32
worry, anxiety and, 40–41, 149

yoga, 291

Zukav, Gary, 283

About the Authors

DEBBIE MAGIDS, PH.D., is a licensed psychologist with a private practice in New York City. She is a specialist in helping people become self-aware, showing them how to discover the hidden thoughts and feelings that drive their behavior so they can change their lives for the better. Dr. Magids's career has been diverse as she has had over ten years' experience as an academic, a clinician, and a professor. She is the author of many articles on self-awareness and psychological issues. Dr. Magids taught at Hunter College for the last six years, in the Department of Educational Foundations and Counseling Programs. As a professor, she has actively guided new professionals into the field of counseling. She has been a member of the American Psychological Association since 1989, and can be seen as a featured guest expert on the *Montel Williams Show*.

NANCY PESKE is a freelance writer, editor, book doctor, and ghostwriter. She is the coauthor of the successful Cinematherapy series as well as *Raising a Sensory Smart Child: The Definitive Handbook for Helping Your Child with Sensory Integration Issues.* She lives in Shorewood, Wisconsin, with her husband and son.